THIS IS A BOOK FOR ALL AMERICANS EVERYWHERE— FILLED WITH THE DRIVING EXCITEMENT OF A MAJOR NOVEL

—a book about the U.S.A. and the way our democratic system works, the grassroots story of free Americans making up their minds and choosing their public officials

—a book written by a foremost American author, filled with the driving excitement of a major novel, the story of people, politics, and how John F. Kennedy was elected

—a book for mothers and fathers, civic groups, women's clubs, church societies, Republicans and Democrats alike

—a book for you, me, and every citizen and his family!

Books by James A. Michener

TALES OF THE SOUTH PACIFIC

- THE FIRES OF SPRING
- THE VOICE OF ASIA
- RETURN TO PARADISE
- THE BRIDGES AT TOKO-RI
- SAYONARA
- THE BRIDGE AT ANDAU
- RASCALS IN PARADISE (with A. Grove Day)
- HAWAII

Published by Bantam Books

☆Report ☆of the ☆County ☆Chairman

James A. Michener

BANTAM BOOKS ☆ ☆ NEW YORK

*This low-priced Bantam Book
has been completely reset in a type face
designed for easy reading and was
printed from new plates. It contains the complete
text of the original hard-cover edition.*
NOT ONE WORD HAS BEEN OMITTED.

REPORT OF THE COUNTY CHAIRMAN

*A Bantam Book / published by arrangement with
Random House, Inc.*

PRINTING HISTORY

*Random House edition published May 1961
Bantam edition published November 1961*

Cover photo by Cornell Capa—Magnum

Bantam Books are published by Bantam Books, Inc. Its trade-mark, consisting of the words "Bantam Books" and the portrayal of a bantam, is registered in the United States Patent Office and in other countries. Marca Registrada. Printed in the United States of America. Bantam Books, Inc., 271 Madison Ave., New York 16, N. Y.

Contents

To

JOHNNY WELSH

practical politician, county chairman,
a dedicated, arrogant, honest man

1

In a Small Room

☒ ☒

Since it seems likely that the 1960 Presidential election will long remain a matter of speculation for historians, I think it might be of interest to have a factual record of the reflections of a citizen who found himself involved in the campaign at the precinct level. The comments that follow are as honest as I can make them and they provide a chart of the alternate hopes and fears with which I followed the course of John F. Kennedy to the Presidency.

The second time I met Kennedy was in Hawaii in the early summer of 1959 during the islands' first political campaign under statehood. At that time I was arguing with myself as to whether or not I should become involved in that highly emotional Hawaiian election, and in a mood of both uncertainty and apprehension I accepted an invitation to a Democratic dinner at which the main speaker was to be the visiting senator from Massachusetts, John Kennedy.

All I can remember of his address was that he quoted most aptly from some of the major documents of American history, and also from some extremely obscure ones, and I recall thinking casually, "It would be nice to have in the White House someone who knows books." Later, in the reception line, I slipped past the young senator unnoticed, but someone whispered in his ear, "That's Michener, the writer," and quickly he stepped forward to catch my disappearing arm, and said most engagingly, "I hoped you would be here. I've always liked your *Fires of Spring.*"

I am sure that the wise whisperer at the senator's elbow had forewarned him that I might be passing through the line, and that I might just possibly prove helpful in lining up Hawaii's delegates to the Democratic convention, then less than a year away. But I doubt if the whisperer could have prompted him to recall so obscure a book as *The Fires of Spring.* As graciously as an author can, when one of his older children is remembered affectionately, I nodded and the senator said, "Some of us are getting together later on. Care to join us?" I replied that unfortunately I had already arranged a date to talk over the forthcoming island election, and I did not see him again.

It was true that I had a minor political meeting that night, but it was one that I could easily have missed, for my presence was not necessary. The real reason I absented myself from the midnight caucus at which Kennedy made a favorable impression upon my Hawaiian friends was a most specific and conscious one, and I remember verbalizing it to myself with more than customary clarity: "This man Kennedy is unusually appealing. He knows what to say to people. And I'm not sure I want to support him for President. Not yet."

For two reasons it was fortunate that I stayed away from that Kennedy caucus to go instead to the meeting where Hawaiian politics were discussed, for the latter turned out to be one of the finest political discussions I was to attend in the islands. It was held at the home of Vincent Esposito on a hillside overlooking Honolulu's mysterious night lights, and there, as we dissected the imminent election—which everyone expected the Democrats to win easily, since they had swept the primaries, but which I felt sure the Republicans would win, because I knew how badly the Democrats were split—I engaged myself to work whole-heartedly for the Democrats, even though I was convinced their cause was hopeless.

In the turbulent weeks that followed I received my initiation into the grief of local politics. The Democrats lost, as I knew they must, but they lost by only two thousand votes, and they might have won had I been able to get the two Democratic factions together a week sooner. Even so, as a result of last-minute efforts which took us to all the islands for speeches and meetings that lasted around the clock, we almost salvaged the victory.

But it eluded us, and in the days that followed I experienced the penalties of losing. Some months earlier in a moment of weakness I had accepted the chairmanship of a public drive for charity funds. Now I was advised that my having championed the Democrats had ruined whatever chances I might have had to collect money from the community, "since everyone with money is a Republican," and it was politely suggested that it might be wiser, and fairer to the charity, if I resigned my chairmanship, which I did.

Friends who had once been rather close, now avoided me. At one dreadful party more than half the guests preferred not to talk with me, and those who did said ugly things. One commented, "Don't you feel a little sick at your stomach when you think that your television speeches could have won the election for the Democrats?" I replied that that's why I had made them, and my questioner looked stunned. "Don't you understand what the Democrats would do to people like you and me?" he asked, and to this I made no reply.

One of my most honest friends, a devoted Republican lady, came to report, "It's widely believed, Jim, that you were temporarily deranged because of change of life. Everybody felt that if you were in complete control you wouldn't have done what you did." I replied that I was in fine health, so my interrogator asked, "Then you really knew what you were doing?" I replied that I had thought things out carefully and had decided that the Democrats would do better for Hawaii than the Republicans. My friend confided, in a burst of the honesty for which I esteemed her, "Well, I'll tell you what I did, Jim Michener. On the night before election I prayed for half an hour that your side would lose so that you would never have to face up to the terrible mistake you came so close to making. And God protected you from yourself and saw to it that the Democrats lost."

More unpleasant were the other friends who explained to the community that I had supported the Democrats only because my wife happened to be a Japanese-American, for in Hawaii many of the younger Japanese were Democrats. "If Michener had been left to himself, he'd never have done this terrible thing," these logicians explained, "but his Japanese wife put fierce pressure on him and he had to knuckle under."

What I learned from losing this Hawaiian election in late July of 1959 was the tension that still ran through American life whenever economics, or social values, or racial problems were concerned. Since both the Republican candidate for governor and his Democratic opponent were Catholics, I fell into the error of assuming that religion no longer played a major role in American politics. Later, when the Republican administration took control, I found that in actual politics the Republicans really did tend to vote against liberal measures and to work for a balanced budget, whereas the Democrats were inclined to support acts which would help the society to move forward, even though such acts might temporarily postpone a balanced budget. And I found that without exception my intellect and my heart and my patriotism and my sense of history inclined me toward the Democratic view. So in foregoing that midnight caucus with Senator Kennedy, I took the first step along the path that was to end in my supporting him most vigorously.

The second reason why I was fortunate in not having met with Kennedy that night was that the Hawaiian election, and the subsequent ostracism I experienced, gave me time to consider exactly what I wanted to do in the 1960 Presidential campaign and to reach an intellectual decision without being unduly influenced by the personality of one of the major contenders. If later I were to support Kennedy, it would be because I had decided intellectually that this was the right thing to do.

Consequently, when the Hawaiian election ended, I shipped aboard a sailboat which was beating its way back from Honolulu to Los Angeles, following its participation in the biennial trans-Pacific yacht race. It was a splendid craft, owned by a congenial sportsman with the unlikely name of Baldwin T. Baldwin. One of the reasons why I undertook this arduous trip was obvious: "You've written so much about the Pacific," I reasoned with myself, "that the least you can do is cross it in a small boat to see what it's really like." The other reason was simple: "I want time to think."

For our skeleton crew back to the mainland we had an extraordinary group of six tough men, professionals most of them, none of whom smoked, drank, took coffee or swore. One was a Mormon lay minister, one a Marine colonel, one a Dutch carpenter who could cook like a Frenchman; two were students from the University of Nebraska. And everyone loved classical music, so that the long night watches when we could get California good-music stations on the radio were the most sought after.

It takes only eleven days to race from California to Honolulu with the wind at one's back. It takes twenty-two days to beat the other way with the wind in one's teeth almost all the journey. Boats scurry north to the latitude of Seattle in hopes of catching a wind blowing down from Alaska, and the rail is under water most of the way. It was a long, tedious, wet trip home and even the professionals were seasick.

It was while I stood at the wheel as our boat headed into the storm that I reached several conclusions. I was about to publish a novel which dealt with Hawaii, and all who had read the galleys had warned me that after it appeared I would no longer be welcome in the islands. "If you think you suffered retaliation because you voted Democratic, wait till this novel hits the fan," they said. Since men understandably prefer to escape animosity, and since I was already paying taxes on a hillside home in one of the loveliest Pennsylvania counties, I concluded that it would be unwarranted to press the issue in Hawaii. There was also a second consideration, more imperative perhaps than the first. In the novel that I was about to release, the main theme was the enviable manner in which Hawaii had been able to assimilate men and women from many different races, and what I wrote was true: these islands today represent a beacon light of hope for all communities who are striving for racial harmony and they are of extraordinary value to the United States because they prove that our nation can attain this harmony. But on the day-to-day operating level at which my wife and I had to live, we met with more racial discrimination in Hawaii than we did in eastern Pennsylvania, and my wife understandably preferred to live permanently in the latter place. For example, when we thought seriously about buying a home in Hawaii we had the bad luck to settle upon one in Kahala, where restricted covenants prevent any Japanese from moving in. The three finest clubs in Honolulu admit no Orientals to membership, and other trivial, but irritating, folk customs prevail which a man in his middle years prefers not to bother about. So, aboard the yacht heading away from Hawaii, a land I had grown to love as the spiritual capital of the world about which I wrote, I decided that my home would henceforth be in Pennsylvania.

I also decided that in the 1960 elections I would work diligently on the local level, but who my candidate would be in the primaries I did not know. I was somewhat in the position of the Kentucky senator who replied, when asked by a reporter what stand he was going to take in a forthcoming election, "I haven't made up my mind, son, but when I do I'm going to be damned bitter about it."

If I felt no bitterness, I did feel a deep commitment. This stemmed, I believe, from a profound love of country that I had developed over the years. I suppose that accidental circumstances have accounted for much of this: I have served my country in two wars; in peacetime I have been involved in many dangerous pursuits relevant to our position in the world; during the Hungarian revolution I was often behind Russian lines; I have undergone three other major revolutions, disaster at sea, and danger in half a dozen different foreign lands. An appalling share of the money I have been able to earn has been handed over to the government. And I have had to learn the operation of the American system in order to teach it at both the high-school and the college level.

But most of all, my strong affection for my country stems from the fact that America has been overly generous to me. As a boy I lived in extreme poverty with a mother who did the cruelest kind of sweatshop work to educate a horde of abandoned children whom she picked up off the streets. But because ours was a generous country, I later on received scholarships and fellowships and traveling funds and good jobs. I was given, at no expense to myself, an excellent education and when I started to write, my countrymen supported me rather better than my native talents might have warranted. I was in truth what I remain today, a very fortunate son of America and as such I was much concerned in my country's politics and was determined to do something about them.

"If I were asked," I said to myself one night as our boat plowed northward to the strains of Beethoven's *Seventh*, "why I want to become involved in the forthcoming election I'd have to say that it was because in my work overseas I've seen at first hand how sadly our reputation has slipped." I recalled the riots in which I had at one time or other been engaged where Asian students calumniated the United States as a fat, weary, selfish, illiterate, perverse war-monger, determined to destroy all the world's revolutionary movements. I recalled how ineffective I had been when I tried to argue with these students, assuring them that the United States was not like that. They would not listen to me because they were convinced that we were a tired and timid nation.

I recalled the disasters our people overseas had led us into by always supporting the reactionary side. It was what one might call the Buick syndrome. I saw it at its best once in Korea when we were about to capture a minor city, and our general said to his staff, "As soon as we take the city, you fellows set up a civil government, and be sure to use for mayor a Korean who is sympathetic to us." When one of his underlings asked how they were to select a mayor he replied, "Pick out one of the men who has a Buick or some other big car." I often reflected upon this rule-of-thumb, and I concluded to my surprise that this Buick syndrome was not a bad way for selecting quickly a temporary mayor who was likely to be inclined toward our side, but it did seem somewhat inadequate as a criterion for selecting a permanent mayor. I suspect that most of our errors abroad have arisen from the fact that in laziness we have allowed temporary arrangements to crystallize into permanent agreements, for to differentiate between the two requires both courage and insight, and these two virtues have often been absent in our foreign representatives.

I recalled also how fragile our international alliances seemed to have become. In England I had read newspapers which frankly suggested that Great Britain enter into anti-American rearrangements. In Pakistan I had seen one of our most trustworthy allies, one that had risked its very existence on our friendship, turning conspicuously away from us. In Hungary I had seen the misery our vacillations had in part occasioned. And in Japan I had watched the growth of a strong intellectual movement against America. Yet our administration and our press seemed indifferent to these shifts, if, indeed, they knew of them.

Finally, I had watched for ten years the often subtle,

sometimes brutal manner in which our national image had been debased by ourselves and our enemies. From a distance we did often seem to be a fat and foolish nation. We seemed to be against the great changes that were sweeping the world. During the McCarthy period we were outspokenly contemptuous of the intellect; in the Little Rock period, antagonistic to anyone who was not white; and in the whole decade, paralyzed by a fear of natural revolution. From abroad we seemed to be a faltering nation, insecure even in those great principles upon which we were founded, and I felt that something had to be done to rectify this national image.

Another decision I reached during the night watches was that I would henceforth, insofar as I was able to determine my own actions, never again make even the slightest concession where race, religion or a man's type of work was concerned. I found myself willing to accept a man whether he was a Negro or not, whether he was a Catholic or not, and whether he belonged to a union or not. In fact, I suppose I was dangerously close to making the error of believing that merely because a man was a Negro, or a Catholic, or a union member he must be a good man; but I felt that if I were to be guilty of error, such an error had this to commend it: on it social progress has often been built and can be built in the future. If one elects to act on the contrary principle, no progress is likely.

If I had been required then to state one short reason why I was about to plunge into national politics I would have said in summary, "Because there is a nation to be won." In those intense days on the bosom of the stormy Pacific I visualized the United States as a rich and lumbering galleon adrift without crew or purpose, and I knew that she could be won by men of vision and determination. In the forthcoming election on many lonely nights I would remind myself stubbornly, "There is a nation to be won," and I knew that I was engaged permanently in the battle to win it. But if I had been asked why I wanted to capture a nation I would have been forced to reply, "Because I want my ideas of justice and accomplishment to prevail." Later I was to discover that many of the men with whom I was to work had exactly the same idea.

Consequently, when I reached California one of the first things I told my wife was, "We're going back to Pennsylvania, and I want to work in the Presidential election."

"Good!" she cried. "This time we'll make sure that Adlai wins."

I remember that I was silent for a few moments. Then I said, "I'm not sure I'm going to work for Adlai in the primaries."

"My God!" she shouted. "Who else is there?"

My wife was a charter member of the Adlai Stevenson Club. In Chicago long before we were married she worked for him when he ran for governor of Illinois. In the 1952 Presidential campaign she not only worked vigorously but contributed her own funds and all that she could cadge from others. When he lost, her friends tell me, she went home and wept. In 1956 we were working in Europe, and I remember that bleak November morning when we staggered in to Paris after a dismal trip from Bordeaux to find that Stevenson had lost again. This time I know she went up to our hotel room and cried. If ever a husband had reason to support Adlai Stevenson for President, I did.

We drove across country to our home in Pennsylvania, and as we rode through one brilliant state after another—California, Arizona, New Mexico, Colorado—we often spoke of how magnificent our nation was. We had each, I think, known the grandeur and the misery of life in America. As I have indicated, in my case the misery came first, in the early years as a small boy who almost never got the playthings a boy would want, with the grandeur coming later, when as an adult I found thrown at me almost everything a man would desire. In my wife's case it was rather the reverse. As the much-loved youngest daughter of a successful Japanese melon grower in eastern Colorado, she grew up in a family where her brothers spoiled her and where the world was good. Then, in a series of dramatic shifts, her older brother died of a ruptured appendix; her father died because a doctor failed to diagnose blood poisoning; her family was swept into one of the worst wartime concentration camps; all their property was confiscated without remuneration; and the burden of holding the family together fell upon my wife. That she survived this series of disasters without impairment of her natural optimism was due to the solid education Japanese parents give their children and to the fact that Antioch College, in southern Ohio, was brave enough to award her a scholarship while she was still in her concentration camp. The college also found her a good job, and she has always felt "that one Antioch in a country offsets four patriotic societies in Southern California." It was inevitable, I suppose, that she came through these experiences without rancor and with a great love for a nation which might make mistakes, but which was generous enough to correct them. It was also inevitable that she would be for Adlai Stevenson.

So as we drove homeward she pressured me. "Who else do the Democrats have that you could possibly vote for in the primaries?" she demanded. "You've lived overseas. You've seen what America really needs. A President with courage to do the right thing. Somebody with brains. Somebody the other nations can respect. A man with determination in the field of social legislation. There's only one man you could possibly support."

Across the country my wife bombarded me with reasons why Adlai Stevenson had to be our next President and why I would be ashamed of myself if I supported anyone else. She made a persuasive case for her candidate and convinced me that she was going to further his candidacy with all her energy, which is phenomenal. By the time I reached Pennsylvania, after refreshing my powerful memories of Nebraska, Iowa, Illinois, Indiana and Ohio, each of which held recollections of happy hours spent there during the last forty years, I was not, perhaps, completely convinced that I was going to come out for Stevenson, but I at least had more than a dozen good reasons to fortify me if I did so decide. The most persuasive argument my wife had used was this: "The people of this country sense that enormous decisions are going to be made in the 1960's. And they know that more than half those decisions will involve foreign relations. They want somebody with brains. Instinctively they know the President ought to be Stevenson. And without General Eisenhower to run against him, Stevenson will win."

"If you had to give me just one reason why I should support Adlai, what would it be?" I asked.

"Because the people sense that he's big enough to do the job."

"Do you think he can get elected?" I pressed.

"This time, yes," she insisted.

When we reached home I spent the better part of one November week locked up in the small room where I usually did my serious work. My dictionaries were in place; my typewriter stood on its stand; and certain objects which have a warm good-luck quality about them stared down at me from their appointed homes. But I did not pitch in to my writing. Instead I sat back and gazed out the window at the lovely Pennsylvania forest which stood stark in the autumn winds. And as I sat there I reviewed the political condition of my nation.

"The fundamental thing," I reasoned, "is that we have got to have a wholly new administration. It musn't be saddled with old policies and old policy-makers. Therefore it's got to be Democratic. This country really needs a Democratic administration."

I thought that it had to be Democratic for these reasons. First, our country had indeed grown somewhat fat and flabby, not as seriously as our enemies abroad preached, but jut enough to give me pause. Second, "It does seem evident to me that we've been standing still insofar as our internal affairs are concerned. Education, new dams, new factories, our general spirit of adventure . . . in nearly everything but roads we need enormous new energy." As a former teacher of economics I was innately supicious of a high interest rate that limited new starts in industry. And I was disturbed at the deterioration of our cities, at the vetoing of bills that would aid housing, health and depressed areas. For all these substantial internal reasons I wanted a Democratic administration. Third, it seemed certain that the Senate and the House of Representatives would be markedly Democratic, for the American people showed no inclination to elect conservative Republicans to those important bodies, and I suspected that our state governors and their legislatures would be increasingly Democratic, for that was apparently the mood of the people. "Therefore," I reasoned, "at this critical period we ought to have a Democratic President, too. I don't like divided responsibilities now, even though it didn't worry me too much during the last six years." Fourth, I was deeply distressed that President Eisenhower had not used the majesty of his office in support of the Supreme Court decision on integrating our schools, and I felt that any of the talked-about Democratic nominees would, if elected President, do so. Fifth, I was even more distressed by the fact that the last eight years of Republican rule had been a period of strong anti-intellectualism, both implied and overt. So far as I knew, President Eisenhower had done nothing to encourage the arts: he not once had attended the theater, or gone to a concert, or commented favorably on books, or entertained anyone but top business and sports leaders who were equally indifferent to the arts. One of the damning charges against the administration was James Reston's analysis of the Presidential visiting list; few men with an artistic or philosophical I.Q. of over 60 had ever appeared on it, and this attitude had insidiously permeated our national life. I myself do not place the arts inordinately high on the scale of national preferences; I have always supposed that people like painters and novelists and college professors came rather far down the list—say, right after efficient druggists or office managers—but they ought to appear somewhere, and much of America's loss of prestige abroad stems from the world's suspicion that Russia cares for the arts and we do not. I therefore concluded that as an artist and an intellectual I was obligated to vote for a change. Finally, and this was of major importance, I was convinced that any one of the principal Democratic contenders was on the whole a better man than Richard Nixon, and that assurance, whether accurate or not, gave me comfort. At the same time, from having talked with numerous Republicans, I knew that within their ranks there was deep dissatisfaction with Nixon and that in 1960 many who had previously voted for Eisenhower did not want to vote for Nixon. Therefore, if we nominated the right man, we had a chance of winning.

But when I had reached the above reassuring conclusions I saw clearly that everything hinged upon the Democrats' selection of their candidate, and so in my somewhat chilly, isolated room I tried to decide who the logical choice was. Alone, and without help from anyone or any printed material, I tried to predict in my own mind what ought to happen and what was likely to happen.

I considered these men in order: Adlai Stevenson, Mennen Williams, Stuart Symington, Hubert Humphrey, Lyndon Johnson and John Kennedy. At no time did I consider Edmund Muskie, Pat Brown or Robert Meyner, for they were all Catholics; and although I was willing to support them, it seemed to me that as such they did not yet have an adequate stature to risk the adversities that overtook Al Smith, at least so far as popular legend reports.

My wife kept reminding me forcefully of the claims of Adlai Stevenson. He had run two honorable campaigns and everything I knew about him suggested that he had grown in the interval since 1956. Having twice sacrificed himself at the altar of the unconquerable legend of General Eisenhower, he merited a third chance against a less popular opponent. My instinctive sense of poetic justice also told me that it was proper that Stevenson should defeat Nixon, since the latter had abused him so badly in the previous campaigns. I recalled particularly how Nixon had ridiculed Stevenson's 1956 suggestion that nuclear tests be halted, even charging him in terms that questioned Stevenson's sanity if not his loyalty. Brains, character, insight, aptitude for the job and the capacity to perform brilliantly Stevenson had. I was not even worried about the William Jennings Bryan third-try jinx. Furthermore, I felt certain that if he won the nomination he would do so without splitting his party wide apart, which had to be a major consideration. Most of all, it seemed to me that my wife was right in one important particular: our peculiar age seemed to call specifically for Stevenson. We needed a President with brains, a man who could provide the nation and the world with the kind of leadership it merited. In fact, there was only one weakness in the candidacy of Adlai Stevenson, but that seemed to me to be absolutely fatal. He could win the respect of the world, the love of his followers, and the nomination. But I was sure he could not win the popular votes that would elect him President. I foresaw that if he was nominated the newspaper editorialists and cartoonists would massacre him. Radio commentators and television pundits would treat him with contempt. And what the big journals of opinion would do to destroy him I could only guess. His campaign would be a debacle, and he would be driven from one extremity to another. His defeat would be predictable by mid-October, and the wolves would never leave his jugular. Furthermore, Richard Nixon, having twice been on a team that had thrashed him soundly, would profit from the aura of victory that would be about his temples from the first day of the campaign until a Republican victory became a reality on November 8.

After reaching this gloomy conclusion, I went back to see if there was any substantial reason why I was wrong in my calculation. Could Adlai Stevenson be elected in 1960? On one side of a sheet of paper on which I should have been writing a novel I listed all the people who my wife argued would vote for him: the intellectuals; businessmen who knew the interest rate was too high; confirmed Democrats; people who sensed that America had been marking time; labor; young people; and all others who might conceivably qualify. In the opposite column I listed those who would probably not vote for him: Catholics, who had shown a marked disinclination to do so in 1952 and 1956; Negroes, who had drifted toward General Eisenhower; women who objected to his divorce; people who were insecure and who instinctively followed what the newspapers and radios told them; all Republicans; and no less than eighty percent of those numerous Democrats who had already voted against him in 1952 and 1956. Furthermore, I concluded that most professional big-city Democratic leaders would be cool to his candidacy, and whereas they might be forced to acquiesce in his nomination, I doubted that they would vigorously support his actual candidacy. In late November of 1959 I decided that Adlai Stevenson could not be elected President, but when I told my wife of my conclusions she refused to believe them and continued to work for her candidate right up to the last minute.

Mennen Williams, the brilliant and likable governor of Michigan, was vulnerable, I thought, because of the administrative troubles he was having in his home state and because he was not well enough known across the country. It seemed to me that any of the other candidates would make a much better showing than he. Furthermore, I had the feeling that Richard Nixon would more or less cut Williams to shreds in public debate, for I knew Nixon's formidable reputation as a debater and I was sure he would use his skill to good purpose in the rough and tumble of an intense campaign.

Stuart Symington perplexed me. Like many other Americans I knew him principally as a participant in the Army-McCarthy hearings, where his performance was hardly sparkling and where he seemed to be a most timorous lion if, indeed, he had any teeth at all. Certainly, what I had seen on television gave me no reassurance about his candidacy. On the other hand, I had done a good deal of work with military people, and they spoke most highly of him, even when they disagreed with his position and he with theirs. I also knew that his published remarks on our military posture made a good deal of sense, and that his general conduct as a senator was far above average. Listening to the comments of others, I found that he made a good impression on people who did not otherwise know much about his career. Women liked him. And I was forced to give him real attention when I heard an old couple affirm, "That man Symington looks like a President should." The last President we had who "looked the way one should" was Warren Gamaliel Harding, and I often reflected painfully, "If the scandals had not overtaken him when they did, he could have been re-elected with ease in 1924 and maybe even in 1928." I always closed such mournful thoughts with this happy conclusion: "Well, then we'd have escaped Coolidge." But in the American democracy it is not inconsequential for a man to look like what he is running for, and if this was true before the days of television, think how much more true it is now. Therefore, at no time did I rule out Stuart Symington as a possibility, even though I would never have chosen him of and by myself. And when my favorite old warhorse Harry Truman came out for him, I gave the Missouri senator very careful reconsideration. I concluded early that he would not be a good candidate for the Presidency itself but that he might make a creditable candidate for the Vice Presidency.

Hubert Humphrey was my wife's second choice for the top position, and during all my reflections I had a fairly constant espousal of his cause at meals. I liked his brilliance. I approved of his voting record. He talked sense and had a certain vitality which I found impressive. My fear was that he would not be able to convince a majority of the general public that he was either qualified or prepared for the job. Early in my considerations I ruled him out for the Presidential nomination and failed to see where he would fit into the Vice Presidential part of the ticket except in the possibility of the Presidential spot's going to Lyndon Johnson. There would be much to be said for a Johnson-Humphrey ticket, and I never counted it out.

As for Lyndon Johnson, the best Democrats I knew in Hawaii were for him, and with me that carried a good deal of weight. Those who knew him said that he owned a powerful brain and knew how to use it. In the early part of 1959 I had met upwards of twenty leading figures from Congress, about one third from the Senate, and judging from what they had told me, if Presidents were elected by Congress, Lyndon Johnson would pretty surely be the next incumbent. In view of what subsequently happened, it would probably be prudent of me not to list the congressmen by name, but their testimony impressed me, and I was four times invited to join one committee or another that was attempting to further his candidacy. I refrained for several reasons. First, I felt that Johnson alone would not be able to enlist labor's whole-hearted support and without such support I did not see how any Democrat could win. Second, I felt that any platform on which Johnson could successfully run would be so watered down in social content that I for one would not care to support it. Third, and this loomed most important to me in late 1959, I suspected that he could not get the nomination without engaging in an intra-mural fight that would paralyze the party for the ensuing Presidential campaign, and this would insure the loss of big cities like Philadelphia and New York, which would inevitably mean the loss of their states and thus the loss of the election. Fourth, I remembered that Johnson had originally won his Senate seat by a mere 87 votes out of a total of nearly one million and I saw little evidence that he would be a good vote-getter across the nation. Opposed to these doubts were rumors that the professional Democratic politicians like Jake Arvey of Illinois and David Lawrence of Pennsylvania were impressed with Johnson and had agreed to back him as a compromise candidate. I suspected therefore that he might be the Presidential nominee, with John Kennedy as his Vice President, and this ticket I would be willing to support with all my energy.

I have left discussion of John Kennedy till last because that's what I did in November of 1959. On the boat trip home I had decided that I could support a Catholic for the Presidency, but that did not mean that I was willing to throw away my party's chances if nominating a Catholic meant that he would recapitulate the misery of the Al Smith campaign of 1928. In fact, the first political speech I ever made was to the assembly of Swarthmore College in the fall of 1928 when, as a junior, I blasted hell out of the complacency of a Quaker college which could profit from the religious freedom under which Quakerism flourished—for few remember that one of the sects which suffered most in colonial days at the hands of bigots was the Quakers, who were beaten and banished and persecuted by devout Protestants—and at the same time vote overwhelmingly against Al Smith because he was a Catholic. As I recall, it was a pretty impassioned speech, dampened somewhat by a senior political-science major who whispered when I sat down, "Stupid, we're not voting against Al Smith because he's a Catholic. We're voting for Herbert Hoover because he's a Quaker." I'm afraid I didn't quite catch his logic, and I remain to this day a little confused. But I did not want John Kennedy to repeat in 1960 the fiasco of 1928. In fact, I didn't yet know who my candidate was to be.

Perplexed by this impasse, I went to a dinner party given by my publisher Bennett Cerf and his partners, and I sat at a table with three gentlemen famous in American letters. In view of what I am about to say, I think it better if I refrain from disclosing two of their names, although they are free to do so if they wish. However, I must state that neither Bennett Cerf nor his partners were present at this particular table when the conversation opened with a discussion of the propriety of electing a Catholic President. The three distinguished gentlemen who shared the table were, and are, noted as American liberals, and I was surprised to find that two of them had the most serious and deep-rooted fears of a Catholic in the Presidency.

Dignitary One said firmly: "I make my living writing books, and I have found that whenever in the United States repressive action is taken against literary works, it's always the Catholic Church that spearheads the censorship. It's against everything I stand for. It's dictatorial, savage in its enmities, all-consuming in its desires, and reactionary in its intentions. I speak from first-hand knowledge of a church that is positively brutal in its lust for power, and it seems to me that to put a member of that church into our highest political office is indeed unwise."

Dignitary Two said more hesitantly: "I've traveled in Spain and Ireland. Have you ever been in Spain on Good Friday? For four days everything shuts down tight. No movies, no music, no games, nothing. The Spanish people don't want this, but the Church does. And on Friday night as dusk falls, the rulers of the city, all the appointed and elected officials, line up, take off their shoes, climb into penitential garb, tie ropes about their necks to which are attached crosses, and parade barefoot through the city dragging these crosses behind them. Why? Because they're holy men? No, they don't give a damn for holiness. They drag those crosses to show the citizenry that they're subservient to the Church. I don't want any church that rules Spain as this one does, no church that has ruined Ireland the way this one has, to get a foothold in the United States. To prevent such a thing I think I would lay down my life."

The gentlemen then asked what my experiences had been with the Church and I replied, "I've recently decided that I could support a Catholic for President, but I must admit that I have persistent doubts about the political influence of the Church. For example, when I was textbook editor for one of the big publishing firms we were visited one day by a priest who showed us credentials entitling him to speak for the hierarchy of the Church in New York City, and he warned us bluntly that unless we stopped using the word *jesuitical* as a pejorative adjective in our books, he would personally see to it that no further book from our company would ever be used in any Catholic college or school."

Dignitary One asked, "Did you use the word *jesuitical* in books that you were trying to sell to Catholic colleges? That doesn't seem intelligent."

"You misunderstand me," I replied. "The word was never used in textbooks because we knew it was pejorative. Another branch of our company had used the word in a book intended for the general public."

"And the Church was threatening you on such a tenuous relationship?"

"Yes. Their pressure was constant and powerful," I replied. "The priest insisted that we drop the word in all future editions of the book he was complaining about."

"Did he specifically say that if you didn't edit it out he would institute the boycott?" the eminent writer pressed.

"Yes."

"Did you cut the word?"

"No," I replied. "As a matter of publishing honor we couldn't."

"Was the boycott enforced?" my interrogator asked.

"I think not, but in all prudence we stopped using the adjective in subsequent books."

The discussion continued for some minutes, and then the fourth man at our table spoke up, and his name I am willing to report: He was Clifton Fadiman, the brilliant essayist and wit, and he said calmly, "Gentlemen, you are talking like idiots. One of these days we shall have a Catholic President and he will probably be a very good man. For every Catholic Spain that you cite, I can cite a Catholic France, where the clergy never successfully interferes. For every repressive Ireland I can cite a Belgium, where the Church's political influence is benevolent. Our Constitution has specific safeguards to protect us from what you fear, and the spirit of our unwritten laws is all in favor of us in any showdown such as you speak of. You," he asked Dignitary One, "were you against the appointment of Frank Murphy to the Supreme Court?"

"Of course not," the distinguished writer said. "I am fearful only of the ascendancy of a Catholic to the highest administrative office. I've seen what they can do as administrators."

"Were you against Al Smith as governor of New York?" Fadiman pursued.

"Of course not," the writer replied. "He was a notable governor. I voted for him."

"You're markedly inconsistent," Fadiman said. "If you truly fear Catholics as much as you claim, you should initiate impeachment proceedings against every Catholic who holds a governmental position." In a quiet, impassioned summary Fadiman then gave as good a defense of religious liberty as I had ever heard, and I sat quiet, marking his thoughts.

But when he finished, a distinguished woman who sat at our table said, "Mr. Fadiman, you make an impassioned plea for the Church that would not recognize a single postulate of your reasoning. I am a Catholic, and a reasonably faithful practicing one, and I assure you from the bottom of my being that no Catholic should ever be President of the United States. The whole tenet of my Church's belief is against democracy, and the exercise of intelligent will, and the freedom of the individual. It's one thing to have a Catholic serve as governor of a subsidiary state, but it's quite a different matter to have the same Catholic serve as supreme magistrate of the land. I do not speak as a theorist. I speak as a Catholic, and I pray God I shall never see one President of this nation."

This burst of reasonable oratory might have stunned some debaters, but Fadiman turned to the lady and in his impressive, quiet manner replied, "This is not a matter of one voter, or one country. It's a matter of an entire world in which we are trying to find centers of reason and stability. All that you say about the Catholic Church in a given situation, or about individual Catholics in their isolated situations, may be true. But the fact remains that we are endeavoring desperately to save a world, and it cannot be saved unless we utilize all the talents of all the people. I am in no way an apologist for the Catholic Church, and I am perfectly happy enjoying the freedoms that I enjoy through not being a member of that church, but I am totally unwilling to proscribe an entire body of people from high office merely because of their religion, which history has proved is a reasonably good religion that yields reasonably good results."

"Fadiman, you're a fool!" the first writer snapped. "We're not talking about high office, as you say. We're talking about the highest office, and all the prerogatives for sentimental indoctrination that it commands. I don't want a Catholic occupying that office and insidiously using it to propagate his faith, whether he does so consciously or unconsciously."

Patiently Fadiman replied, "The office of the Presidency could be corrupted by a Catholic only if the entire body of our nation were disposed to let that happen. And we are not. I would protest. So would Michener. So would you. And so would this good Catholic here."

"But," cried the Catholic woman, "the Irish priests who rule us, they would not protest. They would use the Catholic President as if he were their toy, and in time they would have the power and not he."

"No," Mr. Fadiman argued, "the safeguards of our nation would not permit this."

"Damn it all, Fadiman," the second writer interrupted. "What we're talking about is this. The other night a boy in my play was in New Haven and he wanted to buy a contraceptive. And he couldn't. And do you know why he couldn't? Because the Catholic Church said he couldn't."

"No," Fadiman reasoned quietly. "That law was passed by a Protestant legislature."

"The hell it was!" the writer growled. "It was passed because the priests of the Catholic Church damned well dictated to the legislature—Protestant or not they never care—what bills they had to pass, and the legislature passed them.

And that's what we're fighting about. No more power to the priests."

"No," Fadiman corrected, "that's not what we're fighting about. We're fighting for a rational nation that uses all its talents, all its built-in safeguards, and all its historical purposes in a time of world crisis."

"Why are you defending the Church so industriously?" one of the writers asked.

"As an act of faith," Fadiman said. "I fear Spain as much as you do, but you don't fight Spain by being even more stupid than Spain is."

At this point Bennett Cerf, smiling at some outrageous story told at another table by Russel Crouse, approached to lead us into another room, and the infectious relaxation of his manner reminded us of the fact that at our table we had perhaps been taking ourselves too seriously. Even so, as we broke up, one of the writers growled, "Fadiman, you haven't convinced me," and three others said the same. I did not join the comment, for he had convinced me.

That night I drove home and in my small room reviewed the situation: "I've fought to defend every civil right that has come under attack in my lifetime. I testified on behalf of each of my friends hauled before the McCarthy Committee. I've tried to write as if all men were my brothers. In Hawaii I've stood for absolute equality, and it would be ridiculous for a man like me to be against a Catholic for President."

I then took out a sheet of paper and wrote down every reason I could think of for not nominating John Kennedy for the Presidency. He was young. There were ugly rumors afloat about his father. I had been told that Jews wouldn't vote for him. He had no administrative experience. He had been pathetically weak on McCarthy. And one of the television shows had claimed he hadn't written the book for which they gave him the Pulitzer Prize. I listed a few other disqualifications that I can't remember now, but which I was sure the Republicans would dig up during an election. Then I added the crusher: "He's a Catholic."

But at this point I thought of the first time I had met the handsome young man from Massachusetts. It had been in the South Pacific, and when the memory of that meeting came back to me I wrote in the other column, "But he's also a hell of a man, and he'd make a good President."

That night I decided to work to the fullest extent of my ability to see that John Kennedy was nominated for the Presidency and elected to it. The first thing I did was to write a brief note to Clifton Fadiman thanking him for his patient reasoning at the Random House party. Next I wrote to Senator Kennedy, volunteering whatever help I might muster. This was well before he had engaged in any primaries.

My reasons for settling upon Kennedy as my choice for the nomination were clear, and once reached were never reconsidered. True, in the twelve months that were to elapse before his election to the Presidency there would be times when I thought he might lose. But there was never a time when I did not want him to win. These were my reasons. First, I considered him a very able man with a brilliant mind, substantial courage, an enormous sense of history, and an attractive personality, cold perhaps but reassuring. Second, I was convinced he would make a much better than average President. Third, I was equally convinced that he would be a great politician, and according to my definition of the Presidency, a politician is needed to hold his party, his legislative program, and his country together. I am very fond of good politicians, for they accomplish more than most of us. Fourth, I was convinced that Kennedy would make a strong attempt to win back the labor, Negro, suburban and Jewish votes that had left the Democratic party to support General Eisenhower. Fifth, I was sure that Kennedy, from having written two good books, knew what the intellectual life was, and I suspected that he would support America's efforts in the arts. Sixth, I knew that violent anti-Catholics would vote against him, but I also supposed that many violent Catholics would vote for him, and that the fringe bigots would thus offset each other. In letters that I wrote at the time I tried to convince my doubting friends that it was safe for the Democratic party to nominate a Catholic "because I am reasonably certain that the bigot votes we lose in the rabid country we will pick right back up in the crackpot city. We will lose Mississippi with its 8 votes, and win New York with its 45, and I call that a good exchange." What I failed to anticipate was the violence of the anti-Catholic resentment not in the rabid southern areas but in the solid central body of our nation. Had I foreseen the anti-Catholic campaign that was to be launched

y otherwise reasonable people and to be supported by
others even more sensible, I might have wavered in my decision. As it was, I went through the primaries, the nominating convention and up to the campaign itself before I
realized what my party was up against. As in so many other
instances, in this case ignorance was bliss. There was also a
final point which impressed me very much when I considered John Kennedy's candidacy: I was convinced he could
win. I thought that he could take the primaries without
disrupting the party. I felt sure he could win the nomination
and hold the bulk of the candidates with him. And I was
very sure that in a general election he could defeat Richard
Nixon. On the night that I wrote to Senator Kennedy volunteering my services I went to bed happy.

And yet the very next night the wisdom of my choice
was challenged. By pure chance a neighbor who loved political discussion invited my wife and me to his home, where
four other couples were present. That meant that there were
twelve of us in the room, and when my wife announced
with some asperity that I was not going to support Adlai
Stevenson the entire room groaned, for the other ten were
strong Stevenson people and in a sense the meeting had been
called to see what could be done to further his candidacy.

"Who you going to support?" one of the men asked.

"Senator Kennedy," I said.

A furious consternation erupted, and except for my wife
each of these ten good Democrats, who in the past had
proved their loyalty by working openly for the party in a
county where Democrats have never been popular, swore,
"If the Democrats nominate a Catholic for President, I'll vote
for Nixon."

Through five or six hours of heated discussion in which
I asked all the questions I was to ask so often in the future
months, each of these ten good liberals hardened his determination and warned me that he spoke not only for
himself but for dozens of couples like those present at our
informal meeting.

I need not repeat the arguments. One of the couples was
Protestant and had traveled in Spain. Two were Jewish and
dreaded the prospect of a repressive Catholic domination.
One wife was a Catholic and hated priests who meddled in
political matters. All were of the opinion that 1960 was
going to be a year in which any likely Democratic candidate

for the Presidency could lick Nixon, "unless the party is stupid enough to put up John Kennedy." As we left, all reiterated their determination to vote for Nixon if that latter dreadful contingency occurred.

On the long drive home I was an abashed political theorist. I had been quite unprepared for the vehemence of these ten people and I wondered if they did indeed speak for many like themselves. I remember going silently to my room and taking out a sheet of clean paper. On it I made a diagram which made me feel much better:

Stevenson Kennedy Undecided Nixon Goldwater

I called my wife and explained my happy discovery. "On the extreme right you have the Barry Goldwater conservatives. They may not like Nixon, but they have no place else to go. On the extreme left you have the Stevensonian liberals. They may not like Kennedy, but if he's nominated they won't have anywhere else to go."

"You think those people were fooling tonight?" she asked.

"No, they weren't fooling. They'll be against Kennedy on New Year's Day. They'll be rabidly against him in the primaries. They'll shout against him at the convention. In August, September and October, they'll be strongly against him, and on November 8 do you know what they'll do?"

"Vote for Kennedy?" my wife asked.

"Right. We mustn't upset them by arguing against their positions now," I cautioned, and thereafter I did everything I could to conciliate the Stevenson people; I knew that no matter what they said, they had no place else to go. They might stay home from the election, but they would never vote for Nixon, no matter how strongly they threatened to do so, because for them to vote for Nixon would require that they jump from one side of the spectrum clear to the other and this men refuse to do, for it seems like a rupture of common sense.

I pointed to the Undecided and said, "These are the Republicans and Democrats who voted for General Eisenhower last time but who don't like Nixon. For them to slide into the Kennedy camp involves no rupture of common sense at all. So all the disaffected Democrats will have to vote for Kennedy, whereas at least half the disaffected Republicans can very easily vote for Kennedy." I pointed to the Undecided again and predicted, "That's where we'll win the election."

My wife argued, "Your diagram doesn't take into account the anti-Catholic vote."

I replied airily, "I explained all that before. The screwballs on one extreme cancel out those on the other."

"Don't you wish it was as simple as that?" she asked on her way to bed.

I refused to dignify her doubt with an answer, but as I looked at my diagram I was assailed by an ugly fear and had my first premonition that John Kennedy might not win this election after all. Suppose that the Republican party had sense enough not to nominate Richard Nixon, who might not win, but Nelson Rockefeller, who most certainly could. What would be the situation then? With some apprehension I altered my diagram and studied its fateful signals:

Stevenson Kennedy Undecided Rockefeller Goldwater

How different the strategy was now. The extreme right would have no place to go, so they'd have to vote for Rockefeller. But what was important was that the Undecided could now slide into the Rockefeller camp with no embarrassment. And I was convinced that a large proportion of Stevensonians could leapfrog over Kennedy and join Rockefeller without insulting their common sense. "With all that support," I said glumly, "Rocky can win!"

Very soberly I went to bed and told my wife, "I've just figured out that if Rockefeller runs against Kennedy, the Republicans will win. If I can see this, I'm sure the Republican bosses can see it, too. So they'll nominate him. How do you think he'll do?"

"I'd vote for him," my wife said without hesitation, and I realized with dismay that so would each of the other ten Stevensonians who had been arguing with me that night.

2

Marking Time

☒ ☒

During the primaries my personal work took me to Mexico, where I had the good luck to form an acquaintanceship with our ambassador, Robert C. Hill, a new type of State Department man with a most aggressive determination to see, to know and to appreciate all of his command. We spent a week together flying in a small plane to the most remote airfields, where Mexicans awaited us with mariachi bands, festivals and dinners. Ambassador Hill was an eye-opener, both to me and to the Mexicans, and he apparently accomplished a good deal for the United States, for wherever we went the crowds immediately recognized him, and favorably. They also asked him embarrassing questions, which he tried to answer in stride, insofar as his orders from Washington would permit.

Apart from getting to know Mr. Hill, the most enjoyable part of the trip came when we were aloft, with only ourselves to worry about and with the forthcoming Presidential election to discuss. Ambassador Hill, naturally, was a Republican. In private life he had been a successful businessman and had been hand-picked by the administration, rather than by the State Department, for the critical Mexico job. He loved politics and was friendly to both Richard Nixon, whom he expected to see in the White House, and to Lyndon Johnson, who was a political hero of his. Robert Hill was never afraid to say what he thought, and we had some vigorous debates.

His entourage on this particular trip was also mainly Republican, which was proper, since he served under a Republican administration, but he did have along with him a hilarious press officer from the Midwest, and this delightful man was an ardent supporter of Hubert Humphrey. I was the other Democrat aboard and the first John Kennedy man that any of the group had met in person. I remember the astonishment that greeted my announcement that Kennedy was going to be our next President.

"He really believes it!" the ambassador's group joked.

We were en route to one of the bleakest areas of Mexico, Santa Margarita Island, off the western coast of Baja California Sur, when the reports of the Wisconsin primary were due. I insisted that Kennedy would defeat Humphrey roundly, and remember taking some bets to that effect. The general consensus was that he would merely squeak through, and I fear that no one in the plane except me thought that whether he won or not he had much chance of either the nomination in July or victory in November.

We had flown on to La Paz, the capital of the great arid state of Baja California Sur, when the radio announced the Wisconsin results. I remember being somewhat stunned, for although Kennedy had won, his margin of victory was much less than I had been predicting. Wisconsin seemed to be a setback, even though Kennedy had contested a primary in another man's backyard. Ambassador Hill and his team had a good deal of fun at my expense, and as on the night I had drawn the diagram showing that Rockefeller could win, I began to wonder if Kennedy had the invincibility that I had accorded him. Then came West Virginia.

I will always think of that West Virginia primary with special affection, for not only did it seal my candidate's chances for the nomination, not only did it exorcise the ghost of Al Smith and the anti-Catholicism he suffered, but it also came when I was far from home and engaged in some of the best political debate I have known. I was in Guatemala with a group of American military personnel who loved politics and who were extraordinarily adept in piecing together data and making deductions therefrom.

Day after day we gathered to discuss the impending conventions, and at each meeting one or another of us would have some special information gleaned in some special way. Adlai Stevenson had lately been through the area and he had said thus. Lyndon Johnson had been visiting Ambassador Hill and he had reported so. Ambassadors from other countries had been of this opinion. An admiral who had flown in from Washington had spent some hours with Nixon, and he offered new data. I doubt if there could have been many places, in those exciting weeks, where the political fortunes of the United States were more vividly and intimately discussed than in Guatemala.

And all we heard or knew confirmed our belief that the West Virginia primary was going to be the critical test. Those who knew the South were convinced that West Virginia's natural anti-Catholic animus would defeat Kennedy. Those who knew Hubert Humphrey were satisfied that he had picked for his maximum effort the one state which was most likely to yield him victory. Finally a group of us gathered one night in Guatemala City to argue politics only, in an orderly way and with each man citing his sources, for a period of about four hours.

The conservative and Republican side was defended by a brilliant naval captain, Jacob Heimark. The shrewd middle-of-the-road position was expressed by the cleverest man of the group, the naval aviator and certificated lawyer, John Meisenheimer. The liberal position was defended by me, while two or three army officers stood by to subject anything said to rigorous analysis. In the exciting months that were to follow I often found myself wishing that I could reconvene that brilliant group of men, who though far from America were yet so conversant with American problems.

As the evening wore on, circumstances required each man to put up or shut up, for clarity demanded that each say exactly what he thought was going to happen. I shall not report what voting preferences Captain Heimark and Lieutenant Meisenheimer expressed, for our meeting did have a kind of confidential nature about it, since we were being brutally frank in our expressions, but I can recall my own avowed position on the eve of the West Virginia primary.

Even though our meeting was held during the days when American newspapers were reporting the likelihood of a 60-40 vote in favor of Humphrey, I argued that Kennedy would win the West Virginia primary by not less than 54 percent of the total vote. My contention was so surprising that two members of the group forced me to bet money on my belief, and after I had done so they asked, "How can you possibly believe that Kennedy will win?"

I remember stopping and trying to reconstruct the reasons why I was so sure that the Massachusetts senator would win, and I recall saying, "I think so because to think any other way would be to admit defeat. And Jack Kennedy is not going to lose either the nomination or the election."

"You call that logical thinking?" Captain Heimark pressed.

"I'm not even sure it should be called thinking, logical or not," I replied. Then gradually the basis for my irrational position became clear to me and I said, "What I mean is this. I'm perfectly willing to agree that the people of West Virginia are bigoted, but I've worked in that state and I know they are not damned fools. In this primary they have no real option. It's Kennedy against Mister Nobody, and Kennedy has got to win because the people of West Virginia will not throw away their votes on a man like Senator Humphrey, who has no real chance."

"But if Kennedy were running against Lyndon Johnson in this primary, who would win?" Captain Heimark probed.

For the first time in the primaries I said something that was slowly penetrating my consciousness: "Captain, if either Lyndon Johnson or Adlai Stevenson were contesting the West Virginia primary, they would probably win, and Jack Kennedy would have no chance for the 1960 nomination. But neither of these men had the guts to contest it, so Kennedy's going to win, and he'll go on to win the nomination, too."

Captain Heimark asked, "And you really think your man will win by 54 percent of the votes cast tomorrow?"

"I suspect he'll win by much more," I said. "But I'm positive he'll win by at least 54 percent." When the votes were counted he had won by 60 percent, and any substantial chance of stopping him in Los Angeles had vanished, although as you will see shortly, I didn't recognize this latter fact at the time.

My next two guesses that night in Guatemala were not so good. As to the Republican nomination, I was forced by the debaters into betting that Nelson Rockefeller would be the choice. When pressed for my reasons I said, "It's perfectly obvious to me that President Eisenhower doesn't want Richard Nixon. You know that, so I must suspect that the general electorate knows it, too. I know that the professionals in the party turned Rockefeller down last Christmas, and I know they don't want him now. But they're not going to commit suicide and turn down a sure winner. Watch! At Chicago they'll swallow their pride and nominate Rocky."

Lieutenant Meisenheimer would have none of this. He argued, "I think it was Boise Penrose of Pennsylvania who said, 'If a real politician ever faces a choice between losing control of his party or losing a specific election, he never hesitates a moment. He'll throw away the election and keep the party.' The professionals will never accept Rockefeller, because he smells too much like Wendell Willkie. I've known some real Republicans who truly hated Roosevelt, but they hated Willkie a lot more, because all Roosevelt did was win elections, whereas Willkie won control of the party."

I countered by pointing out that friends had told me the same thing about the professionals in 1952: "They'll never turn down Taft and take Eisenhower." I pointed out that in the end they had been forced to do just that.

Lieutenant Meisenheimer replied, "But General Eisenhower was in every respect a special case. Besides, Taft couldn't have won. Nixon can."

My third prediction was that if Rockefeller did not win the nomination he would certainly accept the Vice Presidency. Again Lieutenant Meisenheimer challenged me with the single most incisive comment I was to hear during the nominating period. As I recall the course of his argument he reasoned, "We must assume that the differences between Nixon and Rockefeller are real. And these differences, being intellectual, constitute irreconcilable elements. Now either Rockefeller is an adventurer or he is not. If he is an adventurer, he'll accept the Vice Presidency, but I'm convinced he's not an adventurer, so as an honest man he will have to reject compromise. The reason I think he's an honest man is that the reports of the Rockefeller brothers practically constitute a platform for the Democratic party, and he is either going to have to rescind every one of those reports, or he is going to have to stand on them. He'll do the latter, I'm quite sure, and if he does that he cannot possibly at the same time accept second place on any team running on the Republican platform. So you can forget Rockefeller as Nixon's Vice President. He cannot possibly accept such a position, not because of vanity but because he is a logical and an honest man.

"Furthermore," Lieutenant Meisenheimer continued, "if Nixon wins in November he'll certainly run again in 1964 and will probably win then, too. In this century the only incumbents to lose at the end of one term were Taft, because Teddy Roosevelt led a splinter party, and Hoover, who got caught in a depression. In 1968 Vice President Rockefeller would be too old to run. Moreover, if he were the Vice President to Richard Nixon's President, he'd find the job unrewarding and stifling, because Nixon's view of the Presidency would surely be much different from Eisenhower's. I doubt that Nixon would permit his Vice President to wind up in 1968 as the inevitable choice for the nomination.

"And finally," Meisenheimer argued, "Rockefeller would not have issued those reports unless he was pretty sure that Nixon would lose in 1960. He knows that Nixon is doomed. His logical game is to sit aside, watch the debacle, and offer himself to the party in 1964."

When Lieutenant Meisenheimer was making these remarks I did not recognize their pertinence, for I responded, "You overlook one thing, John. Nixon running with Rockefeller might possibly win the election. Nixon without will surely lose. Now if the old professionals know that their side lost simply because Rockefeller refused to lend a hand, he will be forever dead in the Republican party. You claim that if he sits to one side and watches Nixon lose, he can then offer himself as an alternative in 1964. If he contributes to the loss of this election every professional will work to destroy him in 1964."

Lieutenant Meisenheimer replied, "Smart politicians take each year as it comes. If Kennedy wins in November, by 1964 the Republicans may be very happy to have Rockefeller on hand, no matter what they thought of him in 1960."

My fourth prediction was one of the few bits of real insight I had during the campaign, and once I stated it, I never reconsidered: "I don't know who is going to be the Democratic nominee. Obviously, when Kennedy wins tomorrow in West Virginia he'll be in front position. But you fellows claim the old professionals in the Democratic party won't have him. If you're right, they won't have Stevenson either, and they know they can't win with Symington. So I suppose it'll have to be Johnson and Kennedy. And I think they'll win."

Captain Heimark asked, "You think that Jack Kennedy will accept second spot on the ticket?"

"Any one of the four leading contenders will accept either first spot or second."

Lieutenant Meisenheimer probed, "You think Johnson would accept second spot to Kennedy?"

"Sure," I said, "and I hope that's the way it works out. Because that ticket might prove to be the very best."

Captain Heimark was not entirely satisfied. "You think that Adlai Stevenson would run in second place with Kennedy?"

"If asked," I said. "Or Kennedy will run in second spot to Stevenson. The difference between my Democrats and your Republicans is that your two top men can't get together to win an election, whereas our four top men will submit themselves to any possible combination in order for the party to win."

Somebody asked slowly, "Let me get this straight. You are saying that in your opinion Lyndon Johnson would accept the Vice Presidency in second place to Jack Kennedy?"

"Certainly," I replied.

Then Lieutenant Meisenheimer asked bluntly, "But tonight, what do you think the ticket will be?"

I thought for some time and said, "I suspect it's going to be Johnson in first spot and Kennedy in second, but I sure hope it works out the other way."

Guatemala illuminated two other aspects of the campaign. Adlai Stevenson had recently passed through Mexico and Latin America, and I was surprised at the manner in which Republicans who might have been disposed to scorn him said, "Stevenson accomplished wonders for the United States down here. No American in recent years has done as much. It's one thing to see Adlai at home, where the press is always hammering him. But it's quite different to see him overseas, where he's about the only American the foreign nations really respect." Listening to many such comments, I began to suspect that Stevenson might have a better chance for the Presidency than I had originally thought, but if he did not win, I hoped that the victorious Democrat, whoever he might be, would find a major place for him in his official family. My wife, of course, exulted, "See! I told you, Adlai's the only candidate of any stature." I replied, somewhat churlishly I'm afraid, "If he could win, I'd be for him."

The second discovery was in some ways more amusing, in others, more ominous. An American wife, normally a loyal Democrat, chuckled, "I hope Rockefeller wins, and I'll tell you why. I want to see the startled look on America's face when he decorates the White House with his personal art collection. Picasso, Jackson Pollock, Feininger and Jack Levine! It's about time we had some art in our life, after the dreadful drabness of the last eight years."

I asked, "Would you, a good Democrat, vote for Rocky against Lyndon Johnson or Jack Kennedy?"

"I sure would," she snapped. "Rocky knows his way around. He's modern. He talks my language, and we've got to get some vitality in the White House. Can't you just imagine Rocky's first musicale? Not Guy Lombardo, not Meyer Davis, not Lawrence Welk, but the Schola Cantorum singing Carl Orff. That I want to see."

I returned to Pennsylvania to find the U-2 incident splashed across the papers, and from the first I took a much more grave attitude toward this than did some of my friends, who found considerable consolation in *Time* magazine, which pointed out that after all the incident merely demonstrated our ability to penetrate Russia.

I had known something of the problems of espionage, and a fundamental understanding of all who occupied themselves with it was that if they were caught by the enemy, their own government would piously wash its hands of the whole affair. When the Eisenhower administration elected to pursue a course counter to historical precedent, I suspected that real trouble would follow, for one of the basic arrangements whereby nations are able to continue talking with one another had been breached. Along these same lines, I was appalled at the reported behavior of the aviator, Francis Powers, and it seemed to me as if a segment of our whole national posture had been willfully jeopardized. Both the government and the man behaved badly, and when Powers' trial eventuated, he proved the sickliness of the situation. As one general observed wryly, "He certainly was no Nathan Hale."

I was on the point of writing to the *New York Times*, advocating that the Paris summit meeting be canceled by us before something worse took place, but my friends dissuaded me from such a course, and I sat back waiting for the time bomb to explode. I remember taking consolation in the fact that at least one of the Republicans' major campaign issues was about to be blown sky-high. They could not, in October, claim that they had brought peace in our time, for now what many of us who worked abroad knew, would become apparent to all: that America was far from true peace and that her international posture had deteriorated badly in the last eight years.

The debacle came, not in the form I had imagined, but worse. With shame I read President Eisenhower's response to Khrushchev's breaking up the summit and found it one of the most tedious and ineffective statements ever made by an American President. Where were the bold challenges that Teddy Roosevelt would have thrown down, the clear logic of right that Woodrow Wilson would have expounded, the ringing call to international decency that Franklin Roosevelt would have uttered, or the pedestrian, honest reaction of Harry Truman? Our nation looked most inadequate that day, and when, a few days later, our President retreated from Paris to Portugal to garner the meaningless plaudits of a commandeered crowd I wondered what our values were.

I took consolation from the fact that although as a nation we had suffered a body blow, the citizens had witnessed what had happened and were in a position to assess the blame.

At this point the Democrats received help from another quarter. Months before, I had been apprehensive about President Eisenhower's intervention in the British elections. London newspapers had cynically termed him "Prime Minister Macmillan's campaign manager," and much of the Labour Party's subsequent hostility to the United States stemmed from this unwarranted intrusion by our President. The only reason why there were no riots in the streets of London was that Englishmen tend to be gentlemen.

But when President Eisenhower tried the same gambit in Japan, seeking again to shore up a conservative party, which sought revision of the Japanese constitution, the roof fell in. Japanese leftists, in their weird snake dances and virulent chants of hatred, proved that they were not bound by the restraints that govern British gentlemen. I am sure that the Japanese did not resent President Eisenhower's intervention any more deeply than had the British; they merely expressed that resentment in more violent ways. At the time I was widely questioned about the Japanese riots and replied consistently, "In the long run they mean very little. Merely that the Japanese won't tolerate outside meddling in their internal political life." When my interrogators expressed amazement at my lack of panic I added, "Watch. At the next election Japan will vote conservative, just as before." And it did.

On the other hand, from the short-range view, the Japanese rioters had struck another lethal blow at Republican campaign claims, for it would now be difficult for that party to argue that it had organized the world into groups that supported us. All too visibly, the world was falling apart if an American President was unable to visit the capital of our nation's principal bastion in the Far East. I remember thinking at the time, "Right now the general public doesn't seem to realize the setbacks we've suffered. But later the pictures they've seen on television will return to their minds, and when the Democrats refer to these matters, the voters will understand." I was convinced that the Republicans had suffered substantially from the events in Paris and Tokyo.

At the same time I had to admit that the Democrats had also absorbed two frightening body blows. When I heard the newscast that John Kennedy, while on tour somewhere in the West, had said something like, "President Eisenhower might have apologized to Khrushchev," I was shocked. The news report was fairly garbled and I remember praying that I had not heard it correctly. This was the kind of unhappy phrase that could plague a candidate right down to the wire. Later, when the clarification came through, I felt that whereas Kennedy had offered an explanation, it did not constitute a justification, and I dreaded the repetitions of that phrase that I was bound to hear through the autumn months.

Even more damaging, I felt, was the French newspaperman's report of his interview with Adlai Stevenson. I recall reading a very brief news story about this on an inside page in the Philadelphia *Inquirer*, and I stopped cold when I saw it, for if what the Frenchman reported had truly been said by Stevenson, it did indeed constitute giving aid and comfort to the enemy on the eve of an important international convention. Specifically, it undercut our nation's bargaining position. I refused to believe that Stevenson had made the remarks attributed to him, but I knew that the fat was in the fire. For the next several days I looked in vain for any follow-up on the story and felt considerable relief when it appeared to have been overlooked. But in politics I am a great believer in Murphy's Law, "If something bad can happen, it will." And before long the Republicans caught up with the damaging article and interrogated the French reporter, who defended the accuracy of the interview as printed; thus they had a vibrant fresh charge that Stevenson was soft on communism. At the time I felt reasonably sure that Mr. Stevenson did not say the things he was quoted as saying, but I also felt certain that he had further disqualified himself as the Democratic candidate. Republican orators would hound him to his political grave, chanting those words from Paris and conjuring up visions and images that would be as deadly as they were unfair.

Casting up the harm done both sides, Paris and Tokyo versus "the apology" and the French "interview," I felt that in superficial damage the four events were just about a stand-off. But when one considered the fundamental nature of the wounds, one found that half the Democratic losses involved only Stevenson, who was not going to be the candidate anyway, while the wound that Kennedy had suffered involved only vague words which could later be explained away. But the damage that the Republicans had suffered was visual. Most of the American electorate had seen on television the appalling events in Paris and the wild-eyed snake-dancers in Tokyo, and these wounds were not peripheral; they struck at the vital posture of the party. On the whole, I faced the nominating conventions with equanimity.

But on May 23 my complacency received a sharp shock. That evening I spoke in New York on the same program with Governor Nelson Rockefeller at a meeting to honor Shigeru Yoshida, the former prime minister of Japan, and it fell to me to speak first. I made a few undistinguished remarks and was followed immediately by the governor, who went out of his way seven times to comment on the brilliance and aptness of what I had said. I thought: "This man's really running for the Presidency. He doesn't know where I stand and he wants to be as congenial as possible." As he spoke, I smiled wanly back at him and fought down the sick feeling that had taken control of my stomach. I thought: "I was absolutely right in

Guatemala. This man's going to get the Republican nomination and he's going to win. Look at that audience!"

As Governor Rockefeller spoke, the large crowd poured out its adulation. When he ended, people surged about the table crying, "We want you for President." I followed him as he moved through the crowd and saw how hundreds of strangers rushed up merely to touch him and to cry, "You're our man, Rocky." There was something terribly electric in the air, the unknown substance from which votes are compounded. I heard him say over and over, "Thank you, fellow. Thank you, fellow." If I ever saw a man running for office, it was Nelson Rockefeller. Finally he gripped my hand and said, "Thank you, fellow. That was a great speech." I thought: "Damn him. He can defeat Kennedy and he knows it."

Later on I rejoined my wife, to find that while I was at the dais, she had been sitting with Emmett Hughes, one of my favorite politicians, the gray eminence of the Rockefeller team. I had first known him as an editor at *Life*, and he was one of the best. He had often worked on my material and I could always tell where he had added something because he had a penchant for alliteration and an uncontrollable fondness for the letter *p*. Often during the time that he wrote Eisenhower's speeches I would listen to the President read off something like "our powerful posture of preparedness," and I would say to myself, "That's my boy, Emmett." He was a tall, prematurely gray, extremely brilliant young man whose book *America, the Vincible* must have outraged the Republican administration, for it was a frontal attack on the Eisenhower foreign and defense policies. Now Hughes was supporting Rockefeller, and they made a formidable team.

That evening I asked Emmett some desultory questions and he replied in kind, and so well did he mask his feelings that I got the impression that he had given up on Rockefeller's chances for the Republican nomination. The very next afternoon the governor released his famous statement concerning the direction in which his party ought to move. It constituted a direct attack on current Republican policies and an oblique attack on Nixon. It was a persuasive document, and it tore the Republican party apart. We were told that when Eisenhower saw it he growled, "Emmett Hughes wrote this." When I read the strong alliterative passages I said the same thing, and we were both right. Then I read the vituperation from Republican headquarters and slowly realized that even though defeat seemed certain if the Republicans nominated Nixon, the professionals were determined to do so and to crush Rockefeller. I could not believe what I was witnessing.

"It looks as if Rocky won't make it," I told my wife.

"That's too bad for the nation," she said. "He'd be a fine President."

"It's good for Kennedy," I replied.

When the conventions were over my optimism waned somewhat. It seemed to me that the Democratic convention had been a rather shabby affair, with Stevenson refusing to run openly yet borrowing help from Mrs. Roosevelt; with Lyndon Johnson trying to cram into a few days the work that should have occupied him over several months; with the disgraceful bumbling of Robert Meyner; with the lackluster keynote speech of Frank Church, which at times grew ludicrous; and most of all with the inept acceptance speech of John Kennedy.

In contrast it seemed to me that the Republicans had got off to a rousing start. President Eisenhower's speech was one of the best I had ever heard him give; it frightened me with its visions of the old soldier stumping the nation in October; he was going to be very persuasive indeed, and I suspected that his old magic would be doubly appealing with its necessary overtones of a President Washington's farewell. Walter Judd's keynote speech, compared to Frank Church's, was a masterpiece, even though its policies dated back to the 1920's. Governor Rockefeller's graceful acceptance of the inevitable was beguiling and gave the picture, at least, of a united party. And I think no one could deny that the acceptance speech of Vice President Nixon was stirring, forceful, and well thought out. He created a most favorable impression on me —I vaguely sensed that he wasn't saying much, but suspected that the details would be filled in later—and when I read that Senator Kennedy had agreed to share the same platform with the Vice President in public debate I told my wife, "Kennedy's gonna be sorry he did that! This Nixon's a born debater. I'm afraid he'll cut our man to pieces." Judging merely from the two acceptance speeches, I had every right to be apprehensive.

My wife, now solidly in the Kennedy camp, argued, "I think Kennedy'll be able to take care of himself." Like all Stevensonians, she had supported her plumed warrior right down to the last six inches of the lists, and when he fell unseated, tears came into her eyes and she did not want to talk. But unlike many of them she then vigorously supported Senator Kennedy and was responsible for gaining him many votes, for she was a tireless and a persuasive campaigner.

My native village contains two women who ought to be copyrighted by George Gallup, because by questioning them he could save a lot of money. They invariably express the average view on everything. I have known them for many years—they were good neighbors of my mother's—and I have rarely known them to express a wrong opinion. If a new play opens in Philadelphia, they go to see it, and next morning the conversation goes something like this.

ME: I hear you went to the theater last night. How was it?
MISS OMWAKE: Interesting play.
ME: How will it do on Broadway?
MRS. DALE: It's bound to flop.
ME: Why? Poor script?
MISS OMWAKE: That leading lady.
ME: Can't she act?
MRS. DALE: She acts very well.
ME: She's not sympathetic?
MRS. DALE: In the second act she wears a purple dress. And what do you suppose she wears for a scarf?
MISS OMWAKE: A yellow scarf!
MRS. DALE: The play won't last a week in New York.

Invariably, the play flops. By some alchemy of mind, these two women isolate the irrelevant truths that illuminate the fundamental ones. They didn't like one automobile because the handles looked like egg cups, and that model was a dismal failure. They don't trust a man because his dog walks sideways, as if it was afraid of being kicked, and sooner or later the man embezzles $50,000. I have never been able to figure out how they know, but they know. They have mysterious pipelines to some deep reservoir of the American spirit, and they report with accuracy the taste of the times.

In 1956 they gave me an exhibition of their political insight when they recited a series of reasons why President Eisenhower was bound to be reëlected: "He never swears in the White House, the way President Truman did. His son was in uniform in Korea, not singing on a public stage the way some people we could name did when their father was in the White House. Besides he has as his Secretary of State a fine Christian gentleman like John Foster Dulles, a real religious man and not a crooked lawyer like Dean Acheson. Mrs. Eisenhower stays home the way she should instead of gallivanting around like Mrs. Roosevelt. And he goes to church on Sunday because you can see the photographs of him on Monday morning in the papers. And he went to Korea, just as he said he would. But most of all, James, if he has served us so faithfully after having suffered a heart attack, the least we can do is vote for him again." For these reasons they were sure he was going to be reëlected, and they even told me by what margin in the electoral college.

Although I had started out reasonably certain that John Kennedy was going to be our next President, the two conventions had shaken me a bit, so I consulted my oracles, and what they told me gave me a positive jolt.

MRS. DALE: Nixon is going to win because President Eisenhower personally selected him, and if he's good enough for the President, he ought to be good enough for the people.

MISS OMWAKE: Senator Kennedy can never win because his wife is not appealing to the average American housewife.

MRS. DALE: But Mrs. Nixon is. She looks like any American woman you would meet anywhere. Our nation would be proud to have a woman like Mrs. Nixon in the White House. She looks like a President's wife.

MISS OMWAKE: Mr. Nixon has been personally trained by the President. He has been responsible for most of the big decisions of the past four years.

MRS. DALE: And the way he stood up to that Khrushchev!

MISS OMWAKE: Wars always come in Democratic administrations, but the Republicans are men of peace.

MRS. DALE: And did you see how orderly everything was at the Republican convention and what a bunch of rabble the Democrats were?

MISS OMWAKE: President Eisenhower personally ended the war in Korea the way he said he would.

MRS. DALE: Mr. Nixon had to work for his money, like an

honest man should. It isn't right for a father who makes his money selling booze to give his sons a million each so that they can lord it over poor folks.

MISS OMWAKE: Mr. Nixon will protect the dollar. He knows the value of money.

MRS. DALE: The Republicans look more gentlemanly than the Democrats. Have you ever compared Ambassador Lodge with Senator Johnson. One is a polished gentleman. The other is a Texas bum.

MISS OMWAKE: President Eisenhower returned dignity to the White House, and Mr. Nixon is very dignified. Mr. Kennedy looks like a boy, and his wife with no hat is worse.

As I listened I became increasingly aware that I was hearing the fundamental issues upon which much of the electorate was going to base its decision and I became afraid. If Miss Omwake and Mrs. Dale spoke for America, and I was satisfied that they did, at least for large segments, this election was bound to be much closer than I had anticipated; and yet as they talked I felt that they were for the first time in many years not telling me all the truth. I charged them with this and finally they spoke of what really troubled them.

MRS. DALE: The truth of the matter is, James, I could never bring myself to vote for a Catholic.

MISS OMWAKE: Don't ask me why, It's a feeling I have.

MRS. DALE: I'll tell you why. I used to be a secretary in Philadelphia. For many years. And week after week we would see in the paper pictures of Denis Cardinal Dougherty. And Cardinal Dougherty was saying, "You can't go to this movie." And Cardinal Dougherty was saying, "All public schools are no good." And Cardinal Dougherty was shouting, "If you do that you'll be damned." James, I just got sick to my stomach of hearing Cardinal Dougherty telling me what to do. Your Senator Kennedy may be as fine a man as you say, but he's a Catholic and he's got to put up with Cardinal Dougherty the same way I had to.

MISS OMWAKE: I would be afraid to tell you how many people in this town feel the way we do.

MRS. DALE: All the Lutherans. Most of the Baptists. Many of the Presbyterians. They all remember Cardinal Dougherty and his arrogant ways.

ME: Then no matter what I say, no matter what Senator Kennedy says, no matter what proofs he gives you, you still won't vote for him because he's a Catholic?

MRS. DALE: That's right. In this world, if you fear something deeply enough, there's probably a reason. And I fear the shadow of Cardinal Dougherty over the White House.

ME: But he's dead.

MRS. DALE: His spirit goes on forever, telling Protestants what they can't do.

I returned home deeply perturbed, and the more I talked with my neighbors, the more determined they became never to vote for a Catholic. Some were German Lutherans, and their historic animosity toward the Catholic Church was understandable. But many were ordinary Protestants with no special animus toward any other religion, yet the specter of a cardinal dominating White House policy was to them positively terrifying. With many of my neighbors I could not even argue. If I spoke of religion they changed the subject, and as the campaign edged toward the starting gun I began to realize that in my early assumption that only the crackpots on the fringes would be affected by the religious issue, I was wrong. Religion was going to be a major issue. This meant that all my assumptions about the election had to be revised, so I retired to my small room and asked myself, "All wishful thinking aside, how does the campaign look now?"

I reasoned, "If the religious issue is as grave as it now seems, the Republicans have a good chance to win. They have an awful lot in their favor. There's peace of a kind. There's prosperity within limits. They're the incumbents, and that helps a lot. They have almost all the newspapers and magazines on their side, and they have a commanding military hero as their leader. If President Eisenhower decides to campaign with full vigor, he'll carry a lot of states, and he seems to be ready for the fight." Things didn't look too good, for in addition to all the above assets, the Republicans had put together an appealing ticket whose second man, Ambassador Lodge, was being heralded by all the newspapers as much stronger than our Lyndon Johnson. Sitting alone with the cold facts I reasoned further, "It looks to me as if they'll be able to hold the Negro votes that went for Eisenhower. The Jews certainly don't like Kennedy. And even Jimmy Hoffa's union is out to beat us, although that might prove to be an asset. What's worse, Nixon got off to a rousing start by hot-footing it out to Hawaii. That was a real smart move, and our side hasn't even started yet."

Summing everything up, I told myself brutally, "The Republicans ought to win. Every major indicator says so, and if Eisenhower and Rockefeller pitch in, their victory is in the bag. Because I know that Nixon will put on a terrific campaign." I sat back with the facts before me and came to this conclusion: "Nixon'll win about 53 percent of the popular vote and about 380 electoral votes." As I now look back at the election, I still think he should have done both.

On the other hand, I was emotionally committed to a Kennedy victory, and at the pit of my stomach—not my brain—I had intimations that some kind of irrational, last-minute miracle would enable us to win. What it might be I could not even guess; but if I was a firm devotee of Murphy's Law I was also a partisan of Mr. Micawber's completely contradictory theory that something good usually turns up. I felt this was particularly true in politics, and on this theory I based my irrational hopes. In the meantime I would work as never before.

The night after I formulated these rather gloomy assessments of the situation, I attended a dinner party, the last purely social affair I would participate in for a long time, and after we had dined, the guests were handed sheets of paper bearing the names of ten states whose votes would be critical in the election. We were required to predict how each state would go, and also what electoral vote the winning candidate would get. Of the ten people present, eight were sure that Nixon would win 300 to 350 electoral votes, and all were sure that he would carry most of the critical states.

My wife judged that Kennedy would win with 300 electoral votes, and she guessed right on almost all the states. I, facing my first public test in the campaign, thought: "This parlor game is not related to fact. This is an act of propaganda. Tonight I commit myself to John Kennedy." Boldly I predicted that he would carry nine of the ten focal states—

I gave him California, Ohio, Indiana . . . everything but Florida—and for my electoral total I splashed down the figures, "410."

"You don't mean you think the Democrats will win 410 electoral votes?" asked my host in astonishment.

"I do!" I snapped. "You don't seem to realize it, but John Kennedy is going to win this election. The popular vote will be close but the electoral vote will be a landslide."

I made these remarks so forcefully that in time I came to believe them. During the campaign, I repeated them a hundred times, in Connecticut, in New York, in Idaho, in Utah and in Indiana. I insisted that Kennedy was going to win handsomely in the electoral college, and the very force of my belief rallied people to my cause. I found assistance where before it did not exist, and to no one during the long campaign did I betray doubt regarding my announced position, to no one, that is, except one night as I was speeding across Pennsylvania accompanied by one of the most incisive young men I had ever encountered. With me rode Robert Kennedy, campaign manager for the senator, and he asked, "All fooling aside, how's it going?"

"Terribly close," I said.

"Will you carry Pennsylvania?" he pressed.

"If we do, it'll be by a whisker," I replied.

"But there is a chance?"

"Yes, there's an honest chance."

"Will you carry your county?" the quiet voice probed.

"No. The religious issue will hurt us badly. We'll lose by about eight thousand. But that's twelve thousand better than last time."

"Good," he said. "Maybe that'll be enough to enable Philadelphia to carry the state."

"How do you see it nationally?" I countered.

"Very close."

"But we will win?" I asked.

"Yes," he replied, and we drove through the long night.

3

My County

☒ ☒

The first thing I had done politically upon returning from the boat trip across the Pacific and the car trip across America was to report to my Bucks County chairman, there to volunteer my services in the forthcoming campaign. Renewing acquaintances was a pleasant job, because for nearly fifty years the chairman had been a personal friend. We had grown up together, had seen many storms, and had reached middle age with some illusions intact.

Johnny Welsh, when I saw him again in the fall of 1959, was a wiry, well-preserved, gray-haired, sharp-tongued politician whose iron will and personal integrity had kept the local Democratic party functioning for more than a quarter of a century. When others of us were working abroad, he and his six sons were at home doing the dirty work of running a complex party organization. When the Democrats were in such low esteem locally that not even candidates could be found, Johnny Welsh ran for office. He made his living selling real estate and insurance, but his real occupation was politics, and he knew more about the workings of my county than any other man alive.

Pennsylvania has the commendable system of placing each county's affairs in the hands of three elected commissioners who in former days were paid $6,500 a year (now $8,500) and of whom one must by law be of the minority party. Thus no matter how strong the Republicans became, and they used to reap about 80 percent of the votes, there was always one paying job for a Democrat, and starting in 1951 Johnny Welsh filled that job. As such he became titular head of the party, and by the exercise of great will power and leadership in 1955 won the county away from the Republicans. This meant there would be two Democratic commissioners, and Johnny Welsh became the boss of one of America's most challenging counties.

He was helped conspicuously, I must confess, by the fact that shortly before the county-wide elections in 1955 the Republican coroner was charged with twenty-five counts of misconduct in office. For this misbehavior the unfortunate coroner went to jail, taking his party with him in defeat. But I do not mean to explain away this stunning Democratic victory solely in terms of an imprisoned coroner. Most of the credit was due to Johnny Welsh, who, as minority commissioner, had so valiantly struggled to build a party.

By 1959 Johnny had run into trouble in the form of a revolt in the southern end of the county, where otherwise loyal Democrats had axed him, so that he not only lost control of the county, but his minority seat on the commission as well. He did not, however, relinquish his leadership of the party, although someone else now stepped forth as titular head. Like everyone else in Bucks County, when I wanted to talk to the head of the Democrats, I went to see Johnny Welsh, who sat like a gray eagle surveying everything with cold caution.

I said, "Johnny, if Senator Kennedy wins the nomination I want to work for his election."

Welsh said, "I thought you were a Republican."

I said, "For many years I was registered that way."

Welsh said, "What's a Republican doing working for Kennedy? You're not a Catholic."

I said, "I think the country needs him."

Welsh said, "Well, if anything turns up later on, I'll let you know."

I said, "All right."

Welsh said, "By the way, did you mean that if Kennedy is not nominated you don't want to help?"

I said, "Kennedy or Johnson, either one."

Welsh said, "Well, who do you think it's going to be?"

I said, "Maybe Johnson and Kennedy, in that order."

Welsh said, "That would be a good ticket, but I hope it's the other way around."

I said, "So do I."

I did not hear from my old friend for many weeks, and I suspected that as a professional he did not entirely relish the participation of an amateur in an important election, but his tardiness in responding gave me an opportunity to study my county better, and all that I saw I loved.

Bucks was one of William Penn's original counties rimming the environs of Philadelphia, and throughout Pennsylvania's history there had always been antagonism between the crowded city and the lush, spacious counties of Bucks, Montgomery, Delaware and Chester. From time to time the central city voted Democratic, but the suburban counties could be depended upon to turn in large Republican majorities. In my youth, in central Bucks County, I grew up without knowing any Democrats. My mother thought there might be some on the edge of town, but she preferred not to speak of them. When I brought my wife home from Chicago, she met my aunts, who had occasion to observe, "We have really never known any Democrats," and when my wife volunteered, "Well, you know one now," there was a painful silence.

As a boy I used to sneak into sex trials that took place in the old courthouse just across the street from our school, for one of the major advantages of living in Doylestown was that it was the county seat with a courthouse where lurid trials were always available. Most exciting of all were the murder cases, and rather early in the game I noticed that one of the real tests of wit between contending lawyers came when our local district attorney tried by one subtle means or another to inform the jury that both the accused murderer and his lawyer were not from clean, God-fearing Bucks County but from corrupt, Devil-worshipping Philadelphia, and from the struggle which the defending lawyers put up trying to prevent this knowledge from becoming public, I could only guess that they acknowledged how prejudicial the comparison was. Well, sooner or later the truth leaked out, and there were very few Philadelphia murderers who got off free in our county.

Bucks County is a rather large county about forty-three miles long by seventeen wide, lying roughly north and south

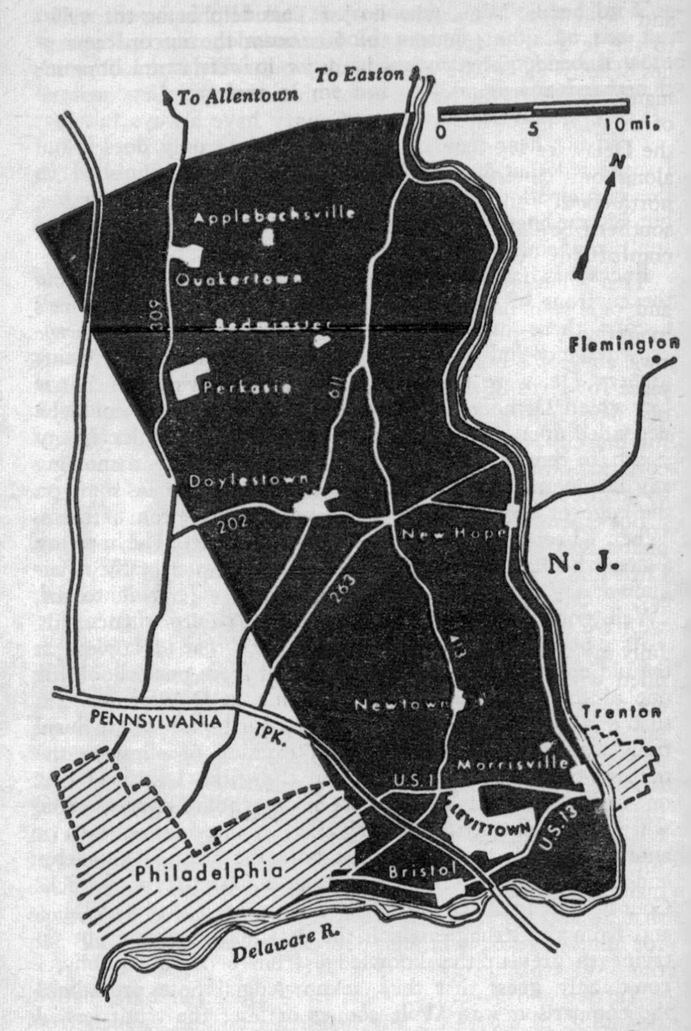

BUCKS COUNTY, *showing the communities mentioned in the report*

and extending from the edge of Philadelphia at the south to the large industrial city of Easton at the north. Since it lies wholly along the right bank of the Delaware, it commands the loveliest stretches of that river's valley, and all of us who grew up in Bucks County have always felt that the Delaware was our special river, for not only does it run along our eastern boundary, but when it has finished its north-south run, it turns abruptly westward to form our southern boundary, too, as if it were determined to tuck us comfortably into place.

This valley is a land of extraordinary beauty. Maple trees and oaks combine with evergreens to lend the forests real majesty. A hundred little streams wind through the meadows, and for a hundred thousand years it has been a resting place for birds in their hurried pursuit of the seasons. In the old days before the gasoline tractor it was a breadbasket for the city, its spacious farms yielding substantial crops of corn and wheat, but now its historic fields are manicured by gentlemen farmers from the surrounding cities.

Bucks County is replete with historic sites. From our hospitable shores General Washington crossed the Delaware on Christmas night to attack the British encamped in New Jersey. Back and forth across our county he marched, so that we have many houses still standing of which one can truthfully say, "George Washington slept here." Our old towns are filled with colonial remnants, and along our country roads are many farms that date back to the time of William Penn, our founding father. It seems only proper that we own one of the world's principal historical museums, and experts come from many parts of the world to study here, for a sense of the past is very strong in Bucks County. Only this morning I was talking with Arthur Eastburn, crafty senior tactician for the Republicans and a man with an astonishing record of maintaining political control of his county, and he told me that he and his father between them had served as lawyers for ninety years, working out of the same office all that time. We are a historic county.

Yet we also have a *nouveau riche* aspect, and the natives despise it. In the 1920's distinguished men and women from New York theatrical and publishing life discovered our magnificent farms, and for the next forty years one after another of the old places fell into alien hands. I was a boy at the time this invasion began and I can remember the bitterness with which we watched the outlanders arrive with their inflated bankrolls and their station wagons: George S. Kaufman, the playwright; S. J. Perelman, who thought he was funny; Pearl Buck, who wrote all those books about China; Oscar Hammerstein, who was mixed up with musical comedies; Moss Hart, who wrote and directed plays . . . we watched them all come and of each we suspected the worst.

But we were powerless to keep them out, for our farms were no longer productive, and in time Bucks County became world famous as a center for intellectual bohemianism, not that Kaufman, Perelman, Buck and Hammerstein ever engaged in any of it. They rather disappointed us by staying properly at home on their farms just as if they had been stuffy Bucks Countians all their lives. It was the hangers-on that made Bucks County, and especially the lovely old town of New Hope, notorious. The area was flooded with artists and writers and revolutionaries and people who never took baths. A disproportionate number of homosexuals arrived and people who read poetry aloud and who listened to high-fidelity music at all hours of the night. Our courthouse in Doylestown began to entertain some rather extraordinary cases, and we natives listened agog as things we had never heard of before unrolled before our judges, as such things sometimes will. A few years ago an outsider wrote a novel about us entitled *The Devil in Bucks County*, and all local patriots branded it scandalous, but there was some truth in it if you restricted its more lurid passages only to the New Hope area.

For one thing we were grateful. The strangers who flooded our county generally kept out of politics, so that although there was a natural animosity between the poor honest residents of the county and the rich debauched strangers who swept in—except that after a while it was the residents who were rich and the strangers who were broke—this animosity never expressed itself in political terms. The county remained Republican, and no man could remember when it had ever voted for a Democratic President.

When I was a boy we took politics seriously. My first memory of a political campaign concerned the 1916 contest between Hughes and Wilson, which occurred when I was nine years old. I remember the joy with which my mother took me into the center of town that Tuesday night while the victorious Republicans paraded with torchlights and a long, horn-honking file of expensive automobiles. We trudged home content that Charles Evans Hughes would be a great President, and my mother explained how good life was going to be, now that the Democrat Wilson had been thrown out.

I also remember that awful Friday night of the same week when my mother, biting her lip to control her tears, hauled me back to the Intelligencer Building, where we stood in the shadows and watched the Democrats celebrate their belated victory. What a grubby lot of people they were, strangers for the most part who had come into town to jeer at the Republicans, who had held their parade prematurely. I remember my mother saying, "Never forget this night, James. Look at them. There isn't a Buick in the lot." Years later, when Franklin D. Roosevelt was elected for the second time she went to bed sick for four days and told me she didn't care if she ever got up.

It was about 1916 that Bucks County fell into the hands of one of the greatest party politicians of our time. Joseph R. Grundy was then a powerful textile-mill owner who lived in Bristol, the industrial center at the southern end of the county, and as a boy I always considered him a man of better than national stature, for I once worked on one of his newspapers and I can remember how we stood at attention when Mr. Grundy stalked in to lay down the editorial line for the next month.

He was a powerfully built man, silent, shrewd, and brilliant in command. I can see him now marching from our newspaper offices over to the courthouse, where every man who worked did so solely because Mr. Grundy had assigned him to the job. I suspect that even the judges were judges because Mr. Grundy had selected them. His word was absolute law, and the two things he hated were Democrats and disloyalty.

He controlled our county with an iron hand until he was in his nineties, and even as I write he is ninety-six and still a major force. During his long reign he gave us as good a government as a benevolent dictatorship can, and it was one remarkably free from open corruption. For example, when the overambitious coroner got into trouble it was widely held that if Mr. Grundy had been younger he never would have allowed this to happen, but whenever a Republican makes such a comment to Johnny Welsh, the Democratic boss observes acidly, "From the time I was a boy, every five years by the clock some leading Republican went to jail for stealing the people blind. If Grundy was so powerful, why didn't he stop that?"

I wouldn't say that Joe Grundy had ever been a hero of mine—I was far too scared of him for that—but I must admit that I felt a glow of local pride when he branched out from Bucks County to become the dictator of Pennsylvania and finally a United States senator. He was also president of the Pennsylvania Manufacturers Association and was held by many to be the most typical president that that organization ever had. When he spoke on economic or political matters there was no uncertainty as to what he meant. So far as I knew, he was against every major bill that even the Republicans had ever brought out since the days of Abraham Lincoln, which is as far back as one can go in that direction. As for Democrats, his stand was forever exemplified by the front page of his *Intelligencer* for November 3, 1948, which remains a museum piece in political reporting.

I suppose even the most jaundiced critic would have to confess that Harry Truman's astonishing victory over Thomas E. Dewey, who had already announced his cabinet, was news. You might not have liked the result, but it was news. Our paper the next day carried big, bold headlines proclaiming the fact that "Dewey Got 12,731 Majority in Bucks County." The lesser headlines detailed how the great victory had been won, and off to one side was the news that Harry Truman had won the Presidency. If the Democrats had won nationally, Bucks County would do its best to ignore the unpleasantness. We had three daily papers in the county and six weeklies, all vigorously Republican.

After the conventions were over, Johnny Welsh called me to his office and said, "The people backing John Kennedy are eager to have each county establish a committee of independents and Republicans who will work for his election. Will you head that committee in this county?"

I replied, "I'm neither an independent nor a Republican."

John observed, "You're not a professional Democrat, either. How about taking the job?"

I agreed and was told that the national committee sponsoring my work would get in touch with me promptly. In the meantime I was to be known as the county chairman of Citizens for Kennedy. I was to hire a hall and establish headquarters immediately, and there would be no funds forthcoming from anywhere. Within a few days I had raised $1,200 and was ready for business.

There then occurred a symbolic event which impressed me at the time; its beneficial effects were to sustain me during the campaign. The county seat of Bucks County is the quiet, beautiful old town which had been my home for more than fifty years. Doylestown was strongly conservative, at times almost 90 percent Republican, and a thoroughly delightful rural community with good schools, fine churches, a new shopping center which everyone said was ruining the town but which everyone also patronized, no heavy industry, and very little trouble of any kind. In 1948 my home town had voted 78 percent for Dewey; in 1956, 75 percent for General Eisenhower.

Main Street in Doylestown is a major United States highway running south and north between Philadelphia and Easton. In the center of town it crosses Court Street, which is a major residential and business street running east and west. At this intersection, and commanding the attention of any motorist or pedestrian who moves in any direction, stands an old office building, whose ground floor is just about the most advantageously situated in town. In mid-August that store was vacated and no new occupants were scheduled to move in until after the election in November. As a temporary political headquarters it was perfect, and I assumed that the Republicans had already paid a deposit on it.

But they never did, and for modest rent we got hold of this fine situation. Here my committee commanded the attention of people and impressed them with the fact that we were really trying to win this election. Hundreds of Republicans stopped by to see us, to ask incredulously, "You really think you have a chance?" And our physical presence at that vital corner, day after day, convinced some that we were serious. Throughout the campaign the Republicans were tardy in almost everything they did. We waited apprehensively for their powerhouse to start rolling, but it never did. We instinctively sensed the next steps they ought to be taking to defeat Kennedy, and often we even discussed them among ourselves so that we could counteract them, but the logical steps were never taken, and we could only conclude that for some reason that we did not know, the Republicans were not throwing their full weight into this campaign.

I am not speaking of the campaign at the local level. Bucks

County combines with Lehigh, to the north, to send one representative to Congress. For the last twenty-six years he has been a Republican, and the local party showed no inclination whatever to let a Democrat take over. They fought a remarkably good fight against a strong Democratic adversary, and they won. But what the party did not do was to support Richard Nixon with the all-or-nothing kind of campaign that we Democrats expected and which we feared would give Nixon the victory. We therefore concluded, perhaps incorrectly, that many Republicans simply did not like their candidate and were not working for him.

This gave me a clue for all my speeches throughout the campaign. Since I addressed mostly Republicans I knew that frontal assaults on their party or their candidate would accomplish nothing, so I consistently pointed out that Richard Nixon was a good man and a respectable candidate. In fact, I was so fair about acknowledging these matters that after my first four talks both my wife and the more ardent Democrats in my audiences protested, "We couldn't tell whether you were for Nixon or Kennedy." This was not an accident, for to the end I kept admitting that Nixon was good, but that in my opinion Kennedy was better. But my most telling blow came whenever I observed casually that "the trouble is that many Republicans just don't like their candidate." Whenever I said this I could see a dozen or so good Republican heads nodding in agreement. Now whether they were nodding for themselves or from their recollections of other Republicans who had expressed antagonisms, I never knew, but I am sure that by this tactic I won over quite a few Republicans. Equally effective was my constant reference to the fact that quite obviously President Eisenhower did not entirely approve of Nixon and never had. Here scores instead of dozens nodded their agreement, and I am sure that this was one of the most damaging situations with which Mr. Nixon had to contend during his campaign. Whether President Eisenhower actually did find his Vice President distasteful or not we will not know until the memoirs of this age are published, but I can certainly report now that an enormous number of voters in the 1960 election thought that Ike distrusted Dick, and a great many—across the nation something like 5,000,000—who had voted for Ike in 1956 were persuaded to vote for Senator Kennedy in 1960, partly because they felt that the Republicans themselves did not wholly accept their own candidate.

On the day we opened our headquarters in Doylestown, Johnny Welsh gave me some bad news. "I've been looking at the registrations from Bedminster," he grumbled, "and they don't look good. Normally the registrations from Bedminster East should be 409 Republicans to 210 Democrats. We always expect to lose that area. This year we got our customary 217 Democrats. But the Republicans turned in an amazing 472. It's that way in all the rural areas. Know what that means?"

I said I guessed it meant that the Republicans had worked harder in combing out registrations than we had. Johnny shook his head. "It means that the Mennonites have allowed their women to register again. Usually churches like the Amish and the Dunkards and the Mennonites don't allow their women to vote. Last time they voted in Bucks County was in 1928 when Al Smith ran. Their churches demanded that they vote against a Catholic. Now thirty-two years later they're voting again, and we're in trouble. Big trouble, maybe."

As I studied my county politically, I found that it was divided into three clear-cut sections. To the north and centering upon fine old towns like Perkasie and Quakertown were the German farmers, most of whom were Republicans. There were, however, several strong enclaves of Democrats, where year after year atypical liberal groups turned in Democratic majorities. Such an area, for example, was the one organized by Mrs. Eva Horne Derr in Applebachsville. Mrs. Derr was a good-looking, hard-working doctor's widow who loved politics and who, because she was a German herself, could talk effectively with the farm people of her district. But for the most part Democrats fared poorly in the north. Since the German sections of Bucks County were to be of unusual importance in this election, I had better speak briefly of these remarkable people. Most were of Lutheran or Mennonite families that had lived in the area for two or three centuries, and all were frugal, honest and law-abiding. Few ever went to jail or onto the poorhouse rolls, for the German community protected its people in patterns of cautious behavior inherited from rural Europe. I had grown up with these Germans—the so-called Pennsylvania Dutch—and many of my schoolboy friends had barely been able to speak English when they first came to school. There were still important sections of our county where day-to-day business was conducted in Pennsylvania Dutch and where a candidate for office was expected to campaign in that hilarious language. Historians have always felt that much of Pennsylvania's colonial greatness stemmed from its German heritage and certainly our county was a conspicuous example of this fact. When I was a boy, it was the vote of these German majorities that determined our politics, and although in recent years their monopoly has been somewhat diluted by the arrival of new populations, any politician would be delinquent who did not consider first the Lutheran and the Mennonite vote. In the jargon of our politics they were often referred to as "the up-county religious."

The central part of the county, focusing upon Doylestown and Newtown, still had many Lutheran families, but it was marked primarily by other Protestant groups and by people of some means who had either inherited farms from their ancestors or who had bought them in recent decades. This area, as might be guessed, was also largely Republican. Outsiders, looking at this richly fortunate sector of the county, rarely realized how backward many parts of the county were. Up till only a few years ago in my part of Bucks County we had one-room rural schools without electricity, running water, or indoor toilets. The teacher, in 1957, had to report to school half an hour early in order to start the wood fire, and in other parts of the county these schools exist even today. I remember one bond issue that was opposed by stalwart German farmers who argued, "If you vote for a consolidated school, it will have a football team, and if it has a football team it'll have to have a band, and the band will have to have uniforms, and when they have their uniforms, you'll have to buy your son a trombone. Do you want to spend your hard-earned money for a trombone?" The bond issue never had a chance and in that area the one-room schools continue even now. Perhaps the essential quality of our rural areas can best be conveyed through the story of a fine old friend of mine who had a farm with Black Angus cattle and a wife who had lost her teeth. My friend had just enough ready cash to either repair the barn so it wouldn't rain on his Black Angus or buy his wife a set of store teeth, and he never hesitated a moment in his choice. Furthermore, our neighborhood warmly supported him on the grounds that a man's first duty was to look after his farm. In fact, the cows got in turn a new roof, a new drinking system, and a new fence before their mistress got her new teeth, and both the farm and the marriage have prospered.

The southern end of our county forms one of the most spectacular areas in the United States and has often served as the subject for editorials and general reflections on the future of our nation. Ten years ago it was merely an exquisite rural area edged by a few small industries. Its major town was Bristol, from which Joseph Grundy dictated in his benevolent way. Then, in 1952, United States Steel decided to build the world's largest continuous-flow steel mill at Morrisville, the location farthest north on the Delaware River to which seagoing ore carriers could come from Venezuela. In order to provide homes for the workmen thus to be employed, the New York builder Levitt and his sons began at the same time to build on empty meadowland a model community which in a few short years would become the tenth largest city in the state. The appalling disruptions caused by this combination of steel and suburbia remade the face of Bucks County. Land speculators acquired fortunes overnight. A hundred service industries suddenly sprang up and some prospered fantastically. Restaurants, stores, schools, newspapers, insurance offices exploded all over the place, and 70,000 new people crowded into the area in the space of a few years. Many, in their previous homes, had belonged to labor unions. Many had been Democrats. Thus our sleepy county overnight became one of the principal examples of the new America. Its growth from 1900 to 1950 had been desultory and had lagged behind the national average, but from 1954 to 1960 it was spectacular.

BUCKS COUNTY POPULATION

Year	Population
1900	71,900
1920	82,476
1930	96,727
1940	107,715
1950	144,620
1960	307,815

I can well recall the shock waves that sped out from lower Bucks when all this began to happen. As was my custom, I dropped around to see Miss Omwake and Mrs. Dale and they gave me this report.

MRS. DALE: It was terrible, James. These awful labor-union people started a strike. They aren't even from Bucks County, just a lot of rubbish hauled in here overnight.

MISS OMWAKE: The five businessmen who were putting up the plant came to Doylestown and got Judge Keller to issue an injunction forbidding the labor-union men to strike. And do you know what those union men did?

MRS. DALE: When Judge Keller's injunction was posted on the door of the building, one of the labor-union men from Philadelphia walked up, read it, started to laugh and ripped it down.

MISS OMWAKE: He said, "Apparently the good judge doesn't know that this sort of thing went out of style ten years ago." And do you know what?

MRS. DALE: The labor-union man got his way. Judge Keller didn't know that the law had been changed. But those labor men did, and they went right ahead with their strike. Imagine, in Bucks County!

MISS OMWAKE: And this Levittown, more than 60,000 people jammed in there like rabbits. They can slap together one of those jerry-built houses in two days. Who could live in a house that was built in two days?

MRS. DALE: They tell us that most of the people who are moving in are either Jews or Italians. Bucks County will just never be the same.

MISS OMWAKE: And they're opening new Catholic churches all over the place.

MRS. DALE: Everyone says the county has been ruined and lots of the fine old families are selling their farms and moving out.

MISS OMWAKE: Yes, a farm that used to sell for $15,000 is now bringing $70,000, so the fine old families are selling.

MRS. DALE: Everybody thinks that within ten more years the central part of the county will be ruined, too.

MISS OMWAKE: But our real estate is going up, too.

MRS. DALE: So now we have unions right here in Bucks County.

MISS OMWAKE: And there's some talk that a whole lot of

these people are Democrats. Imagine, right in Mr. Grundy's back yard, and they're Democrats.

In my long life in Bucks County, without question the most exciting single phenomenon has been this metamorphosis of the southern end of the county. The contempt with which my area viewed these changes is only barely suggested by the conversation of Mrs. Dale and Miss Omwake. Later you will see what a sardonic revenge the good people of my county took on the intruders, but for the moment let us consider only the political repercussions.

Overnight Bucks County was transformed from a Republican county to one in which the Democrats had an outside chance. The vote in several recent elections indicates the wide opportunity for fluctuation:

BUCKS COUNTY VOTE

Year	*Type*	*Rep.*	*Dem.*	*Rep. %*
1948	Presidential	29,411	16,655	64
1951	County	23,947	12,603	67
1952	Presidental	40,753	24,301	63
1955	County	31,353	33,237	49
1956	Presidential	59,862	38,541	61
1959	County	45,751	35,903	56

I was told by a man who was present that after the 1955 vote Mr. Grundy stormed up to Doylestown to a meeting of the Republican central committee. Striding into the room he said, "You, you, and you are fired." When the stunned politicians asked why, Grundy snapped, "Because your places are going to be taken by the three best young Republicans in Levittown." When the committee protested that they didn't know any Republicans in Levittown, Grundy is supposed to have cried, "Find them, and we'll meet here again tomorrow. Now go home." Steered by Mr. Grundy's firm hand, the Republicans made strong inroads into the Levittown area, and as the 1960 Presidential race began, the county-wide situation stood thus: Republican registrations 76,354; Democratic registrations 59,559. It therefore looked as if the Republicans ought to win by about 17,000 votes, or 56 percent. On the other hand, the Democrats were working harder than ever, so that in early September my reasoning was that whereas John Kennedy had almost no chance of carrying the county, we could hope that his margin of defeat would be held to about 2,000, which would represent an enormous victory and might enable Democratic majorities in Philadelphia and Pittsburgh to hold Pennsylvania's 32 votes for Kennedy.

But when I reported my hopeful conclusions to Johnny Welsh, he shook his head gravely and said, "I wish I knew what the up-county religious are going to do."

4

The Flood

When I agreed to head the Bucks County Citizens for Kennedy Committee, the fact was routinely reported in a wide sampling of newspapers, and within three days I began to receive the first trickle of that flood of mail which was to characterize the campaign. I can forget the endless speeches, the hopeful conversations, and the great good will which I found on every side. But I will not be able to forget the deluge of anti-Catholic mail that I received.

Usually the letters began, "Did you know that the Catholic Church . . ." and ended with a miserable recital of lies, historic fact, sexual indecency and legitimate comment on Church excesses in Spain or Venezuela. Quotations from scholarly works gave the whole a cloak of respectability, and if one wanted to indulge in anti-Catholic hatreds, here was inviting material upon which to feed.

During the first week I received eleven such letters, and it may be interesting to specify where they originated. Five had been mailed from outside Pennsylvania; four had been mailed from the state but outside Bucks County; two were from my own county. It is noteworthy that during the entire campaign I did not receive one anonymous letter on this subject. All were signed and all contained return addresses.

Of my first eleven, four were from private individuals; four were from committees of one kind or another; and three were from specific churches. As autumn progressed, an increasingly higher percentage of my mail came direct from churches. Only two letters came from the South. None came from anyone that I knew personally, but several dozen came from people who began, "From reading your books I almost feel as if I know you, and I was shocked this morning to find that a man who seems to be as intelligent as you are could be blind to the terrible thing you are doing in helping to put the Pope in our White House."

Without exception, each of the many letters contained pamphlets defaming the Catholic Church, and it was surprising how little duplication there was. I gave most of them away to convince unbelieving friends that an anti-Catholic campaign was under way, but I suppose I must have received upwards of eighty different items.

They fell into three distinct types. First came the relatively honest summary of civil intrusions made by the Church in such countries as Spain, Ireland and Colombia. I never objected to these compilations, nor to the people who sent them out, for they represented an intellectually respectable charge against the Church, and if any voter was sufficiently frightened by the recital of facts contained in these reports, I felt that he ought not to vote for John Kennedy. Later in the campaign I was especially glad that I had never inveighed against such publications, because the Roman Catholic bishops in Puerto Rico very obligingly proved that the fundamental political charge made against the Church was true. Some of my Democratic friends circulated the current rumor that Republicans must have paid the Puerto Rican bishops to release their bombshell at the precise moment when it would damage Kennedy most, but rabid anti-Catholics effectively killed that charge; ingeniously they explained that Cardinal Spellman had ordered the Puerto Rican churchmen to act as they did so as to kill Kennedy's chances for the Presidency, because if, when Pope John died, the United States already had a Catholic President, the cardinals would be loath to elect Spellman Pope because that would place too much of the Church's power in American hands. But if Kennedy lost, the cardinals would almost have to elect Spellman in order to keep the American Catholics happy. Therefore, Cardinal

Spellman was determined to defeat Kennedy so as to further his own interests.

The second category contained numerous pamphlets not founded on fact but consisting mostly of ranting, rodomontade and bigotry. One of the most impressive carried a cover showing a fat and apparently venal bishop on his throne, with "The Rest of Us" kneeling abjectly and kissing his foot. Most of these pamphlets made a good deal of this foot-kissing routine as something especially subversive. They also played up supposedly lurid details of the confessional. A characteristic of the material in this second category was its repeated assertion that in all Catholic countries priests immediately took over the schools, the newspapers, and the civil government. No mention was ever made of countries like France or Belgium, or Canada or Mexico, where the religious problem had been fought, by Catholics, to reasonable solutions. I suppose that most votes that were changed by the religious issue were influenced by this segment of the material. Certainly whenever I finished reading some of it I felt obligated to rush out and shoot the first Catholic I encountered. Such material injected into the bloodstream of democracy was persuasive and fearfully poisonous.

One of the pamphlets most widely circulated in Bucks County showed a trio of priests supervising the following tortures of Protestants: one victim was being crucified upside down; another was being hauled aloft by his hands twisted behind his back while weights were applied to his feet; a third was stretched prone while water was being forced into him; a fourth had his bare feet in a fire while another fire was about to be pushed into his stomach; and the last was having his skin peeled off by a smiling assistant armed with a butcher knife. The text pointed out, among other things, that Congressman John W. McCormack of Massachusetts had personally forced the federal government to give his church "more than thirty millions of dollars of taxpayers' funds."

The third category offered a redundant procession of lurid confessions of one-time Catholics who had fled from either the priesthood or the nunnery. For some reason which I do not fully understand, unless it is that the Church has always stressed a kind of secret ritualism, there seems to be an insatiable desire on the part of Protestants to know what goes on within the hierarchy. All of the confessions that I received dated back to the nineteenth century, but they appeared to be as popular now as they must have been a hundred years ago. So far as I can recall, I received none in which the fugitive had fled the terrors of the Church in this century, although I suppose that such confessions must exist. Probably it is the nineteenth-century masterpieces that report the best horrors. I read about ten of these case histories and got the clear impression that the Catholic Church was well rid of some rather stupid characters and that the Protestants had been gulled. As a matter of fact, I think a good case could be made for the theory that all these authors were in reality counter-agents spuriously expelled by the Catholics to confuse the enemy. On the other hand, if one wanted to feed his bigotry, I must admit that some of the passages of these confessions were calculated to provide nourishment for hatred and confusion.

There was a sub-category of this third group that merits special mention. These were the confessions of nuns who had fled the almost indescribable terrors of convent life, they claimed. These books were downright salacious and had obviously been composed with that effect in mind. *Maria Monk*, which was exceptionally popular during the election, is an old nineteenth-century classic, written so far as I know by a London hack, who offered the public a clever barrage of sexual titillation. One advertisement for this old worthy claimed: "See for yourself how innocent girls are trapped and imprisoned inside dark convents. How young priests visit them at night and force their attentions upon them. How the unwanted babies are strangled and thrown into wells. Live again the horrors of the Catholic Church with Maria Monk. In her own words."

A typical selection of anti-Catholic books which could be ordered by mail was circulated throughout Bucks County at the height of the election. Some of the titles were:

The Catholic Church Unmasked
House of Death and Gates of Hell
Why I Left the Church of Rome
My Pilgrimage to Lourdes
The Priest, the Woman and the Confessional
Abolish the Nunneries and Save the Girls
I Married a Monk
Convent Life Unveiled
My Life in the Convent
Maria Monk
The Convent Horror
The Menace of Rome

What infuriated me personally, as head of a committee trying to elect John Kennedy, was that the dissemination of material in all the above categories, from the factual to the obscene, was paid for by personal contributions which were made for a political purpose and which were tax exempt! If a hard-working Democrat wanted to give me $100 to help the Democratic side of the campaign, it cost him $100 to do so, and it was not tax exempt. But if some addle-brained Republican wanted to get in savage blows, and there is evidence that some did, he could give $100 to any of the churches peddling this filth and, depending upon his income tax bracket, he might gain a rebate of $50 to $70 and clobber the Democrats at the same time. I know of no single electoral practice in my lifetime that was as unfair and dangerous as this.

Let me state quickly that in Bucks County, at least, the formal Republican party took no part in this vicious campaign. One district chairman circulated a pamphlet in which a Catholic priest explained why Kennedy should not be elected, but as soon as we protested he stopped. That single individuals did make financial contributions cannot be questioned, for the churches involved could not possibly have maintained their vastly increased publishing programs without additional financial help. That this insane program ultimately reacted against the Republicans and helped elect a Catholic President was one of the ironic twists of political fate, so I suppose I ought not object. But I do. Religious hatreds ought not be propagated at all, but certainly not on a tax-exempt basis. In fact, one of the most violent of the churches involved in peddling this material mistakenly sent me during the campaign a letter pleading for additional funds, this time to underwrite their legal right to continue distributing the discredited *Oath of the Knights of Columbus*. In its letter soliciting funds the church specifically stated, "Your offering can be deducted from your income tax."

When this avalanche of hate literature began to hit Bucks County I was unable to guess what practical effect it was having, and I consulted with Mrs. Eva Horne Derr, the lively state committeewoman from the northern end of the county. She was a non-hysterical type of woman whose German father had been justice of the peace, postmaster and leading Democrat at Applebachsville for thirty years. On his death Eva, one of seven children, had taken his place in many respects, acquiring elective office and a high place in Democratic councils. Her greatest sorrow was that most of her family had turned Republican. Eva was a devout Lutheran and one of her brothers was a thirty-third-degree Mason, as were many Protestants in northern Bucks.

She reported, "This religious business is going to damage the Democrats. We hear stories of ministers instructing their congregations to vote Republican."

"They won't obey, will they?" I asked.

Eva looked at me as though I weren't too bright and said, "Let me tell you a story. Two months ago I had ideas like yours. Schoolbook stuff. Separation of church and state. Sacredness of the ballot box and all that stuff. Then I accompanied the officers on the registration drive."

She stopped, shook her head in disgust and started to laugh. "What happened?" I asked.

"We went to this one old lady; she'd lived in the same house for sixty-eight years and had never voted. This time she wanted to vote and the traveling registrar says, 'How do you wish to register?' 'Lutheran,' she says, and even Mr. Ziegler, he's the Republican county chairman, had to laugh and he said, 'We don't mean your religion. We mean how you're going to vote.' And the old lady snaps, 'I'm going to vote Lutheran. Reverend Himmelright told me to.'"

"You think we'll run into a lot of that?" I asked.

"That I'm not afraid of," Mrs. Derr said. "What worries me is the fact that many of my registered Democrats won't talk with me. They've decided they can't vote for a Catholic."

When I heard enough of these reports, I convened several meetings to discuss what we should do, and in mid-September we agreed upon this procedure: "We must respect the fact that in our county a lot of people are either Lutheran or Mennonite, and the historic position of their churches has always been to fight Rome. For us to term these people bigots would be historically wrong. They were against Rome when I was a boy. They'll be against it when I'm a ghost. Furthermore, to charge them with bigotry would be politically unwise, for the Democrats among them might leave our party and never come back. Therefore at our public meetings we won't use that word.

"As for the ministers who preach against Senator Kennedy, what can we do? We won't fight them. We won't argue with them. If your minister gives a sermon like that, sit there and take it and next week go out and work a little harder for Kennedy.

"We can take consolation in this. Religious intolerance has already gained for the other side all the votes it's going to deliver, and I don't think that anything you or I say will win back a single one of those votes, so don't worry about them. Argue with nobody.

"But from now on, you watch. A little more of this anti-Catholic smear stuff and a lot of uncommitted people who might have voted Republican are going to vote for us, simply because they're sickened by the filthy material that's being shoveled into this county. And sensitive Catholics who voted Republican the last two times are going to be driven back to our side. We've lost all we're going to lose, and from here on out it's got to be pure profit for us."

One worker asked in a hesitant voice, "Should we show this filthy material to Catholics who haven't seen any of it yet?"

I thought about this a long time and asked, "Are you a Catholic?"

"Yes," the woman said.

"Are you personally mad about the stuff you've seen?"

"Yes," she replied.

"Well, if you honestly resent it, I suppose it wouldn't do any harm for you to tell your friends," I counseled.

Later, however, one of our overly zealous workers pasted a selection of the worst anti-Catholic pamphlets on the windows of one of our offices with a sign that read, "This is what we're up against." As soon as I heard of this, I ordered the sign and the anti-Catholic material taken down. "You may not use such material in this campaign," I said.

"You mean we can't fight back?" my workers asked.

"Such filth fights right back by itself," I argued, and I still believe I was right, yet even I had to smile at one placard I saw: "A Quaker beat a Catholic in 1928; it'll happen again in 1960."

The major breakthrough on the religious problem, in our area at least, came with the Norman Vincent Peale–Daniel Poling report of the anti-Catholic convention in Washington. The storm that broke over this unsavory and ill-advised performance both surprised and pleased me. The newspapers of the country quickly identified the dangers represented by this meeting. They underscored its secret nature and questioned its impartial motives. What had been planned as a body blow to the Democrats was quickly transformed into a very dangerous situation for the Republicans, who as a party had probably not been involved in convening the regrettable convocation of Catholic-haters.

On the other hand, we in Bucks County remembered that Dr. Daniel Poling was an avowed Republican partisan who had once stood for election as mayor of Philadelphia on the Republican ticket, and Dr. Norman Vincent Peale had frequently been identified with Republican causes. For these two gentlemen to pose as impartial arbiters of a sensitive political question seemed to me an improper intrusion of religion into politics. But when the storm erupted, I was impressed by the dignity with which Dr. Poling conducted himself. It was he who had broken the controversial story of Representative Kennedy's withdrawal from the dedication of an inter-faith chapel honoring the four chaplains who had given their lives in the North Atlantic in World War II. According to Poling, whose son was one of those chaplains, Kennedy had agreed to participate but had then refused, under direct pressure from Cardinal Dougherty. I could respect Poling's firm position, even though it hurt my candidate.

But Dr. Peale's performance I found undignified. When newspapers around the country, properly mindful of the sensibilities of their Catholic readers, started to cancel the Peale column—the Philadelphia *Inquirer* was one of the first—the good doctor quickly issued an apology for his fumbling performance, and did so through the agency of the business firm that distributed his column. Then he confessed ineptly to his church that he hadn't known what he was doing, didn't mean what he had done, and had been made a fool of by people smarter than he. I felt ashamed for a man I had once vigorously defended on radio and whom I liked personally, yet I had to be grateful to him, and shall always remain so, for in our area at least he helped us counteract religious prejudice and thus proved instrumental in the election of Senator Kennedy.

What was equally important, he inadvertently introduced some humor into an ugly question; for in subsequent weeks, whenever the religious issue arose at any meeting that I was addressing, I always remarked that the audience would forgive me if I avoided making a fool of myself, as Dr. Norman

Vincent Peale had done. Always there was hearty laughter. I then made a few comments about the fact that I could respect a man like Dr. Poling, who stated frankly that he did not want to see John F. Kennedy elected President of the United States. I always said, "There must be a lot of us in the audience tonight who feel exactly as Dr. Poling feels, and that's a perfectly honorable stand to take. I'm certainly not going to try to argue down an honest religious conviction. But if you're just vaguely afraid of this Catholic question, if you've heard a lot of rumors and read a lot of the hate literature that's being circulated, remember that Dr. Peale apologized for bringing such matters up. Don't make the same silly mistake that he made." Sometimes I quoted the nifty that Adlai Stevenson is supposed to have started: "In this campaign it seems as if each party has a patron saint. Personally I must admit that I find St. Paul appealing and St. Peale appalling." Always in our meetings we acknowledged the honest fears of those who could not vote for a Catholic, and we approached the others with humor. In the long run we accomplished some good.

That one part of my analysis of this religious problem was correct—namely, that during the first few weeks the Democrats had lost all the votes they were going to lose because of religious bigotry and that from there on the issue would only aid them—was proved shortly after the Peale-Poling fiasco when I received on the same day from two highly placed Republicans personal appeals that I get in touch with Senator Kennedy and "try to persuade him to get the Democrats off the religious issue." It seemed to me there were two errors in this approach. I did not know Senator Kennedy personally and thus could have no influence upon his actions even if one supposed that he were guilty. More importantly, it was intellectual effrontery of the worst sort to suggest that a man who stood to lose the Presidency of the United States because of his religion had somehow "introduced the religious issue." For the life of me I could not understand how my correspondents had reached the conclusion that Kennedy was to blame for the eruption of the religious question, and I concluded what now seems to be even more clear than it was then, that the Republican high command had awakened belatedly to the fact that this issue might inflame the big cities and cost Richard Nixon the Presidency. The fact that each of my correspondents was a good friend whom I respected led me to respond as follows:

"Curiously enough your letter asking me to see what I could do to persuade Jack Kennedy to soft-pedal the religious issue was one of two I received that day from men high in the councils of the Republican party, and from what I can see here in Bucks County, we would all be wise to get both parties off this Thirty-Years'-War kick. Right now it looks to lots of us as if it were going to hurt the Republicans grievously, because people around here credit them with having launched the whole affair and then crying quits when the going got rough. Whether that reflects the truth or not I cannot say, but it does seem to me that after the Peale-Poling fiasco, and the miserable manner in which those Republican apologists have tried to climb down, the Republicans can only lose votes from here on in, and I would not like to see our side win merely because of the old Rum-Romanism-Rebellion error which once before won us an election."

So far I have written as if the religious prejudices of our county were restricted to the rural northern areas, but that is not true and I must now correct faulty impressions. Much of the most virulent religious propaganda circulated only in the industrial areas of the southern end, but here its impact was fortunately diminished by the Fair Campaign Practices Committee, which had been called into being partially as a result of the racial fires that had some years before ravaged this area.

The committee was headed by an unusual young man, John J. Malloy, who taught philosophy at La Salle, a Catholic college in Philadelphia. I suppose that Professor Malloy was a Democrat, but he was energetically supported by Republican associates who worked to keep our election free from the grosser forms of abuse. I say that Malloy was unusual because at first glance he was a strait-laced, serious young student who weighed his words cautiously and seemed even a little ponderous; but as any evening wore on he displayed a riotous sense of humor, and one of the reasons why we were able to keep the religious fury under some kind of control was that Professor Malloy could always be counted upon to report in detail his latest outrageous experience.

"We were called into Bristol the other day to check on a woman who was peddling the worst pamphlet we've seen so far. The cover showed 'Protestant' on a medieval rack, his arms broken, fire applied to his feet, and his intestines being unrolled onto a wheel. Smiling evilly was a mitred figure called 'Catholic.' The text was worse than the illustration and proved that positively hellish things would happen if anyone dared to vote for Kennedy.

"Our problem was, 'How can we get copies of the pamphlet from the woman herself?' I solved it by dressing inconspicuously and finding out where she was peddling the stuff. I sidled up and asked, 'You got any more of those Catholic books?' She smiled warmly and said, 'Take one. It may save our nation.' When I had it safely in my hands I said, 'Madam, I'm chairman of the Fair Campaign Practices Committee, and we're trying to see that this is a clean election.'

"The woman grabbed me by the arm and said eagerly, 'You're doing a wonderful job, young man. Keep it up. The one thing we all want is a good clean election.'

"I told her, 'You don't seem to understand. We want to see religion kept out of politics.'

"Again she grabbed me enthusiastically and said, 'So do I! That's why I can't understand how these damned Catholics have the nerve to run one of their men for President.' "

A more serious case developed when a distraught woman came to Malloy's headquarters and said, "I need guidance. My husband and I are fighting over the election." Professor Malloy explained, "We're not allowed to go into family problems, or political ones either. My assistant here likes one of the candidates and I like the other, but we work together harmoniously. You and your husband ought . . ."

"You don't understand," the woman said. "My minister warned us in church last Sunday that if we voted for John Kennedy we would live to see the day when Protestants were crucified in Levittown shopping center. And my husband says that if I vote for Nixon we'll all starve. What am I going to do?"

The men in the office laughed and said, "Under the circumstances, you better just not vote."

"But I have to," she said. "I'm already registered."

Malloy and his assistant again laughed at the irrational story, then asked out of curiosity, "Who told you about Protestants' being crucified?"

"Our minister," she repeated firmly.

"You certainly didn't hear any minister say that," Malloy pressed.

"In his sermon," the woman insisted. "Last Sunday."

She took Malloy to the parsonage, where she introduced him to a perfectly normal, college-educated clergyman of one of the great standard sects. When the woman had left, Malloy asked the clergyman, "Certainly, Reverend, you didn't tell your congregation that if John Kennedy is elected President, Protestants will be crucified in Levittown plaza."

"Of course I did," the clergyman replied.

"You don't believe it, do you?" Malloy probed.

"Why, of course. It says so right here in the book," and the minister produced a real horror, composed of old wood cuts, lurid text, and quotations from long-forgotten Catholic prelates. It was a terrifying document, which assured its readers that rack and pinion were just around the corner waiting to be presided over by fat and ghoulish priests who were lusting for Protestant blood.

"Now really, Reverend," Malloy pleaded, "you can't believe this nonsense."

"It all happened," the minister argued.

"Yes, but this incident took place in 1350 and this one in the 1500's," Malloy pointed out. "You're not using those events as evidence for today, are you?"

"It happened," the minister repeated stubbornly. "I preach only the truth."

"Do you remember that it was the Protestant church that hanged the witches in America? Do you suppose that if Nixon is elected, the Protestants will hang witches in Levittown plaza?"

The minister pondered this for a moment, then said brightly, "Ah yes, but the Protestants didn't hang their people for political reasons." To the end of the campaign, this minister continued preaching in his weekly sermons that if John Kennedy were elected, there would be public crucifixions throughout Bucks County, and there was no legal agency that could stop him.

Malloy says, "But the big day in our committee's history came when one of our Republican members rushed in triumphantly and threw a handbill down on my desk. 'Hooray!' he shouted. 'Now we've caught the Democrats doing it too!' The offensive handbill, crudely printed by some means that was never determined, said simply, 'Nix on Nixon. He's a

Quaker.' And a phrase was added to imply that all Quakers were communists. The handbill had been widely distributed and was a clear infraction of federal law in that it bore no identification of its source.

"We never did find out who issued it," Malloy reported. "And of all the hate literature we saw in this campaign, this was the only piece that broke any law. All the rest bore some indication of origin and were thus legal."

The file of filthy material that Malloy assembled is shocking. It had enormous circulation and apparently a good deal of influence. The reason its poison was not even more effective was that Malloy and his people tracked down all individuals who were distributing it in the lower end of the county and tried to dissuade them from doing so. Even more important, Malloy, instead of ranting about the menacing stuff, laughed at it, and in the end he had all of us laughing at it, too.

During the campaign I was much impressed by the sequence of newspaper stories seeking to prove that in the 1928 campaign the religious issue had not played a major role in the defeat of Al Smith. These writers argued that no Democrat could have defeated Hoover in 1928, that Smith's stand on Prohibition condemned him to certain defeat, and that the man's uncouth habits made him totally unpalatable. Of the major reasons for his loss, argued these pundits, his religion was the least important.

Challenged by these articles, I kept careful record of the impact of religion on the election in my county, and in the last chapter I shall record my conclusions. Here I need only say that the religious issue permeated every meeting I conducted. It influenced Republicans and Democrats alike. Ministers preached politics publicly and churches distributed the most vicious electioneering materials. Practically no one I met escaped the pressure of this overriding problem and, in my county at least, both parties were ultimately forced to make their major calculations with the religious question a foremost consideration. From what I could see, no man among us was clever enough to have judged accurately at the beginning what the ultimate effect of the religious question was going to be.

I can, however, recall what I thought from week to week, because I spent long hours arguing the question both in private meetings and in public sessions, and the record of my confusion probably reflects the national norm.

Before any of the primaries, I judged that the religious question would not be too important and that the bigots on one fringe would exactly counterbalance the bigots on the other. After the Wisconsin primary I thought there was some evidence that in a national election Kennedy might be helped slightly by an unusually large Catholic vote. After the West Virginia primary I was convinced that the religious question had been magnified out of proportion, a position which I held almost into September.

Just before the campaign began, my talks with Miss Omwake and Mrs. Dale showed me how wrong my earlier calculations had been; but even so, when the flood of anti-Catholic literature began to reach my desk, I was unprepared for its magnitude and virulence. I then found that hundreds of Democrats in Bucks County, if not thousands, were going to vote against Kennedy, and for a while I thought this trend, magnified across the nation, would lose us the election.

The Peale-Poling fiasco proved that there were countermeasures that could be taken and that in the long run the religious issue might hurt the Republicans more than the Democrats. In October, talks I had with leaders in other states made me think that the large cities were going to turn in unusually high Democratic majorities partially because the Catholics had been made fighting mad.

In the first week of November, as I shall explain later, I was repelled by the religious bigotry I saw operating in one part of the United States far from my own county, and for a while I feared that it might cost Kennedy the election. No one could underestimate the effect of the religious hatred that I experienced that night.

But on the evening before the election I thought that Senator Kennedy's utilization of the television film taken of his confrontation with the Baptist ministers in Texas was superb electioneering. Somehow those few feet of film wrapped up the whole religious issue and enabled the Democrats to salvage at least something from the wreckage.

If, thirty years from now, all of this can be explained away in clever articles which prove that religion played no significant role in the 1960 election, it seems to me that the writers of that age will have to blind themselves to what actually happened.

5

The Turning Point

☒ ☒

The 1960 campaign began poorly for the Democrats. The conspicuous advantages with which Vice President Nixon started as a result of the Chicago convention grew when the rump session of Congress flatly rejected most of the Democratic program. My friends all considered the Democratic setback rather more seriously than I did. They pointed out that the Republicans could cry to the nation, "See! Johnson was in control of the Senate and Rayburn of the House, yet Kennedy was able to accomplish nothing. It proves he's only a boy." They felt that these charges would be damaging.

I saw it rather differently. I saw John Kennedy battling for some very progressive legislation. I saw him making speeches that looked fine on the record. And I saw him frustrated at every move by the threat of a Republican Presidential veto. It seemed to me that it was he, and not Nixon, who was making points to be used in the forthcoming campaign. It is true that he did not stand forth as a successful leader, and it is true that he was defeated on each major point, often by Democratic votes, but he did appear as a gallant fighter and after the session ended no one could be in doubt as to where he stood. I can't speak for the other Democratic county chairmen, but I am certain that insofar as I was concerned, he made my job infinitely easier. After the Congressional showing I was able to use as my constant peroration: "The only important difference between these two good men is this. If you want better health bills, vote for Kennedy. He has proved that he will recommend such bills to Congress and that he will sign them when they're passed. If you don't want health measures, vote for the Republicans. They've proved that they'll veto them." Down the long list of necessary legislative measures I went, one by one, and in every instance there was on the record the fact that John Kennedy favored such bills, plus the supposition that he would sign them if President, and there was likewise the record and the supposition that a Republican President would veto them. I believe that such arguments won many undecided voters to the Democratic column.

Since the structure of my county made it inevitable that the majority of people in any audience I addressed would have to be Republicans, it was only sensible for me to avoid attacking their candidate. Again and again I admitted that Richard Nixon was a good man, that people who really hated the Catholic Church had a right to vote Republican, that the slippage in our foreign reputation started ten or twelve years ago and was thus not chargeable only to the Eisenhower regime, and that if the President were free to run again, he would surely be reëlected. Of course, I was entitled to needle the opposition on this last point, always explaining that only the petty vengeance of men who hated Roosevelt had produced the law that prohibited President Eisenhower from seeking and winning a third term. "But since we can't have Mr. Eisenhower, we are forced to choose between two younger men, and between these two I really think almost every sensible criterion favors Senator Kennedy." When pressed about his lack of experience as contrasted to Richard Nixon's, I always replied, "Senator Kennedy has had more experience in Congress than Abraham Lincoln had when he was elected. And fourteen years more than General Eisenhower had when he was made President." I am not sure that these were the best answers, but they were the best I could think of.

From the first day of September until Election Day I made no fewer than three speeches every day. I toured my county from one end to another, and often I limped at nine or ten o'clock at night into some cold hall where eight Democrats were gathered. At times it seemed foolish to be wasting my energies in this fruitless task, but the next night I would report to another hall where nine hundred people were waiting, most of them Republicans, eager to talk politics, and I would sit very quiet as I was being introduced, hoping that I might have something fresh to say.

I don't believe that one should write about American politics until he has had this humbling experience of actually beating the backwoods for votes, for in pursuing people one comes face to face with the ultimate problems of American life. Believe me, the people I met knew what questions they wanted answered, and in the course of my travels I suppose I was asked about every single plank in the Democratic platform. I had started out in September not knowing very much about it; by November, I was a walking expert.

As the weeks rolled by, with twenty and sometimes thirty meetings each week, I fell into a kind of stupor built upon unrolling highways down which my car traveled of its own accord, cold dinners at which I arrived late, faces bursting with probing queries and question-and-answer periods that sometimes extended for three hours. In the mornings my wife and I conducted coffee hours, at which all were invited to discuss the campaign; and dulled as my senses were, I always seemed to revive whenever we could get together a handful of people who really wanted to exchange ideas.

Up and down the county I tried to be rock-bottom honest in my replies. I confessed always how close I thought the popular vote would be; there must be many thousands of people in eastern Pennsylvania who heard me argue, "We are not looking for mass conversions here. We do not expect at the end of this meeting that Nixon people will storm out into the lobby, tear off their buttons and jump on them. If you stand at the door when this meeting ends and ask the first ninety-nine visitors what they thought of the talk and if these ninety-nine say, 'He didn't impress me a bit,' I won't be embarrassed at all. For if you asked the hundredth and he says, 'What he said makes sense. I may vote for Kennedy,' then this meeting has been a tremendous success. Because if that one man shifts from Nixon to Kennedy he represents one percent of the vote, and I assure you that one percent of the vote is going to win this election. So get out and win that one percent."

I lost my voice and spoke like a rattle, and the results we were getting were so pitifully inadequate that I began to wonder why I was wasting my time. A special burden which all Democratic speakers had to bear in this early period of the campaign was the member of the audience who jumped to his feet in the question-and-answer period to say in a loud clear voice, "I'm a Stevenson man, and frankly I can't see John Kennedy. I don't know whether to vote for Nixon or just stay home."

When I had heard this about a hundred times, for Philadelphia had been the only major city that went for Stevenson in 1956, I had a private meeting with my wife, who remained the most ardent Stevenson admirer I knew. She counseled, "Remember what you told me a year ago. Don't fight these people. They've got to make three distinct jumps before they'll be any help to us. First they threaten, 'I'll vote for Nixon,' and if they do, they cost us two votes. A little later they'll say, 'I'll stay home.' This is a lot better, because although we lose their vote, they don't penalize us double. Later they'll come around to, 'I'll vote for Kennedy, but I won't work for him.' Well, that's as much as you can hope for. But some, like me, will ultimately say, 'Of course Kennedy's the better man. I'll help.' Let's try to lead them step by step to the light, just as you said."

I'm afraid I never had much success with my Stevensonian hecklers, for although I was patient, and although I tried to do everything reasonable, I suspect I was never able to hide my contempt for people who thought that their tastes were so refined that in a time of national crisis neither Richard Nixon nor John Kennedy was worthy of their support. This pose of superiority seemed to me such a negation of democracy—such a refusal to look at the record where a very average Chester Arthur suddenly thrown into the Presidency gave a fine account of himself or where a Hugo Black, projected onto the Supreme Court after a Ku Klux membership, transformed himself into one of the finest justices of our day—that I had to hold it in contempt. One night, after I had been severely heckled by Stevenson supporters, I said somewhat angrily, "Look, Mr. Stevenson is going to be in Philadelphia on October 19. Go hear him, please, and you'll hear him tell you himself that you ought to transfer your allegiance to Kennedy."

One heckler argued, "He'll never say that in public. How can you, an intelligent man, support John Kennedy?"

Tired, I snapped, "How can you, if you supported Adlai Stevenson, now ignore the qualities of John Kennedy and still dare to call yourself intelligent?" I suspect I lost a vote, but I felt better.

My wife and I often discussed this phenomenon, and once I asked her, "Can you comprehend how anyone who voted for the idealism of Adlai Stevenson could now adopt the pose of not voting at all?" To my relief she said that such a posture was incomprehensible. But out of this searching for a way to handle the disgruntled Democrats, I did fashion a speech which went a long way to assuage hurt feelings. To such hecklers I confessed, "Good as John Kennedy is, he's no superman. He's not as brainy as Adlai Stevenson. He doesn't know as much about military affairs as Stuart Symington. He certainly doesn't know as much about running the Senate as Lyndon Johnson. And if any of you in the audience supported any one of those three at the convention, you know I'm telling the truth. But I'm also telling the truth when I say that all things considered, John Kennedy is the best man available. He's going to be elected. And he's going to be a great President."

Almost every day during the campaign somebody would ask, either in perplexity or with intent to insult, "Why would a man like you get mixed up in politics?" I never got accustomed to this question, nor can I yet absorb it without anger. There were two disturbing parts to the query, each insulting to the nation. The first lay in the phrase "a man like you." At the beginning I used to embarrass my questioners by retorting, "What kind of man do you think I am?" And they would usually reply, "Well, a writer. You could live anywhere you wish. You don't owe anybody anything." There were so many good answers to this part of the question that I never had the nerve to use any of them. They all sounded too much like something Ben Franklin might have written or that George Washington might have copied in his chapbook as a boy. I still wouldn't know how to answer that basic question without sounding like part of the Declaration of Independence, so I let it ride.

The second part of the query, "get mixed up in politics," seemed especially insulting. At first I responded, "If politics was good enough for Aristotle and Cicero and Edmund Burke and Alexander Hamilton and Woodrow Wilson, it's certainly good enough for me." But such an answer was more dignified than the question merited, so in the later weeks I said simply, "I happen to be convinced that John Kennedy is going to make a great President." Usually my questioners were satisfied with this reply, even though I wasn't.

I must confess that in the early days of the campaign, with everything apparently going against us, with a cold in my chest, and with endless miles before me at the close of each meeting, I became momentarily depressed. The Stevenson supporters were openly implying that my candidate was inadequate, and the religious bigots were hammering us from all sides. Several dozen of my helpers reported that their ministers were haranguing them in church, and all the newspapers in our area were reporting fresh Republican triumphs. I had been working mainly in Republican areas, and what the papers claimed was borne out by my experience.

And then late one night as I was driving home alone from a labor-union meeting in Bristol, I stopped at an all-night coffee stand, where a group of ordinary workmen were hanging around waiting for whatever it is that comes along a lonely road at two in the morning. They saw the Kennedy-Johnson sticker on my car and started asking me questions. Why was I for Kennedy? Was I a Catholic? What did I think of the Forand Bill? Would he raise taxes? Would he get the $1.25 minimum wage bill through if he was President? What about Kennedy's brother and Hoffa?

The night wore on and others drifted in and out of the conversation, and as our exchange of ideas progressed, I realized that not since the days in Guatemala had I had so fine a political discourse. These men knew. They understood what was happening in this election. They pinpointed one problem after another, and some of the best of the group were for Nixon, and they knew why. We talked for about two hours, and I left that coffee shack positively elated. That my countrymen knew as much as these men did about our political system was a tribute to our nation. No one asked, "Why is a guy like you in politics?" But four asked, "What can I do to help?" And three made cash contributions to what I was already doing.

As I drove home I took with me a heartening view of

the election. I saw fairly clearly that if John Kennedy could speak sensibly to such people, if he could get across to them the things he believed in, there was a good chance that he could win. On this hope I existed during the dark days. And I must say, looking back on the election, that the best speakers I heard during the campaign, insofar as honest political reasoning was concerned, were the labor-union men. Invariably they cited specific legislation, specific courses of action, specific legislators. They made more sense than anyone else I heard. True, they were the best men from our best unions. They were shrewdly trained political experts, and whenever I found that one of the speakers on my program was a union man, I relaxed. I knew I could depend upon him to talk facts; I was left free to indulge in generalizations.

A corollary to this coffee-stand discovery came during our first big meeting in Bristol, when we were trying with no great success to kick off the campaign. The dais was rather high and this kept our table of speakers—and a rather distinguished group it was, too, with a governor and a senator—rather far above the crowd of some 800 diners. Before it came my turn to speak I saw that two attractive Negro girls had come to the meeting and either by someone else's design or by their own timidity had taken a table totally apart from the white people. I waited for some minutes for someone in the audience to perceive what had happened, but nobody did, and I thought, "You're in this campaign because you say you believe certain things. Prove it." So I left the head table, climbed down into the audience and went over to the two girls. "Look," I said, "I refuse to address a Democratic meeting when two pretty colored girls like you are sitting alone." They looked up at me and laughed. "I mean it," I said. "I'm not going to open my mouth till you join in with the crowd. Let's go."

What I was doing, as will be explained later, was a good deal more inflammatory than it may seem in words, for not long ago in this area Negroes, trying to move into Levittown, had evoked an international race-relations scandal and tempers had not yet fully subsided. I took the girls by the arm and led them to a table where a small collection of Levittowners sat. "Should we?" the girls whispered.

"You damned well should," I said. "That's one thing this election is all about."

I seated the girls and introduced them. The Levittowners seemed pleased to have them, and during the remainder of the campaign the Negro girls from Bristol and their white confreres from Levittown were among the best workers the Democratic party had. I was therefore doubly appreciative, a few weeks later, when Robert Kennedy, speaking in the same hall, but to a much larger crowd, insisted upon exiting through the kitchen so that he could talk with the Negro waiters. "We need your help," he said simply. "Please help us all you can."

From such ground-level experiences I developed a concept which the leaders of the Democratic party had apparently adopted years before: that to succeed, the Democrats must win the allegiance of many diverse groups, and that doing this takes precedence over any other tactical consideration. Starting from a solid base of people who vote Democratic automatically—many Republicans do the same—the party must enlist the liberals, who are notoriously swing voters and must be lured with solid proof of performance, labor, the intellectuals, Negroes, Jews, and the Catholics of the big cities. My wife, who was a distinguished pioneer worker in the field of race relations, screams in protest whenever anyone refers to "the Negro vote," and I am not here referring to such a vote or to "the Catholic vote," or to any other kind of vote that one can rely on automatically. But at the same time I think it naïve to adopt the position that people of similar interests do not vote in similar patterns if they receive similar impulses. I would reject the idea that the Democratic party was the prescribed home of Negroes, Jews and Catholics, for that is patently not true, but I do believe, for example, that people who tend to have the experiences that Negroes today have can find their hopes best cared for in my party.

I was disturbed when, on a visit to one of America's most distinguished Jews, I found that he had assembled a small group of men well known in America, ostensibly for a social gathering but principally to discuss some documents which had fallen into his hands. Most of the men present were Republicans, and some were extremely highly placed. The situation was a simple one: "By means which are of no concern to anyone here, we have acquired photostatic copies of letters written by the German ambassador in London to Herr von Ribbentrop in Berlin just prior to World

War II. Presumably these papers were found by American researchers in the German archives after the death of Hitler."

"What do they relate to?" someone asked.

"They report the German ambassador's conversations with the American ambassador, Joseph P. Kennedy."

A hush fell over the group, and I remember muttering under my breath, "Oh hell! That's all we need."

The nature of the reports was made sickeningly specific. "If they are widely publicized," the self-appointed chairman observed, "I doubt if any New York Jews would dare to vote Democratic, and if Kennedy doesn't carry this state, Nixon is elected. What should we do?"

The discussion proceeded for several hours. One group felt that a late-October advertisement in one of the leading New York papers, simply setting forth the facts, would accomplish the defeat of John Kennedy. Others felt that under no circumstances should the documents be used. "They'd probably backfire and assure his election," these men argued.

I was much impressed by the level-headed analysis offered by one of America's leading public-relations men, and a man totally committed to the election of Richard Nixon. "Don't touch these papers," this gentleman argued. "If you did use them, and I were a Democrat, I'd charge you with having forged them. Next I'd charge you with trying to fasten the sins of the father, supposing they were sins, on the son, and this would gain sympathy for Kennedy. Finally I'd advise Kennedy to put Abe Ribicoff on television with a ringing denouncement of the whole damned trick, and you'd lose more votes than you'd get."

"No," reasoned a profound Jewish patriot. "You would lose some votes, but remember that the Jews have suffered terribly because of opinions like the ones represented in these documents, and if those opinions were circulated, no self-respecting Jew could vote for anyone even remotely related to them."

The discussion grew vigorous, and always the public-relations man insisted that the plan was not practical because it simply would not yield the desired results. "It's sure to backfire," he argued.

My opinion was asked and I said, "Seems to me I read hints about this in Drew Pearson's column. Looks as if the Democrats are building a backfire so as to control the blaze if anyone ignites the subject later in the campaign. But even more important, Joseph Kennedy has denied he ever said what the Germans attributed to him. Doesn't this destroy the papers completely?"

Insofar as this particular afternoon was concerned, the matter was settled by a sage Jew, who gave new reasons: "When I first read those documents my blood boiled, and I wanted to publish them from the housetops, but prudence as an American citizen warned me that to do so would be folly. If it were generally believed that the Jews were strong enough, even in their minority, to defeat John Kennedy for the Presidency, we would not consequently reap any rewards from the Republicans. We would be hated additionally merely because we were so strong. And those who hated us would be right in doing so, for we would have abused in the political field what ought to be a power merely in the religious field. Therefore we should under no circumstances use these documents during this election, for to do so would be imprudent. But if what Michener says is true, and if the documents are false, then to use them would be corrupt."

Someone snapped, "That's a fine speech. But the brutal fact is that where the Catholic Church becomes powerful, liberal Jews have a hard time."

It fell to me to answer this argument: "As has been pointed out, I'm openly working for Jack Kennedy. At the same time I'm one of the leaders of a population-control movement. And as a novelist I frequently find myself opposed to the more repressive measures of the Church. But I don't find working for Kennedy and working for population-control mutually incompatible. I know from my textbook experience that the Church makes it difficult for Jewish liberals and for all other liberals, too. But one opposes this sort of thing step by step in his quarrel with the hierarchy, not in fighting with individual Catholics. I'm much impressed with the sign I saw in the Milan Cathedral which said, 'Bicycle riding forbidden in this church.' But the kids rode their bicycles up and down the aisles nevertheless."

"What's the point of that story?" someone asked.

"Simply that in America we take Catholicism too seriously. Here it's a young religion shepherded by a bunch of overly eager Irishmen. In Italy kids ride bicycles up and down the aisles. I believe that in about fifty years we'll have settled down, and American Catholicism will have settled down, to comfortable European patterns. The best way I know to speed the process is to elect John Kennedy President. He's probably as anti-clerical as I am."

A wise observer said, "You don't elect a President in order to reform a church."

I replied, "But if he's the better man, and if you can help adjust a church to American life at the same time, then it's a logical bargain."

As good Republicans, they did not agree that Senator Kennedy was the better man, and during the rest of the campaign I sat on needles waiting for the New York Jews to publish their German documents. Had they done so, they might have made it impossible for Kennedy to carry New York City, and of course its loss would have cost him the state and the Presidency.

So all in all, the early weeks of the campaign were not pleasant, but I felt that even though the Republicans were off to the better start, something was bound to happen that would get us rolling. What it would be I could not guess. I think I relied principally on some eruption in the field of foreign relations which would disclose to the electorate our nation's precarious position in contrast to the roseate picture being painted by the administration; but even the prospects of such a development gave me little real solace, and in this mood I approached the night of September 26, when the first of the televised debates was to occur. I had already explained to my wife that Nixon would probably trounce Kennedy in formal argument, and it was with no expectancy of triumph that we sat down early that Monday evening to watch the first debate. To me it was just another dangerous hurdle that could not be sidestepped.

When the cameras disclosed the austere concrete walls I gasped and thought, "It's like a setting for a Franz Kafka play." And when one of the lenses wandered over to pick up Richard Nixon I gasped again. He seemed like a ghost. I thought, "My God, he lost weight in that hospital."

The unreality of the night increased when the camera time and again picked up that fantastic row of heads belonging to the nameless and faceless reporters. This indeed was a Kafka movie I was watching, with the ponderous voices of the newsmen intoning their impersonal and generalized questions. The setting, the row of heads, and one of the actors formed the components of a burial, and I felt sure that it was my candidate who was going to be interred.

And then he started to speak. In short, sharp, incisive sentences he hacked away at his major themes. America must move ahead. We are not doing enough. We need much new legislation. At the end of his opening statement I sighed with at least momentary relief and whispered, "It's good he went first. Public got a chance to see him before Nixon clobbers him."

Then came the Vice President, and I was shocked at the emptiness, at the foolish oratory, at the lack of specifics. Where was the fire of the acceptance speech at Chicago? Where was the fighter, the dominator? I simply could not believe that I was looking at Richard Nixon.

Now came the questions to Kennedy, and in the manner that was to become famous he started punching out his answers. His right hand jabbed at the hearts of his listeners. He stood erect, his shoulders and chin leaning just a little forward. He kept referring to things in numbered series. He spoke with rapidity and force, and best of all, what he said made good sense. Along with seventy million other Americans, I sat up.

When the camera flashed back to Mr. Nixon, his face was drawn and streaked. Bubbles of perspiration rested on his chin and twice he tried vainly to wipe them away. His voice was silken where it should have been hard. He said, "I agree," where he should have waged war. He fumbled, failed and frowned. It was a performance that I shall never forget, for I doubt if any other viewer in the nation was as astonished by the complete collapse of a public figure as I was on that first night.

I went to bed scarcely able to believe what I had seen. Suddenly the prospect of victory was very bright before me, for it seemed as if all America must have discovered what I had discovered, that John Kennedy was not only a match for Richard Nixon; he was measurably superior in command of facts, in forthrightness, in ability to reason, and in his willingness to talk sense to the American people. But I was in for a surprise.

On Tuesday morning I had to go to New York, and while there I bought every newspaper I could find, even going to the Times Square special newsstand where I was able to purchase about a dozen out-of-town papers to savor the reports of Kennedy's triumph. To my astonishment all the papers said that the debate had been a draw. Many implied that Nixon had won because of his superior statesmanship. One Associated Press story was particularly infuriating. It said that practically no one's opinion had been modified by the debate. I got so mad at this that I went into a bar and spread that paper out before me and read every word of the report. What it said in its opening paragraphs was what the headlines proclaimed: that practically no one's opinion was in any way modified by what the contestants had said, but farther down in the story, when I read the actual city-by-city reports, I found that everyone whose opinion had been changed had changed from Nixon to Kennedy.

"What the hell!" I cried to the bartender. "Look at it for yourself. Practically nobody's opinion was changed, but everybody who did change went over to Kennedy. That's one percent of the vote, and one percent will win this election. We're in!"

It is a matter of record that I carried this newspaper up and down Bucks County, reading the actual news story and not the headline. There it was. A few people had changed to Kennedy. They could not have been so blind as not to see what I saw on that television screen. Of course Kennedy had won the first debate, and of course all America knew it.

Prior to the fourth debate almost all news stories contained some phrase like this: "As is universally acknowledged, Jack Kennedy won the first debate by a wide margin. . . ." It was certainly not universally acknowledged until long after the event. But by then everyone had to admit that Nixon had lost, and panic had set in at Republican headquarters. I treasured the comment of the Republican committeeman who met Nixon two days after the first debate. "Has anyone told him?" he asked the aides.

The break that I had prayed for had come, and it had come from a quarter that I least expected. I can only say, as a field worker, that it was both appropriate and deeply moving that Jack Kennedy got his campaign off the ground solely by virtue of his own character, his own force of mind, and his own dedication to common sense. Like a million other volunteers in this election, I worked desperately hard to elect Senator Kennedy, but all that I and all that the million others did would have accomplished nothing if in that first debate Kennedy himself hadn't taken command and shown the American electorate that a real man was running for the Presidency.

I think I can testify to the climactic importance of this first debate, because in the days before the confrontation it was very difficult for me to get others to work for Senator Kennedy, and we struggled along with one office and one paid secretary. Immediately after the debate we received funds from heaven knows where to open four additional offices, each with at least one paid secretary and some with three. We got phone calls volunteering services. We got automobiles and posters. We received checks through the mail and a steady stream of visitors. In Bucks County, where it used to take courage to be a Democrat, we had five thriving volunteer offices open seven days a week. In each area we had two or three meetings every day. I kept on a kind of merry-go-round, dashing from one to the next and on to the next. And now wherever I went I could say, with full assurance of recognition, "You saw how our candidate won the debate. That's the way he's going to win the election." Where before I had usually been greeted with amused tolerance, I was now greeted compassionately. People seriously wanted to know why I was for Kennedy, and one night before a large crowd, I told them.

I said, "Some years ago I was working in Djakarta, the capital of Indonesia. It was one of the most difficult cities in the world to work in, because in a few short years its population had exploded from 300,000 to nearly 3,000,000. It was hot, stuffy, crowded, and shot through with ugly bickering between the Indonesians and their former colonial overlords, the Dutch. It was the only place I have been where incoming planeloads of travelers simply couldn't find any place to stay and so slept sitting up in chairs in the airport.

"One afternoon we got a cablegram advising us that this congressman was dropping in for a visit, and we assumed that he was just another junketing legislator out for a free trip around the world. But we couldn't find out what committee he was on, or what his business was. We expected that he would be rather difficult to deal with. Anyway, we went out to the airport and off the battered-up plane stepped a young man who looked as if he'd been on a five-day drunk. He was unshaved, rumpled, had sweat rings under his arms and a shock of uncombed hair. He said briefly, 'I'm Jack Kennedy, of Massachusetts.' And before we could ask what he was doing on such a junket, he said that he wanted to meet some labor-union people, some newspaper editors, some policemen and some soldiers. He didn't demand to see the ambassador or the prime minister or anyone else. He told us that he was merely a congressman, traveling around the world on his own money and his own time in order to see what was going on.

"In the next days Jack Kennedy dug into Indonesia as I have seen few strangers ever dig into a new terrain, so that when he left he was a stranger no longer, and he was prepared to deal with the problem of Indonesia if it ever came up in the Congress. As his plane flew off, a girl from our embassy said wistfully, 'If he keeps this up, someday he's going to be a senator from Massachusetts.' I explained to her that there wasn't a chance, since that state already had a fine senior senator, Leverett Saltonstall and that it had just elected a fine junior senator, grandson of one of the best men who had ever served in the Senate. I explained that with this new young man secure in his job, Kennedy would have to be content with being a representative, 'because,' I pointed out, 'the new senator's name is Henry Cabot Lodge, and with a name like that he'll never be defeated.'

"You know what Kennedy did to Lodge in that election, and you know what he's going to do to him in this one, too. Well, I now knew Kennedy's name, and I started following his work in the Senate. He stood for things that I stood for. With some courage he voted for bills that were unpopular in his own state, but which were necessary for the nation. I found out that he was an excellent writer and that he had a fine sense of history. And of course I knew that during the war he had performed with unusual gallantry.

"To sum it all up, the more I studied John Kennedy the more convinced I became that he had the makings of a superb political leader with the social conscience of a Franklin Delano Roosevelt, the intellectual capacity of a Woodrow Wilson, and the down-to-earth political know-how of a Harry Truman. I promise you that not once since I made that first decision have I had cause to review or regret my choice. His opponents say he is a young man. Neither he nor I can fight the calendar, but I say he has the makings of a great man, and neither his opponents nor the record can successfully challenge that contention. Without any qualification, without any suppression of my own inner feelings or fears, without any hesitation I recommend John Kennedy to you as your next President. Neither you nor I will be disappointed in his performance."

Because Kennedy himself had triumphed in the debates and demonstrated to the electorate that there was substance behind such claims as I made in my nightly speeches, it was now possible to convince a few people each time that he had the makings of a fine President, but I must repeat that so far as those of us were concerned who worked at the grass-roots level, it was Kennedy himself, and only Kennedy, who won the election. At the end of the campaign I was to conclude that it was Nixon who had lost the election, rather than Kennedy who had won it, but that's another story on which I'll comment later.

6
Suburbia

If it were not for its southern end, Bucks County would be of no special political interest. It would merely duplicate hundreds of other semi-rural counties across the nation. But in our southern section three highways form an important triangle, and what goes on inside involves the very future of our nation.

U. S. Route 1 is the oldest and most famous of our national highways, running from the northern tip of Maine south to Key West. It was the great road of our colonial days, linking Boston and Richmond, and today remains a major thoroughfare down our eastern coastline. On its way from Trenton to Philadelphia it forms the northwestern side of the triangle about which I am speaking.

Along another route from Trenton to Philadelphia runs U. S. Route 13, a highway of no special significance, except that after it leaves Philadelphia it does form the main road down the Delmarva Peninsula, which is historic. As it crosses Bucks County it forms the eastern boundary of our triangle.

The southern boundary is appropriately the newest road in the county, the majestic multi-lane Pennsylvania Turnpike as it sweeps westward from New York to Chicago. Its broad concrete ribbons and its stylish overpasses speak of the future.

Nestled within these three highways is Levittown, that extraordinary collection of 17,000 brand-new homes built in one six-year spurt. In 1952, when General Eisenhower was first elected President, Levittown did not exist. Work had begun and a few families had moved into the outskirts, but the sprawling complex of homes and roads was only in the planning stage. In 1960, a mere eight years later, Levittown was a city of some 70,000 people, and everyone who lived there had moved in from somewhere else. In their youth, most of these newcomers, many from Catholic and Jewish families, had been Democrats, and it was supposed that when they settled down to the pleasant routines of Bucks County life they would continue to vote Democratic.

But sociological and political changes of considerable magnitude were in progress, and when families who had been reared in the tight confines of a city reached the countryside they expanded in unforeseen ways, a principal one being that they no longer wanted to observe their inherited patterns of social or political behavior. When they saw suburbia with its hint of golf courses, private swimming clubs, rural marketing and Sunday drives through the countryside, they received the subtle impression that, in the words of one Levittowner, "if we lived in a nice clean area like this we were supposed to vote Republican." And in all the nation's suburbias they began to do so with startling force. Sociologists described these new voting patterns as "the revolt of the lace-curtain Irish," but the effect was equally pronounced in Protestant and Jewish families of similar background. I watched various parts of the United States undergo this change and it is not accurate to brush it off as merely "the real-estate complex." Other substantial factors were operating.

Many of the younger couples consisted of a man who had served in World War II, which had certainly disrupted his traditional patterns, married to a girl who had had to work while waiting for her fiancé or who had been forced to care for a houseful of children without the help of a husband. Like her soldier partner, this young wife knew that the old patterns of allegiance were shattered. Together these couples honestly wanted something better than they had known in the past. They no longer wanted the social revolution represented by the Democrats; they longed for the quiet respectability of American middle-class life, and they felt, in astonishing numbers, that this could be obtained only by voting the Republican ticket.

They were also subject to the new suburban mores which claimed, "Now that you have a good home, you're entitled to vote Republican. To do otherwise would be an anachronism." Many Levittowners were to tell me of friends who had argued, "You can't vote Democratic. You would betray your class." For these reasons, in 1956 Levittown, which according to the inherited tradition of its residents should have voted Democratic by not less than 60-40, turned in only 9,689 votes for Stevenson and nearly three hundred more, 9,954, for Eisenhower. Having thus failed to gain even a 50-50 split in this important segment of Democratic territory, Stevenson had no hope of carrying the county, for the northern sections remained overwhelmingly Republican.

But by 1960 the young Jewish and Catholic newcomers to suburbia, plus thousands of their Protestant neighbors who had felt that with a new home they were obligated to have a new party also, had begun to reconsider what they had gained with their Republican vote and what they had lost, and there was a general feeling that they had somehow defrauded themselves. Certainly, wherever I went in suburbia I found people ready to reconsider their basic political allegiances.

In dealing with the 1960 election I can speak only of Bucks County's suburbia, which was the only one I knew well, and I do not argue that its reaction was typical, for of all the suburbias that had a right to feel that a Republican vote did not necessarily insure happiness on earth, the Bucks County suburbanites had the most legitimate cause for outrage.

For Bucks County's Levittown doesn't really exist. It is a city of 70,000, but it has no entity. There is not even a place legally called Levittown, for when the vast suburbia started to evolve, the canny old-time citizens of Bucks County quickly realized that here was going to be a source of economic and political power, so instead of allowing the new community to coalesce naturally into a major city, four small political entities within the county each stubbornly held onto its inherited portion of the new city.

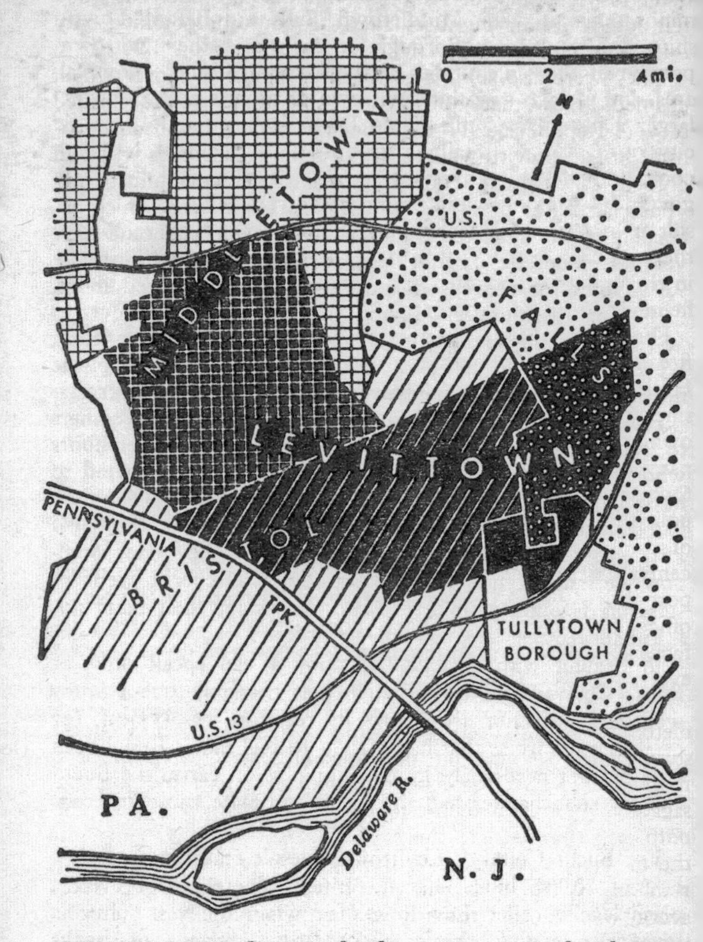

LEVITTOWN, *showing why the city is not a city but the tag end of four different political units: Middletown, Falls and Bristol Townships, and Tullytown Borough*

Therefore what is called Levittown today is actually a random collection of four fragments of four otherwise rather minor political units; Middletown, Falls and Bristol Townships, and Tullytown Borough. In each case, the Levittown portion of the old unit lies at the extremity of the physical area, and in each case the Levittown portion is politically the larger half of the unit. Thus Levittown, in appearance a city of 70,000, is actually a group of four contiguous rural communities, each governed in a separate manner and all governed as if they were unimportant rural villages. The result is governmental chaos, and the Philadelphian who fled the pressures of the city in order to find reasonable solitude in the country quickly found himself enmeshed in problems he never dreamed of before.

For example, since there is no Levittown, there is no city fire company. Not long ago a house caught fire in Quincy Hollow, only 150 yards from the Bristol fire company, but since Quincy Hollow is not in Bristol, the distraught home owners had to wait until their own Middletown fire company, situated miles away, could stagger to the scene. Levittown has four fire companies, each with its own rules, four police forces, four postal systems, four school systems. Some of the segments have kindergartens; others don't. It has no central library, no trash collection, no park system, no main post office with its superior services (although one branch office calls itself Levittown), no equalized tax system. In fact, it is as disgraceful a plan for government as I have ever seen, and I am amazed that it is tolerated.

The problem is not simple. The old-time residents of Middletown, Falls, Bristol Townships and Tullytown, in sponsoring and perpetuating this appalling system, have been motivated in part by economic greed, in part by political sagacity. As long as each established governing unit can hold onto its proportionate share of the stillborn city, some of the old-timers are going to have good political jobs, and all residents of the areas will profit from the higher tax rolls accruing to the old townships. On the other hand, the old-timers have a good point when they say, "Sure, the Levittowners want to incorporate into their own city, but when they do so they want to take in the best industrial areas of Middletown, Bristol, Falls and Tullytown and leave us with no tax base at all. Never!" Finally, it must be admitted that a good many Levittowners, having tasted life in the never-

never land of a suburbia that looks like a city but has the old-fashioned laws of a hamlet, prefer to keep it that way. They argue, "Why make ourselves into a city to be governed by people who want schools and libraries and big fire companies and parks? All that means taxation. We're getting along pretty well the way we are, so let's leave it that way."

So Levittown, this monstrous construction that doesn't officially exist, staggers from one compromise to the next, an object lesson in frustration. If the old-time people of Bucks County resented the intrusion of this sprawling suburbia in their lush farm lands, they have wreaked the vengeance I referred to earlier.

It is interesting to the Levittowners who want to do something about this confusion to observe that when the Levitts built their next city, in New Jersey, they avoided the glaring errors of their Bucks County experience. Explains one local leader, "In New Jersey the Levitts insisted upon complete incorporation before sinking a spade. School districts, fire districts, health districts are all unified. And most important of all, I think, in each area they mixed housing of different economic levels. Here in Bucks County all families who can afford an $18,000 home live together, usually on a little rise from which they can look down on all of us who have to live in $9,000 homes. Much of our trouble here stems from that arbitrary separation of the economic groups."

When I started work trying to line up votes for Senator Kennedy, all I knew about Levittown were the rumors that circulated in my end of the county. This gossip leveled five charges at Levittown. It was a rural slum with people crowded together like rabbits. It was filled with undesirable elements from the big cities, which meant Jews and Catholics with special emphasis on Italians. Unions were known to be strong and engaged in evil work. The area was crawling with communists who had even dared to name a public school after J. Robert Oppenheimer. And it was suspected that a good many Levittowners registered as Republican for social reasons but surreptitiously voted Democratic.

Sane people assured me of these things, and I can honestly state that I never heard any other estimate of the area, except that in 1957 Levittown exploded in a vicious outburst of racial intolerance when a Negro family named Myers attempted to move into the Dogwood area, only to find itself embattled and the center of riots. At that time some of my up-county friends said approvingly, "Those Levittowners must be all right. Like everybody else they're trying to protect their homes." From these conflicting bits of evidence I decided that I knew nothing about this huge suburbia that had erupted in my backyard.

I was therefore pleased when residents of the area called me on the telephone early in September to invite me to a Levittown political meeting. The instructions they gave were intricate, for the area has no over-all street plan, yet sensible, for all the streets in any one area begin with the same letter. I was to go to 69 Queen Anne Road in the Quincy Hollow District, where I would meet the couple who would feed me before the meeting. While I was looking for the address I noticed with approval the neat plantings of arborvitae and yew at the corners of the blocks, and the beautiful utilization of Pfitzer and Andorra juniper throughout. "This may be a slum," I mused, "but it's the best-kept one I ever saw."

The houses were neat and well cared for. Enough variation had been introduced to avoid monotony, and paint was everywhere in evidence. Driveways were trimmed and such automobiles as I saw tended to be new. Lawns were a special feature and I wondered who cut them, the husbands or the wives. Since it was just before dinner hour, there were many children playing across the broad yards and I thought: "I've been in a whole lot of suburbs that didn't look this good."

I finally found the "Q" roads and pulled up before 69 Queen Anne Road and walked up the drive. The door was opened by a very pretty housewife in her twenties. "I'm Penny Young," she said, "and this is my husband Reuben." A tall, good-looking man came forward from the kitchen to introduce his son and daughter, and for the first time in the campaign I sat down in a Levittown house. It was commodious, well planned, with a clever upstairs and downstairs arrangement. It was, I discovered later, a Jubilee, which sold originally for $11,000. I was to find that whenever I went to a meeting in Levittown I was told, "We're going to the Jeffersons'. They live in a Country Clubber." This was like saying in the Navy, "Jefferson's a commander." That told you immediately what pay he got, what his prerogatives were, and where he stood in the social hierarchy. The titles in Levittown went from Ranchers ($9,000) through Jubilees ($11,700) and on up to Country Clubbers ($18,000—except those with air-conditioned finished attics, which were a lofty $20,000).

"If the Reuben Youngs are typical Jubilees," I thought, "Levittown has nothing to worry about." Reuben worked as a sales engineer, while his pretty wife helped run the Levittown Players, where she was studying for a role in their next production, *My Sister Eileen.* Penny was from Richmond, Virginia, and very early in our acquaintanceship, which became close since I often used their house as headquarters, indicated some of the political tensions that existed in suburbia.

"When Reuben said he was going to run for justice of the peace, I thought it was just another job," she explained one night, "but as the time for voting approached, people used to call me on the telephone and say, 'We don't want you damned Jews taking over a decent county. Go home.' You have no idea how terrible it was. On my way to the polls a carload of men drove past shouting, 'We don't want kike votes here.' I was glad when Reuben lost. Then tempers subsided."

Mr. Young laughs about the affair. "It takes time for people who have lived in an area all their lives to accept newcomers. I remember when Levittown . . ." He stopped to explain. "You understand that although there is no Levittown, we continue to use the word. It's as if it symbolized what might come to pass in the future. Anyway, when Levittown conducted a plebiscite to see whether Negroes should be allowed in the community or not it was specifically understood that Jews couldn't vote. The conductors of the plebiscite said, 'Jews are no better than niggers. We know how they'd vote so their opinion doesn't count.' " Young laughed at the memory.

"Now everything's so much better," Penny said.

When dinner was served I got the feeling that here was a family that had consciously sought the good life in suburbia and had found it. The children were healthy. The parents had established fast friendships with their neighbors. The air was clean and the lawns were neat. Not a single rumor I had heard about Levittown was true, and everything I had hoped to find here was present: the happiness of people who were living better than they used to.

After dinner the politicians of the area gathered, hard-headed young men who were determined to do what they could to help elect Jack Kennedy President. Some were Catholic, some were Jewish, but most were ordinary Anglo-Saxon Protestants. Some were union members and some were not. Most were Democrats, but a few were Republicans who wanted to see a change. And when they were gathered, hell broke loose and I realized that I was in over my head, for I had been summoned to Levittown by the dissidents who had been unable to find a place within the regular Democratic party.

Milton Berkes, an extremely clever young man with the quickest mind I encountered in the area, gave the problem simply: "In 1952, when Levittown was just an idea, a lot of us saw an opportunity to make Bucks County a vital cog in the new Democratic party that we knew would arise. The Fairless Steel operation brought in a lot of bright young laboring people who already knew politics. Then, when the communities started to form, some 70,000 citizens piled in from outside areas, and the future of the Democratic party seemed assured. But what happened?"

The explanation that followed came from so many diverse voices and in such bitter tones that I will not endeavor to specify who said what. The story was this: "In 1955 we worked like demons to overthrow the Republican party in Bucks County, and thanks to Coroner Ferris, who was on his way to jail, we elected two Democratic supervisors, which automatically made Johnny Welsh chairman. We thought, 'With Welsh in command, for the first time in history we'll build a powerful party.' But our dream was very short-lived."

It is difficult to describe what happened next. Levittowners gave this as the true version: "We found that our votes were wanted but nothing more. The regular Democratic party, centered in the upper end of the county, was pathologically afraid of anyone from Levittown. It was suspicious of Jews. And it despised lbor. Time after time we pleaded with the regular party for patronage, some kind of power, some kind of recognition. But we were rebuffed and got nowhere."

Here I must interrupt to say that as soon as I heard these complaints I thought: "Good heavens! I'm back in Hawaii!" Every ugly situation that had shattered the Democratic party in the islands was operating to achieve the same result in Bucks County, and I often felt as if my work in Hawaii had been an indoctrination course for a similar fight in Bucks County. Later I was to find that the same forces operated in suburbias all across the land, and that my experience was in no way unusual. Nevertheless, I took the protests directly to Johnny Welsh, the uncrowned head of the party. He listened and replied: "What they say happened is true, but the reasons they give are altogether wrong. They stormed into our county from Philadelphia and decided that we older men who had kept the party together for three decades when there was really very little hope were a bunch of dopes. They wanted to be Democrats, sure, but they wanted to start right at the top. They were never willing to labor in the vineyards."

Later, when in an effort to heal the wounds between the rural areas and suburbia I chided the latter members with being unwilling to labor in the vineyards, the Levittowners exploded: "Johnny Welsh always uses that phrase. But do you know what he means by it? When you labor in his vineyard you're supposed to kowtow to everything he wants. You're supposed to work in the dark. And you're supposed to get neither patronage nor position while doing it."

To this charge Welsh replied: "Let them earn their patronage and position by four or five years of honest work. In my day the apprenticeship period was ten years before you opened your trap. They want to step right in at the head of the class."

A Levittowner responded with more foresight than he knew: "Republicans fear the southern end of the county just as much as the Democrats. Last election the smart young Republicans from Levittown ganged together and put across one of their leaders, Ed Boyer, as county commissioner, and now he's chairman of the commissioners. The old-line Republicans hate this and sooner or later they'll try to knock his ears off, because they hate Levittowners almost as much as they do Democrats."

A special complaint of the Levittowners was that the regular organization, most of it reared in central and upper sections of the county, refused to work with labor. Said Russ Thompson, then president of Local 4889 of the Steelworkers Union, "The regular Democrats are notorious for their antilabor animus. We simply can't get a hearing with them."

To all such complaints a highly placed Democrat at county headquarters snapped, "I haven't leveled with you, Michener. The simple fact is that Levittown is filled with communists. The F.B.I. keeps track of quite a few agitators down there and at the first start of trouble, in they go to concentration camps. That's what we're really fighting." When I asked for particulars my informant said, "Don't you know that some of the very people you've been talking with are the ones who helped niggers move into Dogwood? And named their school the J. Robert Oppenheimer School? You have no idea how far such people will go. But you do know what they did to Johnny Welsh in 1959. Such men stop at nothing."

I asked Milt Berkes what had happened in the 1959 election and he said, "After we pleaded with Welsh for representation equal to our voting strength and after we got nowhere, we had to challenge him. He ignored us. So even though he was senior county commissioner and head of the party, we said, 'Welsh, we're going to throw you out of office.' He laughed at us as if we were children, so we went to work. We got out an enormous vote, all instructed to cut Johnny Welsh off the ticket. I suppose you know what happened."

"I know he's not county commissioner any longer," I said.

"You bet he isn't," Berkes said. "He never knew what hit him. When the votes were counted everybody on the ticket had done well but little Johnny. He was cut to shreds and was even voted out of the county chairmanship. For three years we warned him, but he wouldn't listen, so we had to show him where the votes were."

The most surprising thing about the painful Bucks County split was that everyone from the southern end of the county still wanted Johnny Welsh to be head of the party. Everyone admitted he was the best-informed and most honest commissioner the county had ever had. Bob Saunders, who had participated in the revolt, told me, "If we had a free choice tomorrow, we'd still want Welsh as our leader. But he would have to operate democratically." Reuben Young was emphatic: "Welsh is the instinctive leader of the party, but he's got to reform." During the campaign I made a dozen overtures to both sides, to see if my independent committee could be the mediating force, but instead of healing old wounds, I succeeded only in tearing open old scars.

The men of suburbia wrote in protest to Washington: "Michener is a stooge personally selected by Johnny Welsh and he will help the regulars lead us to defeat." Icy John Welsh said, "Jim, you're being used by a group of men who don't give a damn about John Kennedy." Insofar as healing the savage breach that tore my party apart was concerned, I accomplished nothing.

But like many previous men caught in similar situations, I consoled myself with the fact that my major job was not to heal political wounds but to help elect a President, and it was reassuring to find that on this common ground I could talk to the two warring factions. This election was extraordinary in that across the nation it was the Democrats who were supposed to be riven apart and the Republicans who were the close-knit team; yet in the actual fighting, it was the Democrats who mysteriously coalesced into a brilliantly led unit, while the Republicans seemed constantly to be coming apart at the seams. I am not sure I understand how this was accomplished, but in my area it was done in part because the warriors of both sides were willing to prosecute the national election intelligently, even though in local matters each was trying to knife the other. I would scarcely have believed such schizoid action possible if I had not participated in it.

Thus in Levittown we had a very strong Kennedy-Johnson unit backed by the regular Democratic party and staffed by a fine young politician who took leave without pay from the Pennsylvania Railroad so that he could round up the vote. Chuck McGrath was able, witty, dedicated, and a mortal enemy of the other faction, the dissident Democrats, that is. It was a privilege to work with him and I suspect he has a bright future in the party.

At the same time, and only a block away, we had a very strong unit housed in a trailer parked on a lot beside the theater. It was staffed by Jack Ford, a shrewd, hard-working young labor leader who had taken leave without pay from the steel plant so that he could fight Republicans eight hours a day and the regular Democratic party the other sixteen. Throughout Levittown these two units worked side by side to produce a huge vote for Kennedy, but if the split had not been so irrevocable, I suspect the vote would have been larger; and if it is not soon mended, I believe the party in Bucks County is doomed to be in the minority for many years to come. Certainly, the Democrats would be foolhardy to go into the 1964 Presidential race with what amounts to two Democratic parties functioning in a key county. On the other hand, whereas such splits are usually fatal to the Republicans, nothing seems able to kill off the Democrats, so perhaps our rough-house, vital, brawling old party will stagger up to 1964 just as split as ever and just as powerful.

Of all my experiences during the campaign, and some that I have yet to describe were pleasant indeed, I appreciated most the opportunities I had to get acquainted with the people of Levittown. I found them alert, good-natured, intelligent and politically aware. Most of the ones I met were Republicans and I often thought, "One of the worst things about being a Democrat is that so many of your political enemies are such delightful people." It was when I heard some of their political beliefs that I realized how deep the chasm was between us.

I spent a good deal of time campaigning in Levittown and many hours thinking about suburbia on my way to and from it. None of the myths about Levittown, of course, were true. I have rarely known a better group of citizens nor one with which I would be more willingly associated. They represent one of the strongest reservoirs in our society and I wish there were a hundred Levittowns across the country instead of only three major ones in Long Island, Bucks County, and New Jersey. I myself would be most happy to live in one, and if in older life I found it necessary to sell the home I now occupy, I would think first of a good Levittown. I don't want the genteel section of some tired old city or the rural chauvinism of some house in which George Washington may have rested. I want the midsummer fires of a Levittown, for here live the people with vitality.

If I wanted to select one couple to represent the new spirit of suburbia I would choose the Jack Wards, who live in a neat Rancher ($9,500 new, two bedrooms, unfinished attic). Jack had been a big six-foot-two character in uniform during World War II on liberty in New Orleans when "I see this gorgeous hunk of womanhood walking past, nearly six feet tall, what a shape and flaming red hair. Right then I said, 'That's for me.'" He forgot all other objectives and won this striking Polish girl from Philadelphia. They now have four children, including twin daughters and a son who is a near genius. The whole family attends the Unitarian Church, which is a story by itself.

Mrs. Ward says, "I was raised a devout Philadelphia Catholic, as prejudiced against every other religion as I could be. My father owned a small business and hated labor unions. Our family fear was the encroachment of Negro families. And then I met this big free-and-easy guy. We courted pretty solidly and he said, 'I want you to meet my family.' So he took me to see them and they were delightful. A big Lithuanian family with wonderful spirit. Then on about the fifth visit Jack's mother said something about loving Jewish cooking. And on the next visit his aunt said something about Jewish holidays, and I stopped dead and asked Jack, 'Are you Jewish?' and he said, 'What else?' And I was terrified. When I told my parents I said, 'I've fallen in love with a Jewish boy,' and what they told me I won't repeat. But Jack's parents were telling him the same thing, so one day we two tall people, a Lithuanian Jew and a Polish redheaded Catholic said, 'This is for the birds,' and we became Unitarians."

Jack Ward had inherited even more prejudices than his wife, for he was from a little town in the Deep South, but when the Myers family of Negroes moved into Levittown and hideous hatreds erupted all over the city, the first man to mount midnight watch to protect the Myers home was Jack Ward. For some weeks he imperiled his social position, and his political as well, but he slugged it out and gained in stature by doing so.

When he moved into Levittown he landed in an area that was 70 percent Republican, but by force of his shaggy-dog personality and acid honesty he became a principal factor in making the area 73 percent Democratic and the most powerful precinct in the county. Politics has become his principal interest. In order to provide him time for electioneering, his wife supplements his salesman's income by working for the Army at Fort Dix, twenty-two miles away.

Of her new life in Levittown, Mrs. Ward says, "Before we came here we were paying $91.50 rent for a dingy, dirty Baltimore row house. Here we pay $88, and much of it is for equity in what amounts to our own house. We have beautiful surroundings, a peach tree in our back yard, a swimming pool only a few blocks away. Our children are outdoors all the time on fine playgrounds. Our son plays on an organized ball team, and as a family we are living rather than just existing. When we talk Levittowners into becoming Democrats we talk from the heart, because we've found the good life."

Two aspects of Levittown impressed me unfavorably. I found the forced segregation of the city into economic areas distasteful, for this causes serious complications, the psychological effects on children being the gravest. Also, in all Levittowns the mature population tends to be of the same age, and this is stifling. How often I wished, during my meetings, that there were occasional old men in the audience who had been through elections much earlier than ones I could remember, or newly married couples with their own special problems. A wide range of interests is a fine base for a democracy such as the one we try to operate.

Politically, everything I had been told about Levittown was wrong. The "lace-curtain Irish" were not certain to vote Republican again. There was a real chance they might return to the Democratic party. The Jewish intellectuals who in 1956 had flirted with Republicanism were willing to discuss this election on its own merits. Voters in suburbia were not going to adhere slavishly to any economic lines of demarcation. Everybody's vote was up for grabs. I spent many hours speculating on what the vote would show in Levittown, and depending upon what my most recent experience had been, I fluctuated between a fear that the area would repeat the unexpected 51-to-49 advantage it had given Eisenhower and a hope that it might move into the Democratic column by about 58 percent. At no time during the campaign did I feel confident of the outcome in this critical area.

But one thing I was sure of. Any party which wants to win suburbia in the future will have to make major concessions. Once-rural counties like Bucks can no longer consign their Levittowns to the outer darkness. Local men who have grown up in the party by slow stages will have to find room for newcomers who are in a hurry, distasteful though that accommodation might be. For the essential nature of suburbia is that its men and women tend to be of the same age, the same interests, and the same determinations. If they ever decide that the Democratic party has no home for them, they will swing sharply Republican. Conversely, if the Republicans fail to make the proper adjustments to absorb them, they will move in droves to the Democrats.

One of the things that reassured me most in this election was the skill with which Senator Kennedy wooed the suburbias, for he accurately sensed that victory could be decided by their swing vote. On the other hand, I was surprised that Nixon and Eisenhower did not stress these areas more, for I believe that at the beginning suburbias were strongly inclined toward the Republicans. With these conflicting speculations shifting back and forth across my mind, I waited anxiously for November 8.

7

The Campaign

☒ ☒

On the first day that I reported to Johnny Welsh's Doylestown headquarters, from which the official Democratic party was directed, I saw lounging in an armchair a man who made me actually stop and stare. I remember thinking: "If a person were writing a political novel he'd have to use that character as the typical hanger-on." The man was apparently in his late fifties, wore a loose-fitting suit, brown shoes that needed polishing, a snap-brim hat which he carried on the back of his head, a waxed mustache and a cigar. He had a big, amiable face, eyes which darted about sizing up all visitors, and a most ingratiating smile.

Johnny Welsh was not in the office at the moment, and this gentleman said, "You're Jim Michener. I want to introduce myself. I'm the only man you'll ever meet who has a bottle of whiskey named after him." With that he dragged out of his right rear pocket a fifth bearing a bright new label reading: "Sam Thompson. Selected from our finest reserves of Superior Quality."

"The name's Sam Thompson," he said, extending a friendly hand.

"What do you do here?" I asked.

"Just hang around and make myself useful," he replied.

Sam was useful in so many ways that I came in time to rely upon him for everything from Scotch tape to advice on electioneering. It was he who decorated the office, working on the principle that "if there's six square inches of empty space anywhere, paste up a picture of Kennedy." It was Sam who arranged for motorcades. He knew where he could find a sound truck. It was he who assured me, "That electrician owes me a favor. He'd better lend us some lights for the campaign or else."

It was also Sam, bland as honey in a bear's mouth, who solved our first big problem for us. In setting up our headquarters we had, as I pointed out earlier, usurped the town's best practical location, and we were congratulating ourselves on having outsmarted the Republicans, when one morning I found to my dismay that right up the street from us they had rented an entire abandoned hotel, had plastered it with Nixon-Lodge signs, and had opened a headquarters which frankly swamped ours. I called Sam and showed him the bad news.

"Something's got to be done about this!" Sam growled. "Look at them! They completely blanket us!"

He stomped off, his old raincoat flapping in the wind, and I wondered what Sam Thompson could do that would in any way frighten the Republican party, but three hours later I noticed to my surprise that the big enemy headquarters had shut down. Later that day they reopened in a small vacant store half a mile from the center of town, where practically nobody could see them. When the forced move had been completed, Sam Thompson came shuffling back to our headquarters and fell into a chair. He was grinning.

"What'd you do, Sam?" I asked.

"Matter of a fire inspection," he replied laconically.

"Are you a fire inspector?" I asked.

"I got real tears in my eyes," Sam replied, ignoring my question. "I told 'em that more than anything else in this campaign we wanted them to have the best headquarters available. But I said it was also necessary to protect them, and if that old hotel caught fire, and if any lives were lost, I'd be the sorriest person in town. I told 'em we certainly didn't want to win any election by burning up good Republicans."

"Didn't they argue back?" I asked, staring at the empty hotel.

"They wanted to," Sam replied, looking up at the ceiling and laughing.

"How did you manage it, Sam?" I asked. But he would never tell.

I did find, however, that it makes a great deal of difference in a national campaign if one's state is controlled by one's own party and if the major cities are also in the right hands. The odds against the Democrats' carrying Pennsylvania were tremendous, and few outside observers gave us much chance, but repeatedly I noticed that whenever we faced a real crisis, there was always some professional politician in Philadelphia or Pittsburgh who could help or there was some state official in Harrisburg who, had he been a Republican, could have intensified our difficulty. I came to the conclusion that Democratic control of the state offices, of Philadelphia and of Pittsburgh were worth at least 200,000 votes, and had these various political offices been in Republican hands I doubt that Kennedy could have won the state.

I also found that in Governor David Lawrence we Democrats had an ally who was firm, intelligent, and dedicated. I found him also to be a very appealing man, even though the opposition had long enjoyed painting him as a "typical ward-heeling politician." I wish he were typical. We understood that Lawrence, a Catholic who had just barely squeaked through in his 1958 race for the governorship, was, of all the professionals who dominated the scene at Los Angeles, the one most afraid of the anti-Catholic vote, because he had seen how powerful it could be in a state like Pennsylvania, which the party felt it must win if the national ticket were to win. We were told that Lawrence had held out to the last, insisting that his fellow Democrats acknowledge the grave risk they were taking, but that when the convention decided to go ahead, it was Lawrence who stood forth as one of the most forceful of Kennedy's supporters.

I shared the speakers' stand several times with Governor Lawrence, and he was a valiant campaigner. I also went to many places where he had preceded me, and the reports were always favorable. For many years he had been the vigorous mayor of Pittsburgh and the unofficial boss of the western part of the state, so I suppose the newspapers were right in labeling him "a typical ward-heeling politician," but whenever I heard the phrase in connection with Dave Lawrence, I thought, "I wish my ward were in such hands." For the thing that impressed me most about Governor Lawrence was that he talked sense. In his speeches that I heard he hammered away at specific legislation, at specific problems. He seemed to have a delicate radar set tuned in to the minds of the people to whom he was talking, and with each group he discussed the things that they were interested in. Not once did I hear him degenerate to either stupidity or prejudice, and I never heard him speak without feeling that he had established a higher standard for me to follow. I don't see how anyone could utter more profound praise for a practicing politician, except that Lawrence, while doing these things, also delivered the vote. Sometimes I suspected that he was able to deliver the vote because he had always done the things of which I have spoken.

What Sam Thompson's connection was with Governor Lawrence I never found out, and perhaps it was better that I didn't, because a few days after the closing of the fire trap in which the Republicans had set up office—to the danger of their life and limb—smiling Sam said, "You know, Jim, every morning when I come down here to work . . ."

"What work do you do, Sam?" I inquired.

"Every morning I see this enormous empty store, right in the heart of Quakertown, at the main crossroads where everybody has to go past."

"Sam, put it out of your mind," I snapped in a rather surly rebuff, for I had found that Sam Thompson could spend unlimited funds on unlimited projects. Some time back he had been propositioning me about a sound truck that could be bought cheap, and I had asked, "Would you buy a whole sound truck to use for six weeks?"

"If it would win an election," he had replied. "And we could keep on using it for the next ten years."

"Forget the sound truck," I had said with ruthless finality. Now I repeated, "The store's out, Sam."

"For you, yes. I know your budget is exhausted . . ."

I remember at the time thinking, "That's an odd use of words. 'The budget is exhausted.' I wonder where Sam heard that?"

". . . but would you have serious objection if I used your name and tried to get the store?"

"Yes I would," I said firmly, "because once you got the

store you'd want money to get the decorations, and there . . . is . . . no . . . money."

Sam bit his lip, looked out into the street and whispered, "The decorations we got." He led me to an old car, the back of which was truly crammed with expensive bunting, photographs of Senator Kennedy, full-sized cut-outs of Lyndon Johnson, and a mouth-watering collection of buttons, posters and stick-ups.

I exploded. For two weeks I'd been searching vainly for just a little helping of the paraphernalia of electioneering. Telegrams to Washington and phoned pleas to Philadelphia had availed me nothing. But here Sam Thompson was with a carload. "I have another station wagon full down the road," he added.

"Where in hell did you get this stuff?" I stormed.

"Remember last week when I was gone for two days?" he asked.

"Where were you?" I asked suspiciously.

"Philadelphia," he replied evenly, "and Washington. I marched into headquarters and told them I was your personal assistant and that you would be damned if you could run a campaign with no posters."

"You mean you conned them into giving you . . ."

"They didn't exactly give it to me," Sam explained. "They were impressed that you felt the lack of material so urgently . . ."

Again I was struck by this wild-eyed politician's use of words, but he continued, ". . . and in each case they wrote out an order for me to take to the warehouse. They were willing to let us have a few things."

"What did you do, forge the figures after you left the main offices?"

"Every warehouse in the world," Sam explained, "has a watchman who is underpaid. With your permission, I gave each of the watchmen five bucks, and if you could later on see your way clear . . ."

In the car and the station wagon Sam must have had four hundred dollars' worth of electioneering devices. I stood looking at them for some time, and while I was standing there he was whispering, "So if you would let me use your name in some creative way in the northern end of the county, we might do miracles with that empty Quakertown store."

"I want to see it first," I replied cautiously. So we rode together through some of the most glorious parts of Bucks County, through the German lands where autumn was rich on the farms and deer were to be seen sifting across the brown fields. How often during that long and perfect autumn was I to think, "This is one of the great counties." How extraordinarily lovely it was in the fall of 1960.

Sam, driving the car, was saying, "In that farm over there, all good Democrats, and I'll bet everyone votes for Nixon." He spotted the various places he knew and it seemed to me that nine tenths of them were Democrats who were determined to vote for the other side. "What are we opening an office up here for?" I asked.

"To give the troops encouragement," Sam explained. "Wait till you see what I have in mind."

When we got to the site, I found that Sam had understated the case. It must have been the biggest single building available in Quakertown, and Minnesota could have held football practice in it. It had, as I recall, some dozen enormous windows, any one of which would have been invaluable as a billboard. It stood at the main corner of the new shopping center, had never yet been occupied, and probably commanded a rent that my committee could not possibly meet.

"Sam," I said, "this is magnificent. This is the kind of headquarters a chairman dreams about. We'd have thousands of people passing here every day, and you can see it from four major highways."

"Wait till you see what I have outlined for the roof!" Sam cried, sensing that he had me on the hook. He took me to an area where he had blocked out two stupendous signs, each of which ran almost half a block. They said simply:

JAMES A. MICHENER
PRESENTS
JOHN F. KENNEDY AND LYNDON B. JOHNSON

I looked at the staggering signs and their inappropriate wording and said sadly, "Sam, it won't do."

"Why not?" he pleaded. "For God's sake, why not?"

"It looks like a theatrical sign. What's this *presents?*"

Sam took me by the arm and said firmly, "Jim, for years guys like me have worked in this northern end of the county with nothing. We've had no money, no candidates, no help. Now you come along, a Bucks County boy, and everybody knows you, and everybody's wondering what you're doing backing Kennedy. This is our big chance, Jim, and I'm determined to make a dent this year. Of a thousand people who pass that store, nine hundred and ninety will be Republicans, and I'm going to convert some of them."

"It won't do," I said with finality, but I was to find that speaking to Sam Thompson with finality and making it final were two far different things.

Still holding onto my arm he whispered, "If we took out the *presents*, could you possibly go for it then?"

"Sam," I explained wearily, "we don't have money for this store."

"I was coming to that," he said easily. "Now if I could arrange to get this store . . . at absolutely no cost to you . . . and if I could arrange to have those signs painted, again at no cost . . ."

"How would you arrange all these things, Sam?" I asked.

"You might prefer not to know," Sam said. "Please, this is our one big chance to make a splash."

On one of my subsequent trips, when Quakertown had the single most dazzling political headquarters in eastern Pennsylvania, with signs that stretched for blocks, dozens of windows flashily displayed, and a bevy of eager people spreading the gospel, I did overhear a man who apparently had something to do with the place asking Sam Thompson if Sam thought the last legal permission that was needed before the premises could open as a store was going to come through on time.

"I have a feeling it'll be here," Sam assured him, and that's all I know about the fifth headquarters we opened. It did the best business of all.

Just as we got things organized in Bucks County, trouble began. It was Friday night, October 7, and my wife had invited a group of neighbors in to hear the second debate. We were preparing to gloat over a second victory when I heard Senator Kennedy state, almost unnecessarily it seemed to me, that he would be willing to surrender Quemoy and Matsu to the Chinese communists. "Oh, I wish he hadn't said that!" I gasped, and I do believe that in the first moment of hearing the statement I recognized how important it was going to become. Certainly Mr. Nixon must have felt the same way, because he jumped in with his disclaimer, and went far beyond the acknowledged administration position, stating that he would engage in war to prevent the loss of Quemoy and Matsu. In the ensuing days we Democrats were pressed very diligently by Republican hecklers, and I lived in constant fear that President Eisenhower would make some simple statement to the effect that Senator Kennedy had imperiled the American position. The President's statement never came, and we were able slowly to repair the damage that had apparently been done.

Because of a trick of history, I was called upon to speak widely on the Quemoy and Matsu incident and did so in many different states, for I happened to be one of a handful of private American citizens who had visited both Quemoy and Matsu. Many had seen Quemoy, but few indeed had ever been to Matsu, and even fewer to both groups. My visit to the Matsus had occurred under unusual and privileged conditions during the height of military tension over the islands, and I had spent a wintry day traversing the tiny and insignificant heap of rocks where the Chinese troops were stationed.

Matsu, as I knew it, was about as indefensible militarily as a pile of rocks could be. It lay under the shadow of land-based batteries and could be neutralized at will. All the natives occupying it could have been evacuated in a couple of old liberty ships. It had no airfield, no substantial batteries of its own, no usable harbor, no worthy installations. Its only use, in time of military crisis, might be as a radar station providing help for American planes bombing the mainland, and it was even doubtful if it could be held for that purpose. The only conceivable way in which it could be held, if the Red Chinese wanted it badly enough, would be for the United States to use atomic bombs delivered from either the Seventh Fleet or from our great bases in Okinawa and Guam, and to do that implied the start of World War III. No one that I knew was ready to launch a nuclear war to save Matsu, which was patently not worth saving . . . so far as military considerations alone were concerned.

Yet when I returned from Matsu to the mainland of Asia I wrote a series of two widely published articles in which I advocated precisely the policy that was later to be supported by Vice President Nixon in the second television debate. I argued that Matsu, inconsequential though it might be from a purely military point of view, represented psychological factors which made it important both to the Formosan Chinese and to the United States. I argued that because of those factors it must be kept from communist hands, even at the cost of war, and even if that war involved nuclear weapons. When it was discovered that I had been on the islands, I was invited to address a segment of the war college on the subject of Matsu, since none of the military then discussing the problem had seen Matsu.

But no sooner had my articles appeared than I was subjected to a barrage of criticism by foreign correspondents working in the area and by most of the military men as well. They pointed out three grave fallacies in my argument: first, there was no conceivable advantage to be gained militarily from holding onto the islands, not even if they were to serve as a radar listening post, because other locations already in American hands were better qualified to perform that function; second, there was no psychological advantage in holding onto these rocks, and no question of face involved for either the Formosan Chinese or for the Americans, because only a few weeks before, our side had voluntarily evacuated the Tachens to the north, which did possess a few military advantages, and they stressed that President Eisenhower himself had approved the Tachen evacuation; third, they told me what I had not known before, namely, that every military leader both in the area and at home had advised against the military defense of the Matsu group. They further believed that two distinct American military and civil missions had already approached Generalissimo Chiang with advice that he get out of the Matsus as swiftly as possible. Later President Eisenhower himself agreed publicly that from a military point of view the islands were indefensible and their occupation inadvisable.

Thus I had already, personally, been completely through the line of reasoning adopted by Mr. Nixon. I had advocated it, argued in defense of it, and found it totally insupportable. Therefore when I gasped at Senator Kennedy's intoduction of the subject it was not because I disagreed with his reasoning, for he was correct in his attitude and I better than most knew it, but it was because I knew that this subject ought not to be discussed in public. I therefore knew there would be trouble for the Democrats, because the Nixon-Michener thesis was a popular one to defend, and an easy one on which to excite patriotic responses, even though it was one hundred percent wrong. How many times during the campaign did I have to answer the heckling question: "How can you be in favor of a man who wants to give away our territory to the communists?" I am quite convinced that in my answer I had truth on my side, but I am also sure that we lost a lot of votes on this Quemoy-Matsu business.

Therefore, imagine my dismay on the third debate when Senator Kennedy suggested that we support anti-Castro rebel forces in Cuba! I had just come from Mexico and Guatemala, where ninety-nine percent of the intellectuals I had met favored Castro as an abstract concept of revolutionary zeal, even though the wiser ones rejected many of the specific actions of Castro the man. One of the reasons why Latin American professors, writers and students like Castro was that he had defended Cuba against what they called "the intrusions by Norteamericanos," and now Senator Kennedy was suggesting further intrusions. Again Mr. Nixon was quick to challenge him on this, and again the Vice President had a popular and an easy cause to defend. As for myself, again I waited with real fear for President Eisenhower to state briefly and bluntly that Mr. Kennedy had spoken intemperately, for such an accusation by the President would have hurt the Democratic campaign most seriously. But again the President remained silent.

In my public meetings I could now count on two surefire embarrassments, and I found myself speaking more and more about Cuba, and it was interesting that again I had started out years ago defending Mr. Nixon's precise position and had been educated away from it both by the truth and by the force of international politics. In short, on the Cuba matter Senator Kennedy was again one hundred percent right and Mr. Nixon completely wrong, although the greater error lay in introducing the subject at all.

I knew that Mr. Nixon was wrong because on one of my long stays in Asia I had lived in Bangkok, the capital of Thailand, when John Peurifoy was our ambassador. Mr. Peurifoy was a close friend of Leonard Lyons, the New York columnist whom I had known for many years, and through Mr. Lyons I met Peurifoy shortly before his tragic death in a Siamese highway accident. Ambassador Peurifoy was not altogether popular with the formal State Department, because he had risen rather rapidly and his feeling that he was not wholly accepted made him more prone to talk about diplomatic matters than the typical career ambassador. What he liked to discuss was the wholly illegal steps whereby the United States joined forces with Guatemalan patriots to throw out of power the communist dictator Jacob Arbenz, who had usurped control of Guatemala. Mr. Peurifoy had been the American agent in this dramatic operation, and it is a pity that he died before committing to paper his memoirs on the subject; from what he intimated to me the action in Guatemala constituted a classic example of how beleaguered democracies can defend themselves against the kind of communist putsch that destroyed Czechoslovakia and Hungary. In other words, in Guatemala the United States had done exactly what Vice President Nixon mistakenly decried as irresponsible, and the free world had subsequently applauded the act. Ambassador Peurifoy, on the other hand, had held that we had intervened quickly, effectively and with the best interests of Guatemala at heart. In so doing we saved a sovereign nation and perhaps a hemisphere.

I was forced to admit that Mr. Nixon was correct in charging that Mr. Kennedy had been imprudent in discussing Cuba's parallel situation in public, but for Mr. Nixon to have implied that what the senator had mentioned was beyond the pale of discussion was downright misleading. Yet at the time, the charge seemed to gain votes for Mr. Nixon; I can testify that I was unsuccessful in arguing with people who accepted Mr. Nixon's charge that Senator Kennedy had been hasty and immature. But as we shall see, I later came to the conclusion that Senator Kennedy's forthright stands on Matsu and Cuba were responsible for his winning critical support in the crucial days of the election.

We were now into the hard-fought central weeks of the campaign and these were the subjects which we were called upon to discuss day after day: First, Kennedy's youth. Initially the electorate was honestly worried about the senator's relative youth, and whereas his deportment on the first debate assured some, many remained skeptical, and there was little I could do to dissuade them from their opinion. In time however I developed the device of stating, "Senator Kennedy is older than Teddy Roosevelt was when he assumed the

Presidency, and it seems to me we need a vigorous young man who will have the energy to attend to the job." I doubt that this reasoning was productive.

Second, Kennedy's inexperience. There was real apprehension about Kennedy's lack of experience. I was able to cite the fact that he had served in the federal government exactly as long as Vice President Nixon, but this was not too effective, because my critics always pointed out that Nixon had had administrative experience, whereas Kennedy had not. Later I retreated to my old device of saying, "Senator Kennedy has had exactly fourteen years more experience in the United States government than President Eisenhower had when he assumed the Presidency." This didn't carry much weight, either.

Third, the likelihood of inflation. One of the most telling charges, at least in Bucks County, was that the election of Senator Kennedy would automatically mean inflation, and I feel that if President Eisenhower had gone on the air midway through the campaign to lambaste Democratic spending, past and future, he might have swung the election, but he was silent. This was the more curious in that during his incumbency he had been so often outspoken on this matter. I used to teach economics and felt that Senator Kennedy's reliance upon increased national product to provide an enhanced tax base which would pay for services and prevent inflation was correct, but I found it difficult to explain this point to my listeners, and I am afraid I lost a lot of votes for the Democrats. Later I struck upon the device of arguing, "Let's put it this way. How many people in this room tonight are living in houses that were not even built eight years ago? On streets that were not paved? How many of your children go to schools that were not in being eight years ago? The economic growth represented in this room alone has added hundreds of thousands of dollars of new wealth which can be taxed by our various governments. Senator Kennedy says that additional growth in the next eight years will provide similar new wealth to be taxed. Certainly, we'll need increased funds, and we'll have increased economic turnover from which to provide them." Even more helpful in debate was another gambit which had the additional merit of arousing laughter: "I sympathize with everyone who fears inflation, and I acknowledge that the Democrats have to fight this evil. But let's not get the problem out of focus. How many of you women remember the election of 1952 when the Republicans carried around that tired old basket of groceries, telling you how the Democrats had allowed the price to creep up. What were the figures they used? 'This basket used to cost $3.00, but under the Democrats it costs $5.00.' Well, the other day we costed out that basket, as the Vice President says, and what do you suppose those same tired vegetables cost today? $6.75! The Republicans didn't want the price of that basket to go up, but it went up because the natural speed of our economy increased, and nobody could stop it. In 1968, after the Democrats have had two terms, that crazy old basket will probably cost $9.00, but you'll be better able to pay $9.00 then than you were to pay the original $3.00, because Senator Kennedy has promised that under his administration the natural speed of our economy will increase sharply." In discussing inflation and gross national product we relied very heavily on the reports of the Rockefeller brothers, for they supported the Democratic cause most wonderfully. At times, if you had listened to me argue the campaign, you might have gotten the impression that Nelson Rockefeller was running for President on the Democratic ticket, for I would quote him on perhaps eight or ten questions in a row. He was most helpful, or rather, to be specific, the reports of his brothers' inquiries were both relevant and cogent, and I often had the twisted feeling that if some Democrat of little stature had been nominated in Los Angeles, with Rockefeller having been nominated in Chicago, I would now be touring Bucks County with almost the same arguments but in defense of a Republican candidate. That Rockefeller would have carried Pennsylvania, and most of the Electoral College, there can be no question in my mind. To prove this, a fair percentage of people who told me they had decided to vote for Kennedy, Republicans and Democrats alike, confided that they would have preferred to vote for Rockefeller. Happy as I was with the nomination of Senator Kennedy, and increasingly impressed as I was with his capacity, I could only assure such people that I was damned glad Rockefeller had been turned down by the Republicans.

Fourth, the charge of socialism. I never paid any attention to the flagrant charges of socialism or complete fiscal irresponsibility brought against the Democrats. I said that I would not dignify such charges by even acknowledging them. Consistently I took the public position that if my questioner felt deeply that the Democrats were socialist revolutionaries he should certainly vote for the Republicans because he would never be happy in my party. I may have lost some votes, but I believe, and often said so publicly, that there were certain votes I didn't want.

Fifth, the question of war. At most meetings I was plagued by the question: "Is it not true that in the last fifty years the Democrats have led us to war three times?" My answer was carefully worked out to play upon the very mentalities that gave credence to such theories, and I tried never to vary it: "Now there's a typically tricky statement if I ever heard one. Why does the Republican party always say 'the last fifty years'? Because they know that if they said the last sixty-two years they'd bring to your attention one of the most indefensible wars any nation ever stumbled into, the Spanish-American War, which was engineered by a Republican President, William McKinley. And if the Republicans go back a hundred years they'll have to include the Civil War, and we know that the Republican party was practically called into being to prosecute that war. As a Democrat I'm eternally grateful that a great Republican President was on hand to fight it, Abraham Lincoln." This invariably produced applause, but had practically no effect on any Republicans present. As one elderly lady plaintively pointed out, "But we're talking about the last fifty years and to go back to William McKinley isn't fair." However, there was an additional peroration which I tried by accident one night, frustrated as I was by the war charge, and to my surprise it worked: "And I would like to point out to my Republican friends that if Franklin D. Roosevelt had not taken this country into war against tyranny, nobody in America would ever have heard of Dwight D. Eisenhower, and the Republicans would never have had a President." This always brought cheers, but for the life of me I do not understand even now what the statement says nor why it seemed so effective an answer to the war charge.

Most of my time was spent carefully arguing the basic facts of the campaign, and for every audience that plagued me with irrelevant questions requiring irrelevant answers, there were a dozen groups of people truly interested in the future of their nation and the probable impact upon that nation of either Kennedy or Nixon. There was a real choosing up of sides, and from what I saw there were many thousands of voters in Pennsylvania who did not commit themselves until fairly late in the campaign.

It was my constant pleasure to meet with these people. I believe a strict count of the homes in which I spoke would reveal that somewhat more than half were Rebublicans, and I could not have been treated more hospitably. This stemmed partly from the fact that I tried most diligently to talk sense. I never claimed that the Democrats would win Bucks County; I said I thought we might squeak by in Pennsylvania. I was sure we would carry New York and Ohio, but I feared for California and Texas. I do not think that at any meeting I conducted I ever failed to tell the truth or to label a personal opinion as merely that. Anyone who followed me about got an honest view of one man's judgment of the campaign. The only doubtful item was my insistence that Kennedy would win 410 electoral votes, but I had claimed this so often that I think I believed it myself.

There was one dreadful night when during a public debate a misguided Republican charged the entire Democratic party with being socialistic and communistically inclined. Fortunately he spoke first, so that when I took the microphone I was able to throw away my notes and launch into the most severe castigation of an opponent I have ever indulged in. Later my wife asked, "But why did you shout?" I replied that sometimes a man feels like shouting because he doesn't want anyone to have the slightest doubt as to where he stands. "Nobody had any doubt," she assured me. "You said the same thing over and over again about a dozen times." I replied that some things merited repetition and she said, "They got it."

But with that exception the Presidential campaign in Bucks County was a reassuring display of honest political difference honestly expressed. The Republican orators hammered Senator Kennedy very sharply, but not, I think, unfairly. I heard not a single smear on Vice President Nixon, except when some young Republicans appeared at one of our rallies with a big sign, "The White House is not for sale." Said our first speaker, "Why don't you tell that to Howard Hughes?"

One of the reasons why there was practically no mudslinging in our national campaign was that a curious turn of affairs engulfed our local politics right at the start. Were I to try, as writer, to set up a situation in a political novel equal to the one that developed as I watched, I could not accept what I saw happen, because it would be far too melodramatic.

The titular head of our party in Bucks County was a white-haired Irishman, John Mulligan from Bristol. He was the kind of politician to whom everybody, at the beginning of a meeting, said, "How're the daughters, John?" He had two beautiful daughters, one at school studying to be a teacher, the other married and in Germany, I believe, and I had known John only a few days before I found myself quite sincerely asking him, "How are the girls, John?" He always smiled happily and told us how they were.

Mulligan had been a ward politician when the pickings were tough and now had a job in the unemployment-compensation department of Governor Lawrence's state political team. He was a gentle man and a gentleman to whom the party strife that kept the northern and southern ends of the county separated was a tragedy. Once during the hardest part of the campaign, when I was drugged for want of sleep, I was maneuvered into uttering harsh words and stamping out of a meeting like a child. It was good, kindly John Mulligan who came after me to say that we must not let things like that happen. I suppose that Mulligan would do almost anything to insure party harmony, but during his incumbency as county chairman he was to experience little of it.

We were sitting in the county office one afternoon, a rather glum group of men, for we had been unable to get the campaign off the ground. Mulligan and the county road commissioner, Oscar Booz, and Sam Thompson were lamenting the fact there wasn't any good issue we could hang onto locally and Mulligan said, "You know, it's funny but I've been through half a dozen campaigns like this and I've found that you can always trust the Republicans to do something that'll solve our problems for us."

"Like what?" Booz asked.

"Like the coroner getting arrested," Mulligan explained. "It broke just before the election and won the county for us."

"Coroners like that don't come along too often," Sam Thompson lamented.

"I have faith that something'll turn up," Mulligan insisted. "As county chairman I have to have faith."

Incredible as it seems, at that moment the phone rang. Mulligan took the call, gasped, and went into a private room.

In a moment he came out, his normally florid face drained of blood, to ask for Oscar Booz. The two consulted in secret for some time, then appeared together. Mulligan's face was still white and I assumed some tragedy had occurred.

"Gentlemen," he said quietly, "I want you to take pencils and paper, because this is too fantastic to digest all at once. Ed Boyer, the Republican chairman of the county commissioners, has just been arrested by the Pennsylvania State Police and charged with extorting $4,000 from a merchant and using part of it to bribe a federal marshal from performing his duties."

We weighed the improbability of such a story's breaking at that particular moment, and when we had digested the enormity of the commissioner's act, as charged, and its woeful timing so far as the election was concerned, nobody spoke for some moments. Finally Sam Thompson observed, "Today I have the feeling that God is a Democrat."

In the weeks that followed, the Boyer case exploded all over the papers, and if two Democratic script writers had set out to compose the perfect case to injure the Republicans, they could not have created a better one than the one that now unfolded. For the two Republican commissioners fell at each other's throats, with outlandish charges and counter-charges. No Democrat was required to say a word beyond John Mulligan's frequently expressed pious hope that the county would promptly clear up the mess, since all decent citizens were outraged by what the two Republican commissioners were disclosing. Boyer charged his fellow Republican commissioner with having personally engineered the plot at the covert direction of the Pennsylvania Manufacturers Association, and after that bombshell I was unable to follow the intricacies of the case, except that whenever local Democrats found themselves cornered during the election they invoked coroners and commissioners, always to loud applause.

There were two aspects of the Boyer case, however, that disturbed me deeply, and had I been asked during the campaign I would have stated so, even though to do so might have worked against my party. Ed Boyer was a strong, able younger man from Levittown, and when he elbowed his way into high Republican ranks there were many disgruntled persons in the northern end of the county who predicted, "Hell, this man Boyer isn't even a native. He grew up in Philadelphia and moved in during the Levittown boom. Mark my words, he's not an old-time Republican of the kind you can trust. We'll rue the day we elected that one." Therefore, when he was apprehended in a suspicious negotiation I am sorry to say that just as many Republicans were glad to see him get caught as Democrats. One good Republican told me, "Well, in one way, it's a blessing. It settles forever the question of electing any more Levittowners to office in this county." And many Democrats felt the same way. Thus both parties lost in the Boyer case, and lost grievously, because it drove yet another wedge between the urban south and rural north, between the newcomers and old-timers.

The second reason why the Boyer case distressed me, and why I never mentioned it, not even when it might have helped my cause to do so, was that he was apprehended on a matter which should never have constituted a crime. Pennsylvania, like many other disturbed areas, had recently started enforcing a long-outmoded Blue Law which curtailed the right of stores to stay open on Sunday. In large measure it was directed against Jewish merchants and gentile supermarket operators who worked in suburban areas, and was another in the long chain of exasperations between the newcomers who wanted to shop in one convenient suburban operation on Sundays and the old-timers who said, "Let 'em come into the town on week-days, like everybody else." The law was unfair, unwise, and unenforceable. It cried out for politicians to make deals with the enforcing agencies so that this store or that could remain open without fear of harassment. The crime that Boyer was charged with was arranging such protection. He claimed he turned the collected funds over to his party. The party insisted that he had not done so but had operated on his own. Regardless of the truth, the law that was involved was a bad one, and I for one was sorry to see Ed Boyer charged with crime because of it. Put more bluntly, I sympathized with him and refused to use his embarrassment to my advantage.

One of the prime values I derived from the campaign was the frequent opportunity I had to share speaking platforms with Pennsylvania's senior senator, Joseph Clark. In the long talks that preceded and followed these affairs I discovered what an admirable man Clark was. Originally a wealthy Republican, he had like Averell Harriman and others discovered that his strong interest in good government and the proper solution of social problems threw him more and more toward the Democratic persuasion, so finally he made the leap. First as mayor of Philadelphia and then as senator he brought distinction to our state, and during the campaign when people spoke, as they often did, with contempt of politics I always cited Pennsylvania's senior senator, and wondered how many men of comparable stature and integrity my questioner associated with in his profession.

I do not mean to stress the senior senator from my state at the expense of his Republican junior, Hugh Scott. I had first met this tall, floridly handsome hatchet man under extraordinary circumstances. I was in the cellar of a Honolulu warehouse looking at some old Japanese prints when the custodian said, "There's a man over in the other corner you might like to meet." I was led through cobwebs to where a man of obvious discernment was bending over a tray full of Chinese ceramics. My guide said, "I want you to meet one of America's foremost experts on Chinese pottery, Senator Hugh Scott, of Pennsylvania."

The senator looked up, smiled ingratiatingly and said, "You're sworn to secrecy. Don't ever tell my constituents."

We had an amiable talk about politics, during which he confided, "The reason I'm down here is that I'm hiding out."

"From what?" I asked with some surprise.

"From the outraged leaders of the Republican party in Pennsylvania," he laughed.

"But I thought the Republican party elected you to the Senate only a week ago."

"Well," he admitted reflectively, "I did win, and on the morning after the election the party issued a statement claiming that my victory proved that the Republican party in Pennsylvania was as vital as ever. In the next edition of the papers I announced that my victory proved no such thing, because the party had fought me in the primaries, had worked against me in the general, had grudgingly contributed only $5,000 to my fund, and noised it around that they didn't want me to win. After the interview I hopped on a plane and here I am, hiding out in Hawaii."

I found the senator a delightful conversationalist, so that when, during this 1960 election, I was invited to debate against him I accepted with pleasure. I knew him to be a very tough campaigner and a man most tricky in debate, but I thought I might be able to hold my own simply because in defending Kennedy I had much more to work on than he had in defending Nixon. I was to be surprised.

When we met at the studio Senator Scott was all smiles and recalled with reminiscent relish our meeting in the Honolulu cellar. Station representatives handed us copies of the innocuous introductions they intended using to get the debate started and asked if we had any changes. I looked at mine. It said nothing and was in no way offensive. Scott looked at his and asked, "Could I make one small change?" A moment later we were on the air and the announcer read my trivial introduction. Then he changed over to the one Scott had rewritten for himself, and out came a slashing attack on the Democrats, a bell-ringing defense of the Republicans. That was only the first blow.

Throughout the debate, whenever I presented carefully chosen and checked figures, Senator Scott amiably destroyed them by smiling at me blandly and saying, "Unfortunately, you are using the wrong figures. The correct ones, which I have here, show exactly the opposite." When I cited accurate accounts of votes in the Senate he, with childlike sincerity, pointed out that he had been there and I was all mixed up again. When I wanted to talk seriously, he trotted out a very funny story, and all in all he paraded every debater's device that would discredit and disarm me. He won by a mile. Nevertheless, I enjoyed fighting with Hugh Scott because he had one clear and apparent aim: to annihilate Democrats, and in a campaign year I can respect such motivation.

But what I particularly enjoyed during the campaign was meeting with others who were working directly on the election, whether they were for Kennedy or Nixon, and I should now like to identify those moments when in the company of such workers I became assured that Kennedy would win. They were three in number, and I remember each with special clarity, although curiously enough I cannot remember who provided the first and perhaps the most substantial of the moments.

I had gone to New York to meet Senator Kennedy in relation to a committee of artists and scientists who wanted the privilege of endorsing his candidacy, and while we were sitting about waiting, a newspaperman whose name I didn't catch, was regaling us with an account of how Lyndon Johnson was conducting his campaign in the South. I had long been an admirer of Johnson and it irritated me considerably when at most of my meetings people pointed out that Ambassador Lodge was so much finer a choice than Johnson for the Vice Presidency and that Lodge was helping his ticket while Johnson was hurting his. This I never believed, and in the later stages of the campaign when the rumors became virulent I had the pleasure of telling Senator Johnson that I was one northern liberal who was convinced that he was adding enormous strength to our ticket. I need not explain, therefore, how thoroughly I enjoyed the following monologue:

"I've been campaigning down South with Senator Johnson, and, man, he does things his own way. He blows into a state capital and first thing he does is convene the two senators and the governor. They all pour big drinks and Johnson says, 'Now, Senator Buford, I understand exactly why you can't find it in your heart to come out for the Democratic ticket in this election, and believe me, I sympathize with you. There are many things about that Los Angeles platform that I can't abide, either, and I appreciate the fact that you have to come back to your people in 19 and 62 for reëlection, and you can't do it if you stand on that platform in this year of 19 and 60. So you certainly aren't going to hear any rebuke from me, because I understand fully the political pressures you're under.'

"Then Good Ol' Lyndon pours everybody another drink and he turns to the other senator and says, 'Baxby, old fellow, I would have been amazed if you had been able to support our national ticket, what with Mr. Kennedy being a Catholic and all that. I appreciate the difficult situation this fact puts you in down here with the churches barking at your heels and the preachers lambasting you on Sunday, and I tell my friends it would be a miracle if the South was reacting any way different from the way they are reacting, and, Baxby, I've frequently cited your case as a case in point. I simply don't see how a God-fearing man can be called upon, not even by his party, to vote against his own conscience nor to advise his neighbors to do so. If a man can't respect the dictates of his own conscience, he's not much of a man, I say.'

"Next the senator from Texas looks directly at the governor of this sovereign state and says, 'Governor Beauregard, I would be the last man in the Democratic party to come to you and ask you to change your beholden opinion about this election. Because I have got to acknowledge that our party has made it very difficult for you men on the local scene, and I will so acknowledge publicly if I'm called upon to do so. I refuse to see how a group of party experts in Washington or New York can expect to interpret for us in the South what we've got to do in the South. How can they be expected to understand our separate and special problems? That's why, Governor Beauregard, you find me so sympathetic, because every problem you are now facing I've had to face in the past, and I know better than most men what is involved. So if you thought that I came to put pressure on you to modify your public statements about the present election, put such thoughts from your mind. I'm a practical politician and I appreciate what you're up against here at home.'

"With this reassurance, repeated several times and in different ways, the first two hours pass. But in the third hour Good Ol' Lyndon pours hisself a third round and he says expansively, 'Now, gentlemen, I most particularly don't want you to feel sorry for me nor for Mr. Kennedy. If we lose the election in November we surely aren't going to be out of work. I'll be reëlected senator and presumably will go back to Washington as majority leader of the Senate with enhanced powers because of the national race. And Mr. Kennedy won't be out of a job either, because he just stays on in the Senate as titular head of the party and as one of the most powerful voices in the nation, and, Senator Buford and Senator Baxby, I just don't see how, if your defection is the cause of our defeat, you're ever going to get one little old bill through that Senate. Governor Beauregard, you say you have to have that new airport and you want to keep the Army base down here. How do you think you're going to get such bills through the Senate if Mr. Kennedy and I are sitting there solely because you didn't produce the vote that would have elected us?'

"There's a long silence, and then Good Ol' Lyndon says expansively, 'Gentlemen, there's a lot of work to be done in this state before November 8 and I feel increasingly that you are the men to see that it gets done.'" The newspapermen stopped, looked at us and said, "If I had to bet right now I'd bet that the only major southern Democrat that fails to speak out publicly for the Kennedy-Johnson ticket will be Harry Byrd. The Democrats are going to carry the Deep South, South Carolina and all of them except Florida, and the man they have to thank for the victory is Lyndon Johnson."

We questioned him on many aspects of the story, but he stood firm: "Johnson is going to carry the South. He's the silent hero of this election and it looks as if he might carry Texas, too." From that exciting moment on I never wavered in my belief that our side would win a majority of the votes in the South. With them, it seemed a good bet that we would win the nation, as well. My view was not popular with northern experts, especially those who felt that Lodge had helped the Republican ticket whereas Johnson had hurt the Democrats, but the more I heard from the South and Texas and the more I watched Ambassador Lodge's amiable fumbling, the more convinced I became that Jack Kennedy's selection of Lyndon Johnson as his running mate had been one of the master strokes of the campaign.

That we were going to win the big industrial states of the North I first became aware under dramatic circumstances. On Saturday, October 22, I was driving my wife to an important rally in northern Connecticut, where I was to speak to the egghead population, and we stopped in a small town to get breakfast. Eagerly we looked for a copy of the *New York Times* so that we could catch up on what had been happening in the big states, but all copies had been sold and we were forced to buy a day-old copy of a paper which we do not normally see in rural Pennsylvania, the tabloid New York *Daily News*, and as we rode toward Connecticut, my wife read me the political dispatches, and after the usual material she said, "Here's something interesting, the first returns in the *Daily News* straw vote for New York. It's been pretty good in the past."

"Don't be worried about the first figures," I assured her. "It's a strongly Republican paper and I think they doctor their figures."

"These are nothing to worry about," she assured me. "It says here that on the basis of the first returns Kennedy leads 51.1 to 48.9."

"What?" I shouted.

"Keep your voice down," she cautioned. "That cop'll think you're nuts. It says here Kennedy 51.1 to Nixon 48.9."

Then it all came to me. "What's happened," I explained carefully, "is that the editors have published only the New

York City figures so that tomorrow when the upstate figures come in heavily Republican they'll be able to headline a big swing to Nixon. It's an old trick they pull every year."

"Very interesting," my wife replied, "but these are mostly upstate figures."

"They're what?" I bellowed. I slowed down and then pulled off to the side of the road, and there I saw for myself that the first upstate figures, from traditionally Republican strongholds, showed that Kennedy not only had hacked President Eisenhower's lead of 1952 and 1956, but was actually ahead. I sat still for a moment, then asked, "Do you know what this means?"

"Explain it to me," my wife said, and we drove on.

All that long day in Connecticut, at all of my speeches, I thought of those tantalizing figures, and the more I thought the more convinced I became that this was an editorial trick. It had to be, so in my speeches I made no reference to what was rather striking political news. When the next day's figures were released they showed, under the headline, "Kennedy Leads in Our Straw Poll by 5 Percent—And That Ain't Hay," that the score had now grown to 52.7 to 47.3 in our favor.

Still I could not believe the evidence of my own eyes, for by all accounts New York was not going to be as easy as that. After all, Nixon, Rockefeller and Eisenhower had all made strong pitches in New York, for it was the great prize, and I knew the fighting for votes was brazen. It was in this mood that I returned to Connecticut for another round of speeches, this time to stay with the state's remarkable Democratic boss, John Bailey of Hartford. After a long evening during which Chester Bowles gave one of the finest expositions of a desirable foreign policy that I have ever heard, we retired to the Bailey study to talk politics and wait for a phone call from New York.

My wife put up to Bailey, who had an impressive record of holding his party together in the face of natural strife, the problem that divided Bucks County. As a fighting liberal she was all for the southern end and outspokenly against the old-line conservatives headed by Johnny Welsh and John Mulligan. Mr. Bailey listened patiently, then laughed. "Mrs. Michener," he said with that icy quality he can bring to bear upon political questions, "when you really work in politics you do just what your husband has done. You never deal with individuals, you deal with the office. That is, you deal with whatever individual is able to hold the office at the moment. If you try to adjudicate on the grounds of natural sympathy each separate fight that comes up, you'll quickly go mad and you'll ruin your party, too.

"Let me tell you what happens to a state chairman every week. A protest committee comes to see you and laments, 'Mr. Bailey, the Democratic party in East Cupcake is being ruined by Francis Finnegan. He's no good. He has no support at all. He's petty. And we don't even think he's a good Democrat. Now why do you keep on doing business with Francis Finnegan?' To such complaints I always say, 'I do business with Francis Finnegan because he's the local chairman. If he's as bad as you say, vote him out of office and I'll do business with you.' And then they invariably say, 'Nobody could vote Francis out of office. He's always elected by a big majority.' And all I can say to that is, 'If he's always elected by such a big majority, how can you say he has no support? Seems to me Francis Finnegan has a hell of a lot of support and is going to keep it. Gentlemen, I do business with Francis because he controls the office.' They go away mad, but if later on they unseat Finnegan in a fair vote, they know that I'll support them now just as I used to support Finnegan. Mrs. Michener, in a party fight always support the office, and if your Mr. Welsh owns the office, he owns your support until such time as somebody else wins the office."

At this point the phone rang and Mr. Bailey, who was already being discussed in Democratic circles as either permanent chairman of the party or postmaster general, or both, spoke quietly and listened to the news from New York. We knew it had to do with the election and we suspected that it was good, because a huge smile began to wreathe his rugged Irish face. He betrayed to us no hint of what the call was about, but when he put down the receiver, at about two o'clock in the morning, he said, "This afternoon the New York *Daily News* is going to report as its latest poll figures, Kennedy better than 55 percent, Nixon less than 45 percent." We cheered and Mr. Bailey said calmly, "On that bit of news I think we can go to bed."

On the way upstairs I asked, "Is Kennedy going to carry Connecticut?"

Mr. Bailey said, "If he doesn't, he has no chance anywhere."

"That strong?" I continued.

The state leader said cautiously, "We think by 30,000. We hope by 60,000. But if you hear on Election Night that he won Connecticut by more than 80,000 you can be sure he'll win the nation."

It is difficult for me even now to explain the joy I experienced as I went to bed that night. John Bailey was the first important politician I had met who felt that his state was secure and that it would serve as bellwether to the nation. He was certainly not overconfident, and he saw many pitfalls ahead, but he was in command of forces that could be relied upon, he felt, to get out every available vote. And now from neighboring New York the news was also good—so good that no Democrat really believed it—and on that hopeful note the Bailey household went to sleep.

The third event which reassured me concerning John Kennedy's chances was of an intellectual nature and of tremendous significance to me and, as events turned out, to many others as well. I was scheduled to speak at a joint Republican-Democratic meeting at the lower end of the county and had just appeared in the hall when an elderly lady, whose name I never knew but who attended many of my speeches and often spoke to me, called me aside and warned, "They're going to murder you tonight, Michener. I thought you might be able to use this."

"What is it?" I asked, as she rummaged through a voluminous handbag.

"A newspaper article," she replied. "To me it seems significant. May turn out to be just the ammunition you need." She passed the crumpled paper to me, then winked and said, "My God, it's exciting to be a Democrat."

On my way to the wings I stopped backstage, in a darkened corner, to study what my partisan had given me, and I must confess that I expected to read about some trivial exposé of Republican corruption in western Kansas. Instead it was the single most important piece of writing that was published during the campaign, and as the old lady had feared, I had missed it. It was Walter Lippmann's column in which he carefully analyzed Vice President Nixon's proposals for dealing with foreign affairs, principally the Nixon plan for endless regional committee meetings. In sharp comment Mr. Lippmann quite demolished the emptiness and the precentiousness of this redundant plan, and when he was through doing so he had an excellent column. But then he added three gratuitous paragraphs which were the most damning comments made against the Republicans during the election, and as I read them in astonished silence I foresaw the impact they would have in the large eastern states:

This revealing speech confirms the impression that has grown stronger since the TV debates began. It is that Mr. Nixon is an indecisive man who lacks that inner conviction and self-confidence which are the mark of the natural leader and governor of men.

This has appeared most clearly in the Quemoy-Matsu affair. Mr. Nixon has exhibited a lack of knowledge of the facts of a great question of war and peace, about which he is supposed to have had first-hand knowledge. In the second debate he did not know what the Eisenhower policy was, and he had to be reëducated for the third debate. This is most significant because it reveals such a weak, infirm, inaccurate grasp of a great issue.

The contrast with Mr. Kennedy has become very sharp. It has been truly impressive to see the precision of Mr. Kennedy's mind, his immense command of the facts, his instinct for the crucial point, his singular lack of demagoguery and sloganeering, his intense concern and interest in the subject itself, the stability and steadfastness of his nerves and his coolness and his courage. And through it all have transpired the recognizable marks of the man who, besides being highly trained, is a natural leader, organizer, and ruler of men.*

I probably read these last three paragraphs aloud not less than fifty times during the remainder of the campaign, for they summarized so perfectly the Democratic position, and each time I did so I was careful to explain that they had been written by a man who had supported General Eisenhower twice, was mainly a Republican, and was published in Republican newspapers. These Lippmann paragraphs had a profound effect in my county, for they made intellectually respectable the claims that many of us had been making with only personal judgment to support them. With the appearance of this Lippmann article I was now in the curious position of constructing my speeches with only Republican citations. On all economic matters I relied upon

* Copyright, 1960. New York Herald Tribune, Inc.

Nelson Rockefeller and on all questions relating to the basic capacity of the Republican candidate I referred only to the New York *Herald Tribune*.

Frequently, when I quoted Lippmann I was asked, "But does he carry any weight across the nation?" And I quickly replied, "Walter Lippmann will probably not influence ten votes in Oklahoma, where they have possibly never heard of him. But in New York, New Jersey and Pennsylvania he will influence hundreds of thousands of votes, and they're the states we have to win." In the intellectual struggle for the votes of big-city and suburban residents who read newspapers, Walter Lippmann's column was the single most powerful comment of the campaign. Without it to support me, for example, I would have gained a very dubious hearing in many parts of Pennsylvania. With it, I had a club of flashing light and one that required almost no exegetical comment from me.

At the same time I was impressed by the fact that Lippmann and others like James Reston and C. L. Sulzberger had arrived at their good opinion of Senator Kennedy mainly because of his willingness to talk sense about such problems as Matsu, Cuba and our position overseas, whereas the Vice President almost invariably took refuge in broad generalities and emotional clichés, and it occurred to me that those slips of Kennedy which at the time had caused me so much anguish were not the first steps to political suicide that I had originally held them to be; they were bold exemplifications of the fact that John Kennedy, if he made what appeared to be a mistake, was willing to stand fast, to bear the brunt of all attacks, and to slug it out with his opponents without retreating to clichés or ambiguities. As is so common with strong men, he was able, by an exhibition of resolute courage, to turn disaster into victory. I do not believe that his force of character would have been evident to men like Lippmann, Reston and Sulzberger unless they had seen his reactions to heavy fire.

The emotional high point of the campaign came for me on an early morning which had little to do with votes or voters. I found myself involved in an impossible schedule, for I had spoken on Tuesday night at a labor rally in the northern end of the county; on Wednesday I had three speeches in Pittsburgh at the opposite end of the state; on Thursday there were three more speeches in Bucks County;

and on Friday three more in Connecticut. I decided to drive to all points, and when my wife heard this she called quits, for her days had been filled with political teas and coffee hours and she had twice gained hilarious attention by sitting on the stage while I addressed large crowds and falling asleep while facing the audience. Under the circumstances I was quite content to have her stay home and get some sleep in bed.

After the labor meeting in Bucks County I started the midnight drive to Pittsburgh, but I had barely entered the turnpike when snow began to fall, the most unseasonal that I could remember, for it was only mid-October and snow was not expected for two months. Nevertheless, down it came while I swore at each flake that hit my windshield. Before long I had to leave the turnpike and seek a place to sleep, intending to rise early and push on in daylight hours to the meetings in Pittsburgh, and as I went to bed the motel keeper assured me, "Half an hour of the big trucks' going by in tomorrow's sunlight will take care of the snow."

In the morning I saw that he had been right, and freshened by a good night's sleep I lit out for Pittsburgh. But as I traveled westward, with the brilliant sun at my back, I saw something that few have seen. Snow lay heavily upon the rolling fields of central Pennsylvania, and this was not uncommon, for the area is visited each winter by many storms. And the trees of autumn were swept with gold and blazing red, and of itself this was not uncommon, for we have some of the East's finest falls. But the two taken in conjunction, the snow and the gold, were beyond compare. My eyes jumped constantly back and forth between the softly folding meadows where the snow lay impeccably white and the rolling hills where the trees stood in painted splendor. Regardless of what one looked at first, his eyes were lured away by the greater beauty elsewhere. Only Brueghel, with his love for snow, could have painted that remarkable scene; the alternating patches of snow and fire would surely have caught his imagination.

I remember thinking at the time, "What a truly glorious country this is. How richly it deserves the best government it can get." At one tunnel there was a delay because of road building and the guard called to me, "You ever see a day like this?"

"Nope," I called back. "They come frequent?"

"Never saw one like this before," he replied.

Then, as the sun grew brighter, the snow began to fade and by the time I approached Pittsburgh it had altogether vanished. For a few hours only it had lain there in perfect beauty, and now it was gone. I had worked in many nations that had once known their hours of dignity and grandeur, and those hours had fled. The citizens who followed in the years of gloom were often able to joke about the change, but in their hearts they knew that the snows had melted and would not return except under far less auspicious conditions. One day, I knew, the snows of history would depart from our American fields, too. They had to. No nation had learned the trick of holding onto them forever, but while they lasted how glorious they were and how imperative it was that they be both recognized and cherished.

On the way back from Pittsburgh I passed through the same tunnel, but now the workmen were absent and there was no guard, yet I could remember his call of the morning before: "You ever see a day like this?" Now it was dusk and there was no day. But I consoled myself with the thought that once in central Pennsylvania I had seen right through to the heart of America. Once I had seen it, for a few hours only, but since many never even dimly perceive it, I was lucky.

I returned home from the Connecticut trip to find Sam Thompson busily engaged in preparation for the impending visit of Senator Kennedy to Levittown. It was scheduled for Saturday, October 29, and Sam was worried. When I inquired why, he explained, "We've just got to get out more people than Nixon had at the same spot yesterday. The national committee says we get 'em out or else. We're working on schools, stores, factories, everything we can think of, but I'm afraid we're headed for disaster."

"Why so?" I asked.

"Nixon had not less than 15,000, honest count," Sam insisted.

"We can beat 15,000!" I said airily. "There's that many'll come from Levittown alone."

"Not so easy," Sam said mournfully. "You forget one thing."

"What?"

"Saturday, October 29, is the first day of hunting season."

This was frightening. A city man wouldn't understand this, but on the first day of hunting season in rural Pennsylvania all normal life stops. Men rise two hours before dawn, pile into their cars, and patrol the back roads till dusk. At night they stumble home and throw a couple of rabbits on the table with the age-old cry of, "There's the meat, Mom!" A self-respecting Bucks County man would allow nothing, not even the future President of the United States, to keep him away from the first day of hunting. On one recent year it fell during a near hurricane and the kill, both of deer and of men, was just about the same as always. I didn't know anyone who stayed home.

"The hell of it is," Sam explained, "not only will the men refuse to show up but they'll have the cars so the women won't be able to show up either. Jim, we'll be lucky if we have 8,000 people there. Something has got to be done."

"Wait a minute," I argued. "Let's not panic. Do you mean to tell me that . . . Look, Sam, this man Kennedy is the most popular Presidential candidate America has seen in years. People throng to see him. If we can't beat the 15,000 that Nixon got . . ."

"They won't throng to see him on the opening day of hunting season. Not in Bucks County. And you know how the papers are going to play this up. Kennedy draws less than half the crowd that Nixon got. Jim, it'll kill us."

"Then we have got to get the crowd down to Levittown. We'll hire buses."

"You know how many buses it'd take to get 15,000 people anywhere?"

"I'm satisfied that we'll get the crowd."

"And I'm satisfied that we won't. If Jesus Christ comes back to earth and expects a big crowd to greet him, he better not come back to Bucks County on the opening day of hunting season."

Sam Thompson left me in gathering gloom, but a few days later he was once more his genial political self. "Thank God," he gasped. "We got the national committee to keep Kennedy out of here on Saturday. He's coming on Sunday!"

"Is Sunday good?" I asked.

"Good?" Sam shouted. "There's a lot of pheasant and rabbit around this year. I see them in all the fields. So the hunters'll have a good day on Saturday. They'll have monopolized the family car, so on Sunday they'll be inclined to pamper the missus and the kids. Jim, we're going to have the damnedest crowd to meet Jack Kennedy that he's ever seen!"

Sunday, October 30, started out as a heavenly day, with untimely soft winds, a bright sun, and a gentleness in the air that simply invited people to drive through the countryside. Sam said, "I told you God's a Democrat."

The senator's appearance was scheduled for one-thirty sharp, and at noon my wife and I pulled into the Levittown shopping area, where an immense plaza had been roped off for the crowd. To our surprise, no fewer than 15,000 people were already in place. I thought, "Sam was right. We're going to have a record turnout."

Johnny Welsh's county committee had arranged for bugle corps, dancing girls, orators and popcorn salesmen. We were also plagued by an influx of intruders from Philadelphia who set up large stands from which they peddled Kennedy buttons at outrageous prices, the profits going not to the campaign committee but into their own pockets. Sam Thompson growled, "The hell of it is that these same jokers were up here last week selling Nixon buttons and making a pile off the Republicans."

Apparently Sam voiced his grievance to the members of one of my committees from Levittown, for shortly thereafter one of my committeemen strode into our office and threw down on the table some forty dollars. "Now we can pay for the buttons and the posters we need," he said proudly.

"Where'd you get the dough?" I asked.

"Selling official peddlers' permits to the hucksters from Philly," he said.

"Who issued the permits?" I asked.

"A guy and I typed them up," he confessed.

"What guy?" I pressed.

"Just a guy I happen to know."

"That's extortion," I warned.

"Those creeps are taking money out of the community," he insisted, but apparently they weren't going to take all of it out. Some time later I saw Sam Thompson and a helpful policeman inspecting all the peddlers to be sure they had licenses. They did.

At one-thirty that Sunday afternoon, 25,000 people were jammed into the plaza to hear Senator Kennedy, but he was late. Senator Clark and I were offered to the crowd without conspicuous success. The sound system didn't work, and we raised the devil. During the campaign I must have used upwards of a hundred and fifty sound systems, and fully half of them didn't work. I often used to wonder, as urgent men in dark suits ran back and forth fixing wires, how we were doing in the space race if we couldn't get a simple sound system to work. Now the typical worried man in a black suit hurried up to assure us that by the time the senator appeared, the system would be working, but Sam Thompson followed with the discouraging news that "this system is owned by a Republican, and he's given orders to sabotage it."

At two-thirty the crowd was at least 30,000, twice what Nixon had been able to draw in the same spot. Senator Kennedy was now an hour overdue and we began to wonder if we could hold the crowd. Senator Clark and I were again offered to the audience with even less success than before, partly because the sound system still didn't work.

At three-thirty the crowd was 35,000 and most of them had been standing for at least two hours. Senator Kennedy was still late, and other speakers were proposed, but the sound system didn't work, so we asked the exhausted bands if they would march again. I don't know what Johnny Welsh paid those musicians, but no instrumentalists ever earned their money more arduously than these. One band with three beautiful drum majorettes must have marched ten miles, and always to the same amount of applause.

At this point Sam Thompson and I counted the crowd. We walked slowly along the front line and counted every person individually. I forget what our figure was, but it must have been about 400. We then walked back through the crowd and counted individually the rows that pushed in behind those in front, and they numbered about 70. In the central plaza there were therefore 28,000 people. On the roads leading into the shopping center there were many others, and on the distant highway, for at least two miles, every spot along the shoulders was jammed. When I say that in Republican Bucks County at least 35,000 came out to see the Democratic candidate I am cautious in my estimate.

At quarter of four that afternoon a helicopter flew over announcing like a voice from heaven, "Senator Kennedy is coming!" Excitement grew and I thought to test the public address system. It still wasn't working but the men assured me that soon it would be. Then, from a distance down the main highway, moved three huge buses carrying the press corps. They were about a mile away and struggling through massed crowds, but they were by far the most impressive aspect of the afternoon, three huge beetles crawling through a maze of ants.

Once we caught sight of the distant touring car in the back of which stood a man waving to enormous crowds. Overhead the helicopter assured us in its ghostly voice, "Senator Kennedy is now leaving the highway. He will soon be with us."

On the plaza the crowd surged forward, but the police kept firm control and Sam Thompson assured me, "Wonderful! They have twenty more motorcycles than they needed for Nixon."

The three big buses turned off the highway and moved purposefully toward the plaza. A way mysteriously opened up and a touring car burst into view. There was the candidate, surrounded by a fantastic mob of squealing, screaming, pushing admirers. He waved mechanically, smiled mechanically, waved again. When policemen tried to control the mob, he warned, "Don't push them." On his own initiative he got out of the car, left the protection of the police, and shook hands with members of the crowd.

A path was made for him to the speakers' stand and he climbed the steps. He recognized no one. Men who had served in the Senate with him he was unable to see. A kind of dumb glaze was over his eyes, his face and possibly his brain. Then he looked at the crowd and quickly whipped off his overcoat, standing forth as a handsome, dedicated man. The crowd screamed. He took the microphone and asked impatiently, without seeing me, "Does this work?"

"I don't think so," I said.

"They never do," he said and put back into his pocket an important typed statement he had planned to make.

"Does this work?" he asked the crowd.

"We can hear," somebody shouted.

He spoke about six sentences, during which I dropped down among the press. Nobody was listening, for nobody could hear. I met Maggie Higgins, tired and worn like Kennedy. "Will Kennedy carry Bucks County?" she asked.

"We're going to cut the margin way down, Maggie," I assured her.

"That's not news," she snapped, and soon all the reporters were piling back into the press buses.

With his speech, such as it had to be, delivered, the senator suddenly came to life. Now he recognized Senator Clark and stopped to chat with the senator's pretty daughter, who was attending Bryn Mawr. He recognized other politicians and shook their hands, but soon the police had formed about him and he was hustled back to his touring car. The cavalcade re-formed and the three huge buses began inching once more through the crowd. Overhead the helicopter announced to the jammed highway, "Senator Kennedy is about to appear." For his next engagement he would be three hours late.

Sam Thompson, watching him go, said, "He'll make a great President. At least he was smart enough not to come to Bucks County on the first day of hunting."

The mind is tantalized by several speculations. In Senator Kennedy's tortuous procession from the center of Philadelphia to Levittown and back he was seen by not less than half a million people. He carried Pennsylvania by only 116,326 votes, and if he had not carried the state, he could have been in trouble. Some overt thing, some specific event in this intense campaign meant the difference between defeat and victory. Could it be that Sam Thompson had been right, and that if Jack Kennedy had made his last great pitch for Pennsylvania's votes on the first day of hunting season only half as many people, or less, would have seen him? Don't forget that both candidates together failed to make an impression during the World Series, and both were edged off the front pages by Nikita Khrushchev's taking off his shoe in the United Nations. Some trivial event possibly made the ultimate difference when the vote was close as it was, and I am at least willing to consider the fact that it might have been Jack Kennedy's sense of timing in coming to Philadelphia and Bucks County. Or, you could say, "Sam Thompson did it."

It should be obvious from what I have so far said that in the natural course of the campaign I developed no antagonism whatever for the Republican candidate, Richard Nixon. In fact, my wife kept heckling me on the long rides home with the persistent question: "Why do you continue to speak well of the enemy?" And each time I replied that I wasn't trying to convince Democrats; I was arguing with Republicans. "Besides," I snapped one night, "I happen to think that Richard Nixon is a pretty good candidate, and if he wins on November 8 I'm not going to cut my throat. The nation will be in fairly good hands."

This bland attitude terminated on the night of October 13, when during the third debate one of the interrogators, Mr. Charles Von Fremd of C.B.S., asked what seemed to me a perfunctory question: "The chairman of the Republican National Committee, Senator Thruston Morton, declared earlier this week that you owed Vice President Nixon and the Republican party a public apology for some rather strong charges made by former President Harry Truman, who bluntly suggested where the Vice President and the Republican party could go. Do you feel that you owe the Vice President an apology?"

Mr. Kennedy's answer was by no stretch of standards brilliant, but it was noteworthy for providing the only flash of humor during the campaign, and even it had modest candlepower. He said: "Well, I must say that Mr. Truman has his method of expressing things. He's been in politics for fifty years. He's been President of the United States. They are not in my style. But I really don't think there's anything I could say to Mr. Truman that's going to cause him, at the age of seventy-six, to change his particular speaking manner. Perhaps Mrs. Truman can but I don't think I can. I'll just have to tell Mr. Morton, if you'd pass that message on to him."

The cameras then turned routinely to Vice President Nixon for what I expected to be a routine additional comment. To my astonishment I heard the Republican candidate for the Presidency actually state: "We all have tempers. I have one. I'm sure Senator Kennedy has one. But when a man's President of the United States he has an obligation not to lose his temper in public.

"One thing I've noted as I've traveled about the country are the tremendous number of children who come out to see the Presidential candidates. I see mothers holding their babies up so they can see a man who might be President of the United States. It makes you realize that whoever is

President is going to be a man that all the children of America will either look up to or will look down to.

"And I can only say that I'm very proud that President Eisenhower has restored dignity and decency and, frankly, good language to the conduct of the President of the United States.

"And I can only hope that, should I win this election, that I could approach President Eisenhower in maintaining the dignity of the office, in seeing to it that whenever any mother or father talks to his child, he can look at the man in the White House and, whatever he may think of his policies, he will say, 'There's a man who maintains the kind of standards personally that I would want my child to follow.' "

When this little sermon ended I jumped from my chair and was mad for the second time in the campaign, the first having been when my party was accused of being procommunist. It seemed to me then, as it does now, incredible that a grown man running for the Presidency in the crucial year of 1960 should seriously put forth as one of his major qualifications the fact that he wanted to be an image toward which children could look with reverence while their mothers beamed. Suddenly the whole shabby performance of the last eight years hit me in the face: the postures in place of the performance; the father image in place of a political leader; the bland reassurances instead of the hard dichotomies; the proliferating clichés in place of the truth. From that moment on I was totally dedicated to the defeat of Richard Nixon as well as to the election of John Kennedy.

I did not dislike Nixon the man, nor did I ever inveigh against him. I even felt that the worst charges brought against him by the Democrats—his campaigning against Jerry Voorhees and Helen Gahagan Douglas—were in a sense irrelevant in that the essence of his charges lay within the bounds of conventional political procedure. But for a serious candidate to keep on offering such patent nonsense to the American people as the claim that President Eisenhower never swore in the White House, whereas it was widely known that both he and Nixon had normal, strong vocabularies, which Nixon exercised with sharp profanity after the third debate had ended, that was too much. It exemplified, I thought, the transparent weakness of Mr.

Nixon insofar as intellectual capacity was concerned. For him to say what he did was ridiculous, but for him to think of offering it as a reason for voting Republican was horrifying.

I was so agitated by this extraordinary performance that I said, before he finished his sentimental oration, "Five million people right now are going to say, 'That nonsense reminds me of Checkers.'" In the days that followed I met dozens of people who had been on the fence who said, "I was for Nixon up to the time he gave that little sermon on profanity. When he was speaking his sanctimonious little essay, all I could think of was Checkers. And that did it."

But whenever my intellect is outraged by something I go in to see Miss Omwake and Mrs. Dale, and this time as usual they set me straight.

MRS. DALE: I thought what Mr. Nixon said about swearing was very fine. After all, James, we don't want another man like Mr. Truman defiling our White House.

MISS OMWAKE: I feel reassured after hearing the debate that if Mr. Nixon is elected he'll set a very fine standard for our young people.

MRS. DALE: He's a fine figure of a man and he will make a very imposing President. After all, passing the laws is somebody else's job. What we need is a man who will lend dignity to the White House.

MISS OMWAKE: Frankly, James, I thought your candidate came very close to defending the awful language of Mr. Truman, and I didn't think it was becoming. Not at all.

ME: Didn't you laugh at the little joke he made. About not being able to do anything with Mr. Truman but maybe Mrs. Truman could?

MISS OMWAKE: I don't think Presidents should joke. After all, one of the reasons why President Eisenhower has been so successful is that he always takes things seriously. I feel sure Mr. Nixon would take things the same way.

ME: Don't you ever feel maybe a President ought to be forceful, too?

MISS OMWAKE: That's for Mr. Dulles and for J. Edgar Hoover to take care of. In a President what you want is stability of character, and frankly I don't think Mr. Kennedy has that. His attitude toward swearing shows that.

ME: You think then that Mr. Nixon will make the better President.

MISS OMWAKE: He'll be just like Mr. Eisenhower.

ME: If President Eisenhower could run again, would you vote for him?

MRS. DALE: Everybody on this street would, James. We're all just sick he can't run again. He seems to be the only man of the bunch who has any ideas about the real role of the President.

ME: You feel he would be reëlected if he did run?

MRS. DALE: By a bigger majority than before. He's the kind of President we want.

ME: And you feel that Mr. Nixon's statement about swearing makes him a lot more like Mr. Eisenhower?

MISS OMWAKE: Oh, yes.

ME: What did you think about his statement on Cuba?

MRS. DALE: Things like that are for men like Mr. Dulles to worry about. The President should occupy himself with other things.

ME: Do you agree with Mrs. Dale that if Mr. Eisenhower ran again he'd be reëlected?

MISS OMWAKE: What a silly question!

ME: Do you think Nixon will win?

MRS. DALE: After his promise not to swear in the White House, I'm sure he'll win. Women will appreciate that kind of gentleman.

In the campaigning that our group did, everyone followed our one inviolable rule: no one was allowed even by implication to cast any aspersion on Dwight Eisenhower, because we knew that the American electorate hungered for him as in the past. Since Senator Kennedy had apparently set for himself the same rule, we witnessed the strange spectacle of an election in which the Democrats damned almost all aspects of the last eight years, in which they paraded the dreadful inefficiencies of an incumbency, in which they pinpointed the errors, the oversights, the lack of resolution and the downright frumpiness of an administration without ever identifying the man who was largely to blame. I think that historians will have a great deal to say about this phenomenon.

I cannot speak for the others, but for myself I followed

this course because I knew that if I did otherwise I would alienate a good eighty percent of my listeners and I would lose votes instead of gain them. I could persuade people that our posture overseas was in perilous condition—and I did so persuade them, for many Republicans told me so—but no oratory that I or Cicero possessed could have convinced my listeners that General Eisenhower ought to bear any of the blame for this deterioration.

It is already obvious that the historians of which I just spoke will deal harshly with Dwight D. Eisenhower's incumbency, for both the concept of the Presidency and the stature of the nation were depreciated in his hands; yet when the last word is written there will remain that incontrovertible spectacle of an engaging man whom the people loved, and whom they were willing to forgive for anything. Even when groups of hard-shell Democrats who knew the facts gathered in the secrecy of their homes, no one dared discuss the overriding fact of the election: if President Eisenhower wanted to, and if he were willing to do the necessary hard work, he could still stampede the voters to Nixon. This was the sword of Damocles that hung over our heads throughout the campaign.

In mid-October I felt, "This is where Ike steps in to knock Jack Kennedy out." He did not do so. In late October I said, "They were wise to hold him back until the last three weeks. Now we get it." For some reason which I will never understand, even if it is explained to me, the President made no move. Then he toured the country on his "non-political" tour and instead of looking fiery, he looked transparent. On the first of November I told my helpers, "I think he's waited too long. I don't think he can capture the nation now."

When he finally did speak, he was enormously impressive and I grew apprehensive that perhaps it was not too late after all and that he might still stampede the voters. I wondered how Kennedy would combat the Presidential attack and watched with admiration when the senator ignored everything Mr. Eisenhower had said and directed attention to the ridiculous figure of the little boy Richard Nixon calling in panic for help from his father. To a large extent, the potential force of the Eisenhower thrust was thus neatly diverted. When the strongest gun of the Republican campaign was finally allowed to fire, the shot that should have reverberated around the nation was turned into an anticlimactic pop. What should have been a master stroke was interpreted by the public as panic. And where there should have been the overwhelming force of Presidential dignity there was a gnawing suspicion of insincerity.

Before our Bucks County audiences we praised the Eisenhower speech but lamented the fact that he had been dragged unwillingly into the fight because of Nixon's last-minute panic over what looked like certain Republican defeat. When Republicans asked, "But didn't you think Ike made a good speech?" I answered, "It was a great speech, but it should have come three weeks earlier when it could have done some good, not as a last-minute improvisation." Many agreed.

In these last vital weeks I got little sleep, for although I was generally optimistic about our chances, the gnawing fears that characterize the last days of any campaign were beginning to eat at me. On Sunday evening, following the senator's tumultuous appearance in Levittown, I conducted three large parties in the area and at each I said, "If the election were to be held next Tuesday, November first, instead of on the eighth, I'm sure Senator Kennedy would win handsomely. But in the next nine days anything can happen, and I'm scared stiff it will. I was in Korea just before Ike won in 1952 with his dramatic promise of 'I will go to Korea,' and I know how phony that whole deal was. I was in North Africa in 1956 when Hungary and the Suez imbroglio helped him win again, and I know how unjust that was. I don't know what's going to happen this year, but something will. And there goes the election to Mr. Nixon."

"What are you worried about, specifically?" someone asked.

"These things," I said. "First, some Catholic bishop somewhere is going to say something that will infuriate the nation. Second, the Chinese Reds will start shelling Matsu or Quemoy. Third, Castro will try to occupy Guantánamo Bay. Fourth, Nikita Khrushchev will announce that he favors the Democrats. Fifth, Jack Kennedy will say something he didn't intend to say. Every night when I go to bed I listen to the midnight news to hear which of these things has happened somewhere in the world. And if all's well, I say to my wife, 'Thank God we got through another day.' "

One of my Republican listeners asked, "Isn't there anything that could happen which would defeat Nixon?"

"Of course!" I said quickly. "Khrushchev could say that he wants to see the Republicans win. Or the Russians might put a man in space and remind us all that what Kennedy's been saying is true. Or Nixon might say something grotesquely wrong. But my experience has been that in the last stages of an election the nation tends to get more and more conservative and looks about wildly for any good reason to vote Republican. So I live from day to day, hoping that we'll get through this twenty-four hours."

"You think it's that close?" a neighbor asked.

"We're involved in an election that could be decided by any chance event that occurs anywhere," I replied. "That's why Kennedy's comments on international affairs make so much sense to me. Because that's the ticklish kind of world we live in."

There were many critics of the campaign who felt that Senator Kennedy was ill advised in letting up as he did during the last week of the election. Such critics are correct in their assumption that the Democratic campaign did in a sense let up, for no new subjects were discussed. But I and many professionals with whom I worked were more than content to have it so. We knew that we were ahead across the nation—at least in the big states like New York and Ohio—and we felt that the only thing that could lick us would be one of the catastrophes that I so desperately feared. If we could only keep from making an error of commission, we could win. So I was well satisfied to see Senator Kennedy let up a little and thus avoid some calamitous error. And each night when I went to bed I whispered again, "Thank God we got through another day."

One morning after such a prayer, I was waiting in my Doylestown headquarters for Sam Thompson, who was to show me some new development in the northern end of the county, when Lester Trauch, the drama expert on our local newspaper, dropped by to see what was going on. I told him I was waiting for that rare old clown, Sam Thompson, and he stepped back. "You've got a hell of a nerve to call Sam Thompson an old clown," he snapped.

"I was speaking of his . . ."

"Don't you know who he is?" Trauch interrupted.

"A man with a whiskey named after him," I replied.

"Well, he was one of the dedicated men in the early experimental theater in the United States," Trauch explained. "Sam Thompson helped Eugene O'Neill put on his plays with the Provincetown Players. Sam was in the original cast of *The Emperor Jones*. He's mentioned in books along with Harry Kemp and George Cram Cook and Susan Glaspell and Edna St. Vincent Millay."

"Sam Thompson?" I gaped.

"Sam Thompson with the little mustache," Trauch insisted. "In the revival of *Emperor Jones* that he brought to Broadway he gave a beginning actor his first role. Who do you suppose that actor was? Moss Hart. Jim, this man's a walking monument to artistic integrity. Did you ever hear about the part he played in the Federal Theater Project?"

It seemed so right, what Trauch was saying. It explained Sam's preposterous sign: "James A. Michener presents John F. Kennedy and Lyndon B. Johnson." It explained his flamboyant fire and his plea to allow the men in the northern end of the county to have one good fling. For Election Night he had already arranged for a parade of one hundred horn-blowing cars.

"How did a man like this ever wind up on a farm in upper Bucks County?" I asked.

"A man has only so much fire," Trauch replied. "Sam used his in helping Eugene O'Neill burn his way into the American theater. After that he retired to Bucks County and became a minor politician."

At this point Sam drove up, and as we headed north I said, "You never told me you were one of the Provincetown wild men," I chided.

He looked at me sideways with a certain pleasure and said, "The first play I was in was with Helen Hayes. We were both ten and we gave *Aladdin and His Wonderful Lamp*. Later I was with her on Broadway."

"How'd you get into politics?" I asked.

"Oh, I've always looked at politics as just another road show," he said grandly. "You need a press agent, a production chief, a star and a master of legerdemain. I got here, actually, after the war. I was in the war, you know."

"World War I?" I asked thoughtlessly.

"Hell no, World War II. I was too old for active service,

of course, but I was sitting in my room one day and the thought came to me, 'The stewards on those big troop transports must make a killing,' so I hurried down to the U. S. Lines and filled out an application. I ended the war as chief steward for the lines."

"Did you make a killing?" I asked.

"Soldiers shoot a lot of crap," Sam said. Then he dropped one hand from the wheel and slapped his leg. "You asking me about how I got here. Some years ago at a political rally a Republican woman made a speech and said it was an outrage that a newcomer like Sam Thompson should be elected to office in a historic county like Bucks."

"What did you say?" I asked, realizing that I was supposed to play the straight man.

"I'm glad you asked that question, Senator," Sam laughed, "because I was able to tell that audience that one of my ancestors was the first sheriff of Cumberland County, Pennsylvania, and that he served as an officer in the French and Indian War, where he distinguished himself at Braddock's defeat by hiding from the Indians behind a big tree and escaping the ambush. I told that dame that I refused my wife permission to join the Daughters of the American Revolution because my family held that all that crowd was newcomers to these parts."

I noticed that we were not driving along the normal road to Quakertown and I asked, "What's the big deal, Sam?"

He said, "I want to show you something I've been working on for fifteen years."

We drove along the wonderful back roads of Bucks County through rural areas where the larch was golden and the oak was red. We passed Dutch houses that had stood beside their streams for two hundred years, each with a barn bigger than itself, for that was the sign of frugality. How beautiful my county was that day, how especially lovely and rural it was, as if there had never been a Levittown nor a Catholic daring to run for the Presidency. It was a timeless land and from the towering oaks fell acorns that would be the trees of the next century.

"This is a land worth fighting for, Sam," I reflected.

"I want you to see what I've been fighting for," he replied, and he drove me to a small hill from whose winding dirt road I could see a considerable depression, down the center of which ran one of our most pleasant streams, the Tohickon. On the sides of the hills were the old farmhouses and in the meadows were cattle that had descended from the time of William Penn.

"For the last fifteen years I've been coming to this hill," Sam said, "dreaming of a lake that would be dammed up down there and of a state park that would preserve this area forever. There are so many people crowding into the valleys, Jim, and so few of the valleys are being kept clean and free for the next generation."

"Sam!" I cried. "Is this the new state park they were writing about in the *Intelligencer* the other day?"

"Yep, we finally got it through," Sam said. "I want you to look at the dam." He drove me down a side road to a very old dam, holding back scarcely a pond, let alone the large lake that was now envisioned. "I think the whole project might have fallen through," he mused, "if we'd allowed this old dam to disappear. As long as it was here it remained a symbol of what could be done."

"It looks pretty new to me," I said, kicking at some of the stones in the way a man does when he's thinking of buying a used car.

"Well, that part is," Sam said. "Three or four years ago I talked our Tohickon Watershed Association into encouraging our Boy Scouts into spending their entire vacation rebuilding this dam. When we got it done, the Scouts scrounged everything, cement, time, money. Well, when we got the dam repaired everybody began to see what might be accomplished if we could get hold of the entire valley." He stood beside the dam and looked upstream. "This'll be the best public park in Pennsylvania," he observed.

I found also that during the years when Sam Thompson was fighting for his park he was also organizing the local township officials throughout the county so that each could be more efficient in his job. Today Bucks County has one of the finest such groups, headed by Sam. He was also energetic whenever schools or libraries needed help, and his round, smiling presence was available when old people went on relief.

One day he told me, "I don't dislike Republicans. It's just that men who build parks are usually Democrats." I replied that I was engaged in this election because I felt that there was a lot of building that needed doing. "I figured that's why you got mixed up in it," Sam said. "That's the real reason for being a Democrat."

I would not like, however, to leave even the slightest touch of sentiment in my last comment about Sam Thompson. A reflection of this sort seems closer to the man: I never saw Sam engage in a single activity but what he first asked, "What angle can we use to get the bastard to see things our way? You know any pressure we can put on him?" The last time I worked with Sam was on the evening before election. He was making plans to get a hundred folding chairs for the victory party which he had arranged for the northern section. I said, "Why don't we just call Otto? I know he's got a lot of chairs."

"No," Sam reflected. "We won't call him direct. That would put us in the beggar's position. Otto's coming up for reelection next year and he's going to need our help. I'll just drop by and sort of ask him how he sees things for next year, and he'll get the point and the son-of-a-bitch'll have to give us those chairs."

8
Barnstormers

☒ ☒

In the waning days of the campaign, when it was obvious that I could accomplish no more in Bucks County, I was invited by headquarters in Washington to participate in a barnstorming tour of areas where the Kennedy candidacy was in serious trouble. I replied that I didn't see offhand what I could accomplish, but I agreed to go.

Early one rainy morning a sleepy-eyed group gathered at the Washington airport and mumbled introductions to one another. Not even the most partial observer could have guessed that the dozen or so people who were perfunctorily shaking hands were shortly to be billed as an extraordinary galaxy of stars from the motion-picture, sport and intellectual worlds. They looked for the most part like a bunch of hungover bums.

One of the group was alert. He was Jerold Hoffberger, a surprising gentleman from Maryland. Part owner of the Baltimore Colts football team and partner in the Baltimore Orioles baseball team, he was properly listed as a sportsman. Managing director of many industries, including some hundred bowling alleys, he could also correctly be billed as an industrialist. And in view of the fact that he was contributing the airplane, the food, and the staff, I suppose he could be classified as either a politician or a philanthropist. The one description we never, never used during our trip was the one that was most accurate. He owned one of the biggest breweries in the South, but we felt that it might be a little indelicate to introduce Jerry Hoffberger to political audiences in dry areas as "the genial beer baron." He was invariably referred to as "a leading Maryland industrialist," although I always suspected that the former might have gained us more votes.

He was a joy, a salty young man, wise in the worlds of business and sport, and he made one of the best impressions of our entire group whenever he said simply, "I am a businessman who believes in high wages and high taxes, because I have seen what both have done for my company and my nation. I am a businessman for Senator Kennedy because I know that this country has got to get started on hundreds of different projects. On the morning that I flew out of Washington my assistant told me that Sparrows Point, the biggest steel producer in our area, had just gone on half time. Do you know what that means to an industrial area? Do you know what is really happening in many parts of our country? Do you know why so many businessmen are going to vote Democratic this year for the first time?" When stubborn Jerry Hoffberger punched away at this theme, people listened, and he provided our tour with much more than the airplane and the sandwiches.

Our chairman was the distinguished Denver lawyer, Byron White, who had graduated from Colorado University when I was teaching in that state, and who was noteworthy in those years for being an all-American football player, a top honor student and a Rhodes scholar. Later, as a Detroit Lion backfield star, he had led the professionals in rushing the ball and had been one of the toughest operators in football. I had known of him in the South Pacific as a much-decorated aide to Admiral Halsey, and if you read the official history of the great naval battles fought off the Philippines, you will find that Lieutenant Whizzer White played a critical role far beyond what his immature years would have entitled him to. In civil life he had become a lawyer and while serving his apprenticeship in Washington had met up with Congressman Jack Kennedy, whose later nomination to the Presidency he had helped engineer. The first major campaign appointment Kennedy made was of

Whizzer White to head the Citizens for Kennedy, which made him my boss.

As a speaker he affected a hesitancy which deluded his listeners into thinking, "He's a nice young man." But when the chips were down he could line out facts faster than John Kennedy in a debate. He had a brilliant mind and a sharp wit. We were not surprised that often during the election he was mentioned for this or that cabinet post. He was a quiet operator, a very knowledgeable politician, and a most pleasant man to be with.

The schedule that Whizzer had outlined for us was, I must say, in the grand tradition of the Democratic party. No time was designated for meals or washing up. There were speeches, short plane hops, more speeches, long plane hops, more speeches, and a distant hotel in which to flop. Each day saw four or five meetings, interviews with press and television, impromptu talks to clubs or boys' homes or supermarkets, and an endless procession of local political aspirants who hoped that we would say something to further their candidacies. It was as grueling a tour as could have been devised, and when at last one staggered to the end, he could say with no fear of successful contradiction that he had campaigned for a President.

Whizzer had an excellent and a typical plan. He said, "Why go into areas that are going to vote Democratic anyway? What help can we provide there? Let's go into all the areas where the sledding is toughest for the local candidates and see what we can accomplish in such places." Consequently, our tour took us to Republican strongholds in Michigan, Illinois, Nebraska, Utah, Idaho, Colorado, Indiana and Kentucky, and wherever we went, our forces were beleaguered like forlorn settlers fighting off the final charge of the surrounding redskins. It was exciting work and we grew to love it.

It would be improper for me to designate any one person as the star of our show, but two people did stand out in the public's mind and each happened to come from Hollywood. The first was Angie Dickinson, a strikingly beautiful young woman with golden blond hair, dark eyes and a truly gamin manner. She had just gained much acclaim for her role in a Frank Sinatra movie and was on her way to Spain for a starring role. She was in huge demand at all studios, having suddenly become what is called "a hot property." Even while on tour with us she was bombarded by telegrams from Hollywood offering tempting new roles.

Angie was a delightful girl to have aboard an airplane. She had a low raucous laugh that quite demoralized serious discussion, which was a boon after the hard work we did. Her sole responsibility was to step off the plane at each stop looking positively delicious, but she had to accomplish this with no sleep, improper food, no dressing room, and not even a place where she could stretch out for a nap. She was the soul of patience and my permanent memory of her was of a sleepy-eyed young girl doing her hair laboriously before each stop, and getting it out of curlers just before the plane landed. Magically she would fluff out her curls, press her dress down with her hands, adjust her coat and step out onto the gangway with a ravishing smile.

But Angie was deceptive. I liked to talk with her because I sensed that young as she was, here was a real old pro who had knocked around Hollywood without getting anywhere, and then suddenly everybody wanted her. She was a girl at that magnificent moment when a career dramatically opens up, and I had known many such girls later in their lives when it had somehow all gone wrong, and how desperately I hoped for Angie that she would meet the right agent, make the right deals, marry the right guy and get some good out of the burgeoning fame that was beginning to surround her.

On our entire trip she was a model of good sportsmanship, a source of constant hilarity. I think she had a touch of Carole Lombard about her, a divine irreverence. And she provided us with much more than beauty. Night after night she surprised the crowds when instead of smiling like a movie star she explained, in her halting manner, "I have come here as a private citizen to tell you that I am working voluntarily for the election of Senator John Kennedy. He is a brilliant leader and a man who will serve this country well. I ask you individually for your vote. Because Senator Kennedy will help us all to build the strong America that we need in the years ahead."

But Angie Dickinson had her breaking point. We made her job of keeping herself beautiful extra difficult by periodically losing her cosmetics case. When this first happened she was the sweet young college girl asking her roommate where her blouse was. At the second occurrence she was more like a *grande dame* of the French court asking where her jewels were. But when we lost her case the third time she shouted like a truck driver, "All right, where in hell is that lousy case?" After that we didn't lose it any more.

She endeared herself to all of us by insisting upon calling Professor Arthur Meier Schlesinger—not a man who unbends easily—"Artie," and after an astonished gasp, the brilliant professor acknowledged his nickname and announced to audiences that he formed the lesser end of the Hollywood-Harvard Axis. "It goes to show," he explained as audiences chuckled, "how wide are the types who support Senator Kennedy." Whenever I dozed on the plane, I was ultimately awakened by Angie Dickinson's deep-throated fishwife's guffaw as she enjoyed the latest preposterous occurrence. When we were so tired that we could not think, we could always hear her tantalizing laugh.

Her male counterpart was the intellectual highlight of the barnstorming tour. I had met him some years before when I was making an appearance in a Chicago television station. I was talking about books on a midnight show, as I recall, and the man to follow me—a personality, they called him—had just released a cowboy-and-Indian picture and was in town to ballyhoo it. The agent who was hauling him around from one station to the next knew the man who was squiring me around and he asked, "Why don't you wait till he makes his pitch, and the four of us can split a beer?"

My man replied, "Who needs a cowboy star?" So we left.

In doing so I missed making friends with a man who surprised all of us. Jeff Chandler must have appeared initially to his audiences as a typical Hollywood star, tall, lean, hawk-faced, silver-haired, expert in projecting himself. But I feel sure that before each night ended the crowd realized that this fellow Chandler was completely outside the pattern. After only one session Whizzer White said, "From here on out, Jeff, you're chairman of this outfit. You talk sense."

Jeff Chandler, the cowboy star, was by all odds the most effective stump speaker we had. He knew the Democratic platform better than I did. He had recently toured Israel with political leaders who had briefed him on what was happening in Europe and the Near East. He had a brilliant grasp of American history and his own theories of how to win an election. Before an audience he had an insinuating logic that won votes, and on the long plane trips he had an inquiring mind that pumped from each of us whatever knowledge we could give him. But what surprised me most was that he had an acid wit, and before each stop he would compose in a relatively few minutes poetic lampoons which he set to music and which he sang before his audiences, stampeding them with his hilarious pinpointing of Republican foibles. Most of the effective speeches were suggested by him, and most of the telling sallies of wit were his.

I had many opportunities to talk with Jeff, and his understanding of what was happening in America was profound. He was generous, helpful and of great force in public argument. He was about as far from the stereotype of a Hollywood star as I could imagine, and he was one of the most solidly liberal men, without a touch of nonsense, that I met during the campaign. It was a privilege to work with him.

His side-kick left us all a little dazed. When the barnstorming tour was being organized I said that I did not want to bother with it unless some major sports figure was along, and Whizzer White came up with a dandy. Stan Musial was a howling success from the moment he joined us. A long, rangy, forty-year-old, handsome Polish boy from the streets of Donora, near Pittsburgh, Stan brought with him a distinguished career on the baseball diamond and a long string of successes in business. He will probably end his life as the richest baseball player in history, but I will always remember him as one of the most hilarious characters I have ever met.

He was also our most important drawing card, outranking even Angie Dickinson and Jeff Chandler, for his name lured men to our meetings, and I was constantly astonished at how the men in the cities we stopped at would crowd the airports to see Stan Musial. He seemed about fifteen years younger than he was, and men who were now quite old remembered him as a beginner in the big leagues. Baseball rather bores me these days, but apparently across the nation it has as great a lure as ever.

Musial loved to recount those outrageous incidents that occur in baseball. He was good at dialect and I formed his most appreciative audience, because I love the homely chatter of American speech. Often at night the plane would echo with my guffaws and Angie Dickinson's gutter laughs as Musial told some innocuous story about an illiterate catcher trying to order a meal in a fancy café. At other times Musial and I would ride alone in some back seat and he would tell me of his youth in Donora and of how he always regretted not having gone to the University of Pittsburgh on the basketball scholarship that had been offered him. "All that I have I got because older men helped me," he said. "That's why I'm for Kennedy. Maybe I could explain it better, but either you get what I'm driving at or you don't."

Stan's political speeches were unforgettable. Jeff Chandler would make some gently disparaging remark about him. He would grin, rise to his feet, bend nearly double over the microphone and wait till the roar of applause stopped. Then he would say, "I played in Denver once about ten years ago. I struck out three times." The crowd would roar with laughter and he would flash that incredible Polish grin at them and they would roar some more. "Tonight I'm not here to play baseball," he would say and they would laugh again. "I'm here to ask you to vote for Senator John F. Kennedy." More shouting and Stan would sit down. I suspect he influenced more votes than any of the rest of us, for he spoke to men who could not otherwise be touched. He was the perpetual youth, the boyhood hero, the clean-cut athlete. The crowds used to surge around Angie and Jeff as popular movie stars. But they stood back a little from Musial. He was the champ, Stan the Man, and if a senator from Massachusetts was good enough for Stan, he was good enough for them.

For me the major surprise of the trip was the Kennedy girls, those slim, beautiful, well-groomed creatures who moved gracefully onstage, made their little speeches, and quite bedazzled everybody. They were potent campaigners and lent our whole operation a class it could not otherwise have attained. People wanted to see them, hoping, I suspect, that they would prove to be harpies whom they could dislike, but when they found them to be normal, good-looking, young American married women, the audiences took them to their hearts. The girls were amazing workers, appearing at three to six meetings each day dispensing charm and warmth at the same time. During the campaign I worked at one time or another with five of the Kennedy girls, three sisters of the senator and two of his sisters-in-law, and I have only respect for the efficient manner in which they corraled the votes.

On our barnstorming tour the senator's sisters did not travel with us but did drift into our operation as their own schedules permitted. We would walk on stage, and there mysteriously would be one of the Kennedy girls who had flown in from another direction and who as soon as we were finished would fly away. They always found time to shake hands with everyone in the hall, if that was practical, and they invariably said to me and the other members of the tour, "We are grateful for the help you are giving us." The phrase never varied and never failed to irritate me. I used to think, "Look, sister, I'm not giving you any help. It's your brother." They must have sensed my reaction, for often, when they had recited their litany, they laughed. I remember them as gracious ladies who never ate or slept or did anything but hurry from town to town, and I know from my own experience that they helped their brother enormously.

The sisters-in-law operated differently, for they became a formal part of our troupe and traveled with us. Teddy's wife, Joan, who flew in from her home in California, was one of the most beautiful women it has been my pleasure to know. A young girl, only recently married to Teddy, she had an enviable figure, a divine face, and a shock of lovely hair. Whenever I saw her I was reminded of an imaginary photograph from some *Life* story about teen-agers who had *not* become delinquents. She was great fun aboard the plane, with a rowdy sense of humor, and when she and Angie got together there was usually a riot. Like Angie, her principal job was to keep herself beautiful under the most trying circumstances, and day after day she stepped forth from the plane in perfect grooming.

Joan Kennedy was by far the best speaker of the Kennedy women. In fact, when she let herself go, she could be quite a rabble-rouser and I got the impression she was a very clever girl. She spoke in a high sweet voice, yet she could impart considerable force into passages that required it. She was a fine campaigner, and one local chairman, who was obviously struck by the quality of her words, asked us, "Does the Kennedy family have a casting bureau where they try out girls before the sons are allowed to marry them?" I suspect America is going to hear a lot more from Joan Kennedy. Certainly, on our trip she was a major asset.

But it was to sister-in-law Ethel, Bobby Kennedy's pert little wife, that I quite lost my heart. We did not begin well. After one of my better speeches Ethel took me aside and looking up at me from her five-feet-one and her hundred pounds said bluntly, "I thought you made a grave mistake tonight, Mr. Michener."

I thought, "Who the hell is this dame to lecture me?" and I was about to turn away.

"What I mean is," she forged ahead, "when you tell the story of Brother Joe's being shot down and killed during the war . . ."

"It's one of the most effective ways to combat charges about Democrats' being soft on communism," I snapped rather gruffly.

"I know that," she interrupted impatiently. "But why is it necessary to say that he was killed while he was bombing Germany? This area has lots of Germans. Why not just say, 'Joe was killed in the war'?"

I had never thought of this, and the more I traveled with Ethel Kennedy the more perceptive I found her. She was one of the most politically sophisticated women I have ever known. Nothing escaped her attention, apparently, and it was a privilege to work with her. On the stage she was forthright and effective. In the plane, in face-to-face analysis of ideas and next steps, she was brilliant. I always thought of her as the pert little wren that lives outside my window and makes the summers lovely. Like the wren, Ethel's excited chatter had an extremely winning quality. She had that rare attribute that makes some women so attractive: she could be wholly feminine and at the same time impressively intelligent.

If she started our acquaintance by jarring me, I ended it by forcing her to gasp. On our last hop I asked, "Ethel, what's your husband's role to be in the new administration?"

She blushed and for once had no ready comment. Here was a subject that must have been discussed often in secret but which was not allowed to be handled in public. She tried to avoid it, then changed her mind and obviously wanted to talk. "What do you think it should be?" she parried.

"I believe that the American public rather expects Jack to

appoint one member of his family to a position of high importance," I reasoned. "They know the Presidency is a lonely job and that he is entitled to one or two men whose personal loyalty he can rely upon."

"Do you think the public would tolerate it?" she pressed.

"They did when Eisenhower appointed his brother to various jobs. And when he brought his son to the White House," I added.

"I wonder," she mused, and it was painfully apparent that she wished to speak further, but I quite ended the conversation by my next observation.

"What must be guarded against," I reflected, "is the fact that you Kennedys have such a large family that within a space of four years some one of you is bound to abuse his position and bring infamy on Jack and the party."

Ethel Kennedy blushed red and tried to reach across the airplane table and slap my face. "How dare you say such a thing?" she cried.

"Because it's happened in all administrations," I said. "Look at the Howard Hughes case right now," I added.

"Damn it all!" she blurted out. "The Kennedys don't behave like that."

"I hope not," I said. "For the sake of the party I hope not."

We rode in silence to New York and to the last great rally in the Coliseum. Before we parted she offered a generous gesture of friendship and I believe that we parted with real respect. Certainly I think much more highly of Bobby Kennedy as a future political power now that I know the forthright, intelligent girl he had the good sense to marry. As Jeff Chandler said in introducing her, "She's the most beautiful mother of seven *I've* ever seen." I would add, "And the sharpest-witted."

The last permanent member of our troupe was Professor Arthur Meier Schlesinger, Jr., one of the powerful brains of the Kennedy team and the dignified panjandrum that Angie Dickinson called "Artie." It fell to Schlesinger to give the talks that established the grave theme of our meetings, that America faced a real choice between the Democrats and the Republicans. With precision he identified exactly what that choice consisted of, as between both the parties and their nominees. It was a constant privilege for me to hear Schlesinger, for I had once studied with his father at Harvard, and much of my understanding of the forces of American history derived from the fact that Schlesinger, Sr., had taught me so well. Now to hear the son applying those same hard principles of morality and logic to the current scene inspired in me a kind of intellectual nostalgia. There is a continuum in history, and here I could witness it in operation, passing along from father's principles to son's applications. I often wondered what the austere old man would have thought if he could have heard little Angie Dickinson cooing, "Artie, you were a sensation tonight. Nobody could understand a damned word you said, but you said it so impressively!" Schlesinger grinned at the accolade, for he was sure that many of the people did understand.

During our trip Schlesinger had two political works of his on the best-seller list, *The Politics of Upheaval*, a study of the Franklin D. Roosevelt years, and his savage analysis of the current campaign, *Kennedy or Nixon: Does It Make Any Difference?* Wherever we went university people and newspapermen wanted to talk with Schlesinger about the latter book and all of us on the tour came to realize that in Schlesinger and men like him the Democratic party had powerful supporters. In fact, much of the strength which had carried the party into control of both houses of Congress by such striking majorities stemmed from the intellectual leadership provided by men like Schlesinger.

To see Arthur, Jr., at work was impressive, for he did what all of us intend doing. Whenever he read a newspaper he tore out relevant stories or bits of data and stuffed them into his pockets. Then when he got near a briefcase, he transferred them all to it, so that at the end of a week he had a small file of specific things that had impressed him or about which he might one day like to write. When it came time to write, a careless man like me would be asking himself, "I wonder where I could get a copy of that disgraceful newspaper story about the hecklers?" But Arthur, Jr., would not have to ask that question. Years before he had foreseen that some day he might want to quote that particular story, so he had it neatly filed away.

The precision of his mind was also noticeable to all who worked with him. One night after an especially difficult time with the religious problem Ethel Kennedy asked me what the distinguishing characteristics of the Mormon faith were, and I explained in rather good detail, I thought, how this strong religion had arisen and particularly how it had prospered in two regions I knew well, Utah and the South Pacific, where it has become a leading force. At this point I thought to ask Schlesinger, "When did Joseph Smith receive his revelation of *The Book of Mormon?*"

Without even an instant's hesitation Schlesinger looked up from a book he was reading and replied, "Smith was born December 23, 1805, in Vermont, but at the age of eleven moved to Ontario County, in New York State. On September 21, 1823, when Smith was eighteen years old, the angel Moroni appeared before him three times to tell him that the sacred book of Mormon was hidden on a hillside near Manchester, but it wasn't until 1827 that Smith dug up the three golden plates on which the book was written in an unknown tongue. Smith also got two magic crystals, Urim and Thummim, which enabled him to translate the writing, but the book itself wasn't published until about 1830." Having provided this, Schlesinger ignored us and went on with his reading.

So that was our troupe: Schlesinger the satiric analyst; Hoffberger the surreptitious brewer; White the Rhodes scholar; Chandler and Musial, the big attractions; Angie Dickinson, the little sweetheart; and Joan and Ethel Kennedy, the extraordinary young women. It was an odd collection, but when they faced the microphones at meeting after meeting, they said something.

There was another member of the troupe, but so far as I know he never once appeared in public, yet he was the strong, hard brain of the operation, and since he represents the kind of young men who surround the Kennedys I had better speak fairly fully of him as I came to know him. Chuck Roche is a Boston newspaperman in his late thirties. I believe he went to Harvard, where he made the acquaintance of Bobby Kennedy, whom he has always helped during political campaigns. Roche is the typical Catholic liberal, a good husband with five children to support, and with a sensitive, shrewd, well-organized mind. I would suppose that he had made somewhat above average marks at Harvard.

He looks like a hundred thousand other guys who could have been named Chuck Roche. In fact, he looks a lot like me, and one of my distinctions is that I have never gone anywhere without somebody's saying, "You know, Mr. Michener, you're the spitting image of so-and-so." All I can say is that the average looks of this nation must be pretty average. Chuck has a big roundish face, wears glasses, has indiscriminate eyes and hair of no distinction. I imagine that wherever he goes people tell him that he looks like so-and-so.

He does not think like this omnipresent so-and-so, however, for he has a driving interest in politics, and I suspect that he knows more about what is going on in the nation than all the rest of us together. He had an unusually realistic view of how states and areas were going to vote, and looking back on what he told me, he was surprisingly accurate. I first met him in a car that whisked us back and forth across Pennsylvania to attend political rallies at which Bobby Kennedy was speaking, and he talked with me of practical matters while Kennedy and my wife did what the newspapermen call "double-doming" in the back. Roche had an idea whereby we might take the edge off the *Saturday Evening Post*'s endorsement of Nixon, and he also wanted to know in brutal, operational terms what was happening in the religious field in Pennsylvania. I happened that day to have received a formal summary of the unfortunate incident in which a Bucks County Republican official had been caught distributing anti-Catholic literature and I said, "I haven't read this yet, Chuck. It's of no use to me. Take it, and if the heat gets too hot, at least you have the evidence." About two weeks later, when the Republicans were making ugly charges against the Democrats, Bobby Kennedy simply cited the Bucks County case. There was an immediate blast from all quarters, with demands for retractions and apologies. At this point Chuck Roche coolly pointed out that he had the evidence and that he preferred not to use it. He advised everyone to cool off, and that was the last we heard officially of the religious issue during the campaign.

It was Chuck's job on the barnstorming tour to know what was happening in each area we visited, and his information network must have been good, for unerringly he told us what to speak about and what to avoid. He also worked with the local politicians and sought advice from them on what we might do that would best help the local ticket. In most Broadway plays about politics there is always the newspaperman with his hat on the back of his head who knows where all the skeletons are buried but nevertheless sticks with the tragic hero until he can stand no more.

Then he makes a grandiloquent statement in defense of American democracy, as it ought to function if it weren't for slobs like the hero, tells the hero to go to hell, gulps a swig of whiskey and exits with his hat still on the back of his head. Chuck Roche could have played that role. I never found out exactly why he had the hard idealism he did, but he honestly felt that his Kennedy team could do a good job running the country. What was immediately important, he had some very good ideas as to how his team could win the election.

He operated wholly behind the scenes. When our plane arrived at some city, Chuck would quietly disappear to talk with the local leaders, while the rest of us piled into convertibles for the long ride into town. The celebrities of our party were supposed to ride sitting on the top edge of the back seats so that the long motorcade would appear as impressive as possible. Arthur Schlesinger and Angie Dickinson rode together, and they made a striking and diverse pair waving to the crowds. I usually rode with Jeff Chandler, and because the crowds wanted to see him and not me, and because I did not want to detract from his reception, I refused to ride anywhere but up front in a normal seat. This amused Schlesinger, who chided, "Have you no pride in the republic of letters? A novelist is as significant as a motion-picture star."

"Not from the back seat of a convertible," I replied and held onto my own plan.

At the big formal meetings our speeches were always the same. Whizzer White made a few observations about the local scene and turned the crowd over to Jeff Chandler, who mixed wry humor with hard political sense. Angie Dickinson was adorable. Stan Musial was as handsome as a young god. And Arthur Schlesinger was powerful in his criticism of the drift of the last eight years. Listening to him talk, I used to wonder why so many newspaper editors hated him and used him as the whipping boy of the liberals who help guide the Democratic party. To me he talked sense, but perhaps I was prejudiced.

I came on next to last, for I could accommodate myself to any exigencies of time or special situations. Thus I was told just before I started speaking, "Ten minutes and stress the patriotism record." If we were running long I'd be told, "Three minutes and try to cover the local boy who's been challenged on his war record." If we had lots of time, I was expected to touch upon five or six basic themes and to wind up the straightforward electioneering, for after me came the Kennedy girls and I suspect that anything we first speakers accomplished was doubled by what these beautiful girls added. At any rate, they wound up the show with a bang and we all climbed into our convertibles for the fast ride back to the airport and the hurried trip to the next town.

I have used the phrase, "I was told." The person who did the telling was Chuck Roche, so we worked in rather close harmony. As a matter of fact, when we got onto the platform Chuck usually sat in the first row of the audience with some local leader to judge how things were going in the set speeches, over which he had no power. Angie Dickinson was going to say what she had prepared and that was that. So was Professor Schlesinger, for he knew that what he said gained votes. But different audiences received these set speeches in different ways, so Chuck, even though he had briefed me before I went on stage, now sat with flash cards advising me on last-minute changes.

He was especially fond of a card marked "Cuba." He had developed the startling fact that any American citizen who lived east of Los Angeles "is closer right now to the communists in Cuba than he is to his fellow Americans in Honolulu." Somehow or other, whenever I repeated this, it made Senator Kennedy's concern over Cuba seem legitimate. Chuck also had cards dealing with inflation, structure of Congress, war record and half a dozen other topics which I was supposed to weave into one coherent speech.

The two best performances I gave involved Chuck in quite different ways. In the first, I ignored him completely, because there was something that welled up within me that I had to disgorge. But in the second, I followed his advice minutely, even though I didn't trust it, and as a result gave a talk which had surprising results. That night Chuck Roche was a very perceptive man.

The time I crossed him up was in Denver, where I had once lived and to which I had often traveled when I was an underpaid teacher in a town fifty-five miles to the north. I had a good speech prepared for Denver, and Chuck had approved it. But on the way to the cavernous auditorium it happened that our car passed by the long-forgotten and now demolished area where the Baker Federal Theater had once stood. And as I saw this old site which had given the impetus to so much of my adult work, I asked the driver to stop and I got out to look at the shadows of the theater in which I had grown up artistically.

In the mid-1930's the Federal Theater Project had operated in Denver a stock company composed of out-of-work actors and directors, and each week for several years this distinguished group of people gave a different play. The public was charged thirty-five cents, as I recall, and the plays they saw were the best that had so far been written. I was working in Greeley, a town to the north of Denver, and regularly each week I drove down to the Baker Federal Theater to see either a classical play or a modern success. I got to know the actors and to anticipate seeing them in different roles. I acquired a sense of drama, and an abiding love for the theater.

I was therefore disgusted when Denver reactionaries began lambasting the Baker Federal as a colossal boon-doggle, a waste of taxpayers' money and an insult to the common sense of the people of Colorado. Every cheap critic of a government that was trying to do something productive and to keep creative people from starving got into the act and earned a few headlines by abusing the concept of government-sponsored art. It made me furious at the time, but I was then impotent to defend the project, and it was killed. I remember when it was closed down, for I thought: "Of all that Colorado has offered me, nothing was more important to my life than this theater. I may never write a play nor act in one, but in this old building I found out what it was all about. It was as valuable to me as the colleges and the libraries." I also remember thinking: "I'm against the people who are killing this theater." I thought of the plays I had seen there. Shaw and O'Neill and Sinclair Lewis, Marc Connelly and authors whose names I had not before known had enriched my life and awakened my sense of the dramatic. But the project was ridiculed and killed by people who possessed a limited view of both government and life.

Now, on a dark night in 1960, as I looked at the old spot where even the tinseled marquee had vanished, I thought: "Somebody estimated the other day that on dramatic works that have been derived from my stories the federal government has collected not less than $10,000,000 in taxes, and on the personal incomes derived from them another $20,000,000 at least. I wonder what it cost to run the Baker Federal Theater during the time I saw it? Probably not over $100,000. Yet it ignited my mind. So for every dollar that the government wasted in 1936, it got back $300 from me alone. What did it get back in imagination and happiness and the illumination of life from all the others who used to sit in the audience for thirty-five cents a night?"

It seemed to me, as I stood there in Denver, that Democrats were people who believed that one dollar spent now on a creative theory of government was likely to be repaid three hundred times over during the later evolution of the nation. Republicans were people who believed that men should dedicate themselves to hard work now, and if any money was left over, it could be spent as creatively as one wished, but such expenditure must not be taken seriously. I wished then that I could have before me all the cynical critics of the Federal Arts Project during those depression years, and I wished that I could show them a balance sheet of what the projects had cost and what they had repaid the nation. For example, I would like to show them Sam Thompson, who had been kept alive by a theater project, and who survived to serve his nation well. Those disgusting, little-souled, lack-vision people, how I would have liked to show them such balance sheets that night.

It was in this mood that I reported to the auditorium where Chuck Roche had an audience of six or seven thousand waiting. But I was so deeply agitated by my personal recollections of the powerful days of my youth in Colorado that I could not even consider the topics Chuck was suggesting, and when I stood before the Coloradans I gave what must have been the least effective talk of the tour.

I began, "The Bible has a magnificent old phrase, 'Let us now praise famous men,' and tonight in the white heat of our campaign I should like to do just that, for in a democracy we sometimes forget the famous men who have made us strong. Colorado had such a man, Senator Ed Costigan, who in his day was one of the most gallant legislators this country had. Costigan grew up in the free spirit of Colorado, and here he developed those theories of government which he was later to advocate so ably in Washington.

"He was a liberal. He was a fighter. He was a visionary.

He was a man who spent hours of his time inculcating in younger men the same idealism that he practiced. In the years that I worked so happily in Colorado, every man of stature that I knew owed his philosophy of government to Ed Costigan. This great man taught Colorado to be free. He initiated the legislation that saw us through the depression and kept us strong. He served both his state and his nation as few men are ever capable of serving.

"All the liberal ideas that have been so important in my life I learned from Ed Costigan. Before I came upon his remarkable career I thought it was proper for men to use the government for narrow purposes. Costigan knew that it should be used for the broadest possible human purposes. He illuminated my life, with insights that have grown constantly stronger the farther away from him I move. He was an adornment to this state, the noblest man you have so far produced.

"Let us therefore do as the Bible suggests and praise famous men. Let us tonight praise Colorado's foremost son, Ed Costigan, the fighting liberal. Because the man I have come here to speak to you about is cast in the mold of Ed Costigan. I couldn't support him if he weren't. If Ed Costigan were alive tonight I feel sure that he would be supporting Jack Kennedy, too, because Kennedy stands for all the broad-gauge human rights that Ed Costigan stood for, and I believe that Kennedy is the true inheritor of that great liberal tradition."

I then went into my set speech and I could see Chuck Roche relax a little, but after the program ended Whizzer White said, "I'll bet not ten people in the audience knew who you were talking about. They forget awfully fast."

But Professor Schlesinger said, "I was deeply impressed that you should have mentioned Ed Costigan. What a great man he was and how we need to remember what he stood for."

White was correct. In our audience of six or seven thousand, hardly five people knew that Colorado had once produced a great man, but those five were leaders of the state, who came up to say, "I was a child of Ed Costigan's. He taught me all I knew." I suspect that if I had spoken differently in Denver I might have won a few more votes to our side, but if I had been the kind of man who could have spoken differently under those circumstances, I would probably never have given a damn about Jack Kennedy in the first place.

In the speech where I allowed Chuck Roche to set the pattern completely, the results were more striking. On our way in from the airport to a small city that I would prefer not to name, the man and woman riding in my convertible explained, "This area is the center of the worst anti-Catholic agitation in the nation. Please keep your mouth shut on the religious issue. If you mention it, our side will be seriously damaged."

I assured them: "Mr. Roche, who is pretty canny on these things, has only two topics which are absolutely forbidden. Eisenhower and religion. You don't have to worry about us."

My escorts sighed and said, "We're both Protestants and we were just afraid that you might be a Catholic and that when you see what they are doing to us, you might blow your stack."

I laughed and said, "I face this every day in my own county and I've learned to keep my stack unblown."

"We're relieved," they sighed. "What you might hit in your talks is the farm problem and Cuba. We seem to be getting some mileage out of them."

I started adjusting my notes to include *farm* and *Cuba*, but when we assembled at the high school auditorium where the rally was to be held, one of the other speakers showed us some literature that had been circulated that day, and it was scurrilous. "Why don't you comment on this?" they asked me.

"I wouldn't touch it," I said. I related what my guides had told me and Jeff Chandler confirmed that his escorts had warned him about the same thing. The community was torn apart by religious strife and any mention of it could only exacerbate feelings more damagingly than they already were.

But as I started to go onto the stage Chuck Roche called me aside and whispered, "Jim, have you seen what they're doing in this town?"

"Don't worry," I assured him. "I've promised not to touch it."

"I think you should," he said grimly.

I was surprised at this and warned, "It can only bring trouble."

He took me by the arm and said, "I don't want to win this town by pussyfooting on this issue. If we have to tear it wide apart, let's do it right now. Are you game?"

"I sure am," I said.

"How will you handle it?" he asked.

"Not with kid gloves," I replied.

We went to Whizzer White, who was in charge, and said, "We're going to tackle the religious question head on."

"You'll lose the area if you do," he warned.

"Some areas you want to lose," Chuck said.

"How do you see it?" I was asked.

"This time we lose," I said. "Maybe we clear the air for next time."

"Go ahead," White said apprehensively.

I will not try to repeat all that I said, because it probably wouldn't read well. I can only report that the words I said in that supercharged air that night were the best I have ever spoken. At another time they might not have been effective, and indeed they weren't really effective in this case, for they were heard in sullen silence, but they were heard. I began in as shocking a way as possible by saying that I was supposed to be the speaker who told funny stories about the election so that people would go home in good humor, but tonight I would not speak of humorous things. I would speak of the most tense and terrible matters that were dividing this community. I said that whether they knew it or not, whether they liked it or not, on November 8 Jack Kennedy was going to win the election, and on November 9 we would all have to face up to the fact that America's next President was going to be a Roman Catholic.

Shock waves spread across the audience and I said quietly, "But it isn't going to be so bad, really." And I mentioned the numerous countries that have had Catholic chiefs of state with no disastrous circumstances: France, Belgium, Italy, Australia. I said, "Those of us who hate Catholicism most forget that both of our neighbors, Mexico to the south and Canada to the north, have often been governed by Catholics, and nothing very serious has happened. In fact," I challenged, "if I were to read off the names of Canada's six finest prime ministers, you wouldn't know which three were Catholic and which three were not, and neither would most Canadians." I assured them that ten years from tonight, looking back upon the fears that gripped them now, they would laugh at their apprehensions.

I said, "The people you see on this platform have been traveling together for some time, in very cramped quarters. We've had no great trouble. Did you know that Jeff Chandler is a Jew? I suppose the Kennedy girls are Catholics. Stan Musial bats left-handed so he could be almost anything. We don't ask. Whizzer White's some kind of Protestant, I think. And I'm a Quaker. That's about as far from Catholicism as you could get. Jack Kennedy believes in priests and music and incense; I believe in no priests at all, silence, and no incense. Furthermore, I'm an officer in a group studying population pressures and we advocate birth control. On this I suppose that Jack Kennedy and I are as far apart as we could be. But that doesn't keep me from supporting Kennedy for President, and Jeff Chandler's different beliefs don't keep him from working for a Catholic. Our nation has got to learn what we have learned on this trip."

I don't believe I have ever spoken in such silence. No one moved, and from the front row Chuck Roche nodded grimly. I said in conclusion, "If there are in this audience any who feel that they positively cannot vote for a Catholic, we understand your position and we listen with sympathy to your fears. If you believe that the election of Jack Kennedy to the Presidency dooms the United States to go the way of Spain or Colombia, then you ought surely to vote against us next week. For I have no hesitancy in saying that if America were threatened with the loss of religious freedom that has overtaken Spain I would resist to the point of death. But I am telling you as a Quaker who has no special love for Catholics that that is not going to happen in America. Under President Kennedy we shall be like Canada, and none of you will be aware that a Catholic is our President. So if you cannot vote for us now, we'll understand. Four years from now we'll come back and ask for your vote again. But don't believe the poison they've been distributing in this community. You're far too sensible for that."

I have rarely received an ovation, but I got one that night, and after the meeting hundreds of people, most of them determined to vote for Nixon, gathered around me and one minister said, "Michener, you have courage." I said, "It was Roche, whom you haven't met, who had the courage." The minister said, "Thank him for me." After the election I checked the vote in this city and Kennedy lost by two to one. Next time he may do better.

The feminine counterpart of Chuck Roche was a perplexing girl. Jane Wheeler was a southern beauty with driving energy and the most unruffled calm I had seen in a long time. She had organized the tour and had been in touch with leading politicians in each of the states we visited; if anything went wrong she took immediate responsibility for correcting it, and she could be a cooing slave driver. Her natural good looks were enhanced by a permanent smile, a chuckling manner of speech, and an alertness that was infectious.

What puzzled me about Jane was that she seemed like a Republican committee woman, and not a Democrat at all. I had been awakened to this problem by a recent research article in which the author pointed out that in the American political system it is Republican women, and not Democrats, who do the most productive campaigning, because they tend to come from homes where it is traditional for women to take an active part in community life, whereas Democratic women tend to come from social groups which expect their women to stay home. The author also claimed that Republican women tend to spend more on their appearance and are thus unembarrassed about appearing in public. And finally, Republican men have learned in business to trust women with important jobs, whereas men who tend to be Democrats have not enjoyed this experience and are inclined not to share responsibility.

At any rate, I had often reflected upon the advantage the Republicans enjoyed in this respect. In Hawaii, for example, there was simply no contest between the two parties insofar as utilizing women was concerned. The Republican women, trained in local society, did a magnificent job of getting out the vote and were one of the strongest political factors in the islands; the Democratic women had not yet mastered the tricks. It was like that across the nation.

But here was Jane Wheeler, a delightful girl who could adjust to any confusion and who was at home in any society, and she was a Democrat. I began to take hope, thinking: "We're getting our own type of clever girl, and pretty soon we'll match the Republicans in this field." But then I vaguely remembered having seen Jane at the Washington airport with her husband kissing her good-bye just before we took off, and I thought: "Mr. Wheeler looked exactly like a Republican."

We were flying over Idaho when this picture of Republican husband kissing Democratic wife good-bye flashed across my mind and I went aft to where Jane was cracking jokes with Stan Musial. "Are you a Republican?" I asked bluntly.

"Yes," Jane replied.

"How come you're on this trip?"

"I saw the light," she said. "This country needs Kennedy."

"When it's all over, will you be a Republican again?"

"I don't think so," she replied. "I wouldn't promise, but like the girl said, I saw the light."

I thought: "We could use a lot more like you. I wish I knew where they were coming from."

After we had been on the trip for some time it occurred to me that I had no idea as to why I had been invited. I asked about this and one of the people who accompanied us to check schedules explained, "We were in the office one day when this character blew in from Bucks County begging us for some materials. He talked very persuasively."

"Was his name Sam Thompson?" I asked.

"That was it! We gave him about ten dollars' worth of stickers and posters."

I thought: "You thought you gave him ten bucks' worth, but he waltzed off with four hundred dollars' worth." Aloud I asked, "But what does Sam Thompson have to do with my being on the trip?"

"Well, after he got the slip permitting him to pick up ten dollars' worth of material he asked to see Bobby Kennedy on a matter of vital importance."

"What was it?" I asked, for I was never able to predict what Sam might consider vital.

"Mr. Thompson told Mr. Kennedy that up in Bucks County he had an assistant who could speak better than Demosthenes. He said that if the party didn't utilize his friend the party damned well deserved to lose. So we checked into the matter, and some of what Mr. Thompson said turned out to be true. He made a good impression."

"You'd be surprised at some of the impressions Sam makes," I said.

On our trip we encountered two shocking situations which served to underline our conception of what we were trying to accomplish in this election. In Boise, Idaho, our plane blew a tire and we were necessarily thrown off schedule. Our local hosts, in a burst of ill-advised generosity, cried, "You can eat here on the ground while they fix the tire. We'll take you to the country club."

They led our motorcade to a lovely spot on the outskirts of town where, as the evil genius who supervises elections had arranged it, the Republican women's club of Boise was having a bridge luncheon. When I saw what we were heading into, I suggested, "Maybe it would be wiser if we ate somewhere else." But the local hosts overrode me and said, "You'll be entirely welcome."

We filed into the club to find that word of our Democratic affiliation had preceded us, for we were met by two rows of attractive women in Nixon hats, jeering at us. I took this to be a standard kind of American horseplay and fell into line by going up to an elderly lady waving a Republican flag and saying, "That Nixon hat looks real cute on you, ma'am." As I started to speak she withdrew as if I were contaminated and cried in a hoarse whisper, "Don't come near me, you Democrat!"

I interpreted this as further horseplay and said, "After the election you come to my club and we'll split a beer," but again she drew back among her friends and cried, "Look at them! Democrats in a decent club." I then realized to my astonishment that this kindly lady meant what she was saying, and that our group *was* contaminating hers.

We sat down in ugly silence while the women at the bridge tables stared at us. Our meal was served and I said to Stan Musial and Jeff Chandler, two men who are certainly not repugnant in appearance, "I don't believe this. Let's apologize to these women for having broken up their party."

From table to table we moved, and I shall never forget the look of honest hatred that greeted us at some of the groups. Three times women drew back from us and called out to their associates, "They're the ones who are going to take it away from us."

I was so appalled at this interpretation of American politics that I asked Chandler, "Did you hear what they said?"

"They said, 'They're the ones who are going to take it away from us.' "

We retreated from the tables and ate our meal in embarrassed silence. My back was to the door, so I didn't see the next incident when it began, but I heard a loud cry from the bridge players and looked over my shoulder to see a waitress coming into the room bearing across her chest the biggest Kennedy banner I had seen that day. She had on a Kennedy hat, a Kennedy button, and carried a Kennedy pennant.

"Oh, no, Edna!" the women cried. "You're not a Democrat, are you?"

She paraded in silence through the crowd, then came to me and said, "I apologize for the way you were treated."

I said, "If you get fired, let us know. We'll get you a job training Marines. They need characters with guts." She completed her parade and left the room. When it came time for us to leave, Jane Wheeler and I walked through the tables to quieten the fears of the bridge players, but again they drew back from us and muttered, "They're the ones who are going to take it away from us."

I cannot be mistaken in what was said, for it was said directly to me four distinct times, and when we got back on the plane we were a very subdued group. Among us were some people of wealth, and some of distinction in various fields, and many with conservative economic principles. It shocked us to think that we were being held up as the contaminators of America, the subversives, the revolutionaries, the idiot fringe. I think that for our party as a whole, the experience in the Boise, Idaho, country club, where we met an unusually attractive group of women who would not speak with us, was the most lasting. It convinced us that John Kennedy simply had to win this election, and it made me, at least, a confirmed liberal until the day I die. I would be appalled at my own degeneration if I should ever come to look upon the representatives of a major American political party as we were looked upon that day. With such attitudes there can be no traffic.

Our second psychological jolt came in the city of Bloomington, Indiana, where for the first time during this campaign I had a chance to see how conservative, if not reactionary, many college students are becoming. By ill chance our motorcade was driven slowly along fraternity row at the University of Indiana, and in the some two or three dozen fraternity and sorority houses—those standard Georgian repositories of respectability and family status—we found not one decorated on behalf of Kennedy and Johnson. All were blatantly for Nixon and Lodge, except for several that were for Barry Goldwater.

This was in good fun, and was accepted as such, for fraternity men tend to come from upper-middle-class families where it is almost obligatory to be Republican if one wants to participate in social life, but we were not prepared for the catcalls and ill-tempered jeers that accompanied our progress through fraternity row. Then, when we reached the center of town where the meeting was to be held, we found that more than half the crowd consisted of these same fraternity and sorority people armed with banners and bugles and a determination to break up the rally.

Several events stand out rather clearly in my mind when I recall that exciting afternoon. The Republican newspaper reporting the event went to classic lengths in partisanship. It said, in effect, that some strangers—no names given—had come in to Bloomington to conduct a Democratic meeting, but that they were ably heckled by "Martin Flynn of Lafayette, former student body president; Tom Huston of Logansport, a member of Governor Harold W. Handley's youth council; Robert Gray of Indianapolis, a varsity debater, and Steve Moberly of Logansport, a student government leader."

The able hecklers, and I grant them that distinction, almost succeeded in breaking up our meeting, but the second memory of the day came when Jeff Chandler got sore and very unwisely invited the whole football team to come up on the stand one at a time or in groups and take us on. At this point I started looking for an escape route, but after an initial movement toward the stand, the hecklers subsided.

By the time I was called upon to try to say something I had my courage back and was angry. Under pressure I delivered my only good line in the campaign: "You seem surprised that one small group like this would include two authors. Everybody who can write is for Kennedy and ninety percent of those who can read." This crack almost launched its own riot, but in the end we got out of town without real trouble.

I was both surprised and distressed during subsequent discussions to discover that on many campuses the abler students are turning quite reactionary and that Barry Goldwater and the *National Review* have substantial followings. There are many reasons for this: the temper of the times; the allure of the Eisenhower administration; the natural dissatisfaction of students with their teachers; the fun of being different; the outspokenness of Senator Goldwater; and the subtle fact that there is no longer any cachet in being a liberal, whereas there is great campus distinction in being an arch conservative. It seems to me that the Democrats ought to address themselves most studiously to this matter, for if they lose the allegiance of collegiate intellectuals they have lost one of the great props that have made and kept them strong. I do not believe that the peculiar coalition of talents which the Democratic party must be can prosper or even exist without a constant replenishment of men like Senators Proxmire, Fulbright, Clark, Douglas and Kennedy, and we had better see to it that their successors are enlisted quickly.

I am quite prepared to write off the well-bred, frightened, bridge-playing women of Boise, Idaho, but I am not willing to surrender to either Nixon or Goldwater the potential young leaders at schools like the University of Indiana.

As for the tour itself and the eight exciting states we visited, it was for me a privilege to meet the local political leaders and to exchange ideas with the various senators, governors and congressmen who sought our help. I was also repeatedly aroused by sights of a part of the world in which I had grown to intellectual maturity: the towering ramparts of the Rockies; the bleak yet alluring flatlands of Wyoming; the rolling hills of Idaho; the vast lake of Utah and the lively mountains surrounding its cities; and the historic evocations of central Illinois, southern Indiana, and Kentucky. It was very good to see these places during a time when our nation was choosing its new administration, and it was sobering to think that every one of these cherished locales was strongly Republican. I wondered if there was indeed an irreparable cleavage between the rural grandeur of our nation and our crowded cities; but no matter how strong the suspicion came that we were a nation somewhat divided, I knew that I was totally committed to the liberalism of the cities rather than to the conservatism of the rural areas I had once known so intimately and loved so well. It was a pity that lands as lovely as Colorado, Wyoming and Utah had to be defeated in 1960, but I was satisfied that it was for the good of the country.

I think all of us on the tour appreciated these matters better because of what we came to call "the day of anguish." We were about to depart from Denver for our longest flight, to Bloomington, Indiana, when just before we climbed into the plane we heard the early-morning radio announcement that Nikita Khrushchev had been arrested, deposed, thrown into jail and replaced by Gyorgy Malenkov. We delayed departure of the plane while Chuck Roche frantically called the Denver papers, and they confirmed the story: "Austrian sources released the details, which had been leaked to them by the Russian embassy."

We climbed aboard the plane as gloomy a crew of people as I was to see during the campaign. For six or seven hours we were out of radio communication and were forced to stew in our own mental juices, which were acid indeed and which ate right to the heart. Chuck convened Schlesinger, White and me and asked what we thought. I led off by saying, "Murphy's Law has swung into operation. I feel sick. I can hear Eisenhower tonight telling the American people, 'See! What Nixon has said all along is true. The pressure we have applied through Ambassador Lodge has worked, and Khrushchev is finished. Our international reputation was never higher, and you can see that Russia's was never lower.' "

"Do you think this could lose the election for us?" Roche asked.

"Yes," I said. "But there is still a chance that we can fight back. How can we give this affair an interpretation that will aid our side?"

Schlesinger suggested that Malenkov was known to be more anti-American than Khrushchev, so that we could honestly claim that instead of proving that the Eisenhower administration had contained Russia and forced Khrushchev to resign, as I believed the Republicans would argue, the fact was that Eisenhower had so messed things up that our relative friend Khrushchev was out and our actual enemy Malenkov was in. I thought this was going to be difficult to sell, but I kept my mouth shut.

Whizzer White thoughtfully pointed out that we had to have our story straight by the time we landed, for reporters would surely be at the airport to heckle us on the dramatic developments. "We've got to tell one story," he insisted, "and it's got to be logical. And the hell of it is that we can't consult anybody before we speak. Now what shall we say?"

It was Chuck Roche who determined our tactical behavior. He said, "When we get off the plane, we play it completely dumb. We don't know what they're talking about and will make no comment until I call Associated Press for an official verification."

Then we repaired to our separate seats to brood about the dismal events of the day. Schlesinger and I discussed Russia for a while, and I felt increasingly sick at my stomach. The thing I feared had happened. The Korea that had won for the Republicans in 1952 and the Suez that had won again in 1956 were about to be reënacted, and a party whose fumbling, bumbling policies had brought us to the edge of catastrophe was once more to be rewarded for its failure with a victory at the polls.

I felt so miserable that I had to be alone and went into the lavatory, where I sat for upwards of an hour with my head in my hands. I wouldn't say that any tears actually came to my eyes, but I was desolate. The prize for which we had worked so hard, the near-victory that we had ripped from the caverns of religious prejudice, the administration of hard-working idealists that might have operated in the next years, rekindling flames of imagination in our nation, all these things were about to be lost because of an irrelevant fluke. I swore and beat my fists together and sat with my misery in the little cubicle, until Stan Musial or one of the gang shouted, "Somebody dead in there?" I wanted to reply that I was, but I got up and rejoined my gloomy crowd. This was the low-water mark of the campaign, and I would not like to live it over again. When I looked at the tense faces of my companions I had to acknowledge to myself how desperately I wanted to win, how disconsolate I would be in defeat.

We landed on schedule in Bloomington, and sure enough two reporters lunged right for me shouting, "You've been in

Asia a good deal, Mr. Michener. How will they take the news about Khrushchev's defeat?" I stalled as we had agreed and the reporters rushed over to Byron White to ask him how the startling news from Russia would affect the election. He also stalled, and over his shoulder I could see Chuck Roche calling Associated Press and talking earnestly. In a moment he hung up the receiver and with no change of expression walked behind me as a radio crew zeroed in to ask me about the election.

In a low, guttural whisper that no one else could hear Chuck said, "Story's a fake."

What an admirable interview I gave that day at the airport in Bloomington! I was expansive. I exuded confidence and I wanted to hug the radio man. There was warmth in my voice as I explained everything, ending with a flourish, "Of course Mr. Kennedy's going to be elected. The whole nation knows that." The day of anguish was over and I knew that victory was ours.

9

What Happened

On November 8, 1960, in Bucks County 125,052 voters went to the polls and supported Mr. Nixon by a score of 67,501 to 57,177, giving him 54 percent of the vote and a majority of more than 10,000. Five resolute citizens wrote in their votes for Adlai Stevenson and one, getting ready for 1964, backed Barry Goldwater. By a clear-cut majority we lost the battle for Bucks County. I also failed to win my own precinct for Kennedy, losing it by 178 to 115. Likewise I lost my township, the vote there being 514 for Nixon and only 289 for Kennedy. And of course my home town of Doylestown voted Republican by its customary 71 percent.

Of the eight states in which I campaigned with the barnstormers and the four where I spoke alone, every district in which I appeared went Republican. Nebraska, Utah, Idaho, Colorado, Indiana and Kentucky all voted for Nixon. In fact, I can think of no area where I worked in which my efforts modified any important segment of the vote and there exists good reason for calling me the Typhoid Mary of the 1960 campaign. Where I went disaster struck.

And yet, when one looks at the facts in Bucks County, one discovers that something extraordinary happened in this crucial county. To understand what it was that took place, let us consider the norm established by five major Pennsylvania counties which, like Bucks, had large German religious groups which were vigorously anti-Catholic as an inherited ecclesiastical principle. In 1956, during the Eisenhower landslide, Adams, Berks, Lancaster, Lebanon and York counties voted Republican by the biggest majority recorded in recent decades, 84,849. In 1960, when across the nation the Republicans fared more poorly by 10,000,000 votes than in 1956, these five German counties raised their Republican margin to 88,440.

But in equally German Bucks County the results were different. In the Eisenhower sweep of 1956 our county had given the Republicans a majority of 59,721 to 38,442, or more than 21,000 votes. In 1960, reversing the trend established by the five German counties, we cut the Republican majority in half, to 10,000. This meant that the majorities built up by Senator Kennedy in Philadelphia and Pittsburgh were not diminished by the number of Republican votes that were expected from Bucks and other similar counties. And on his big-city majorities Kennedy was thus able to win the state.

If one isolates the votes of suburbia, he finds that the area gave Kennedy an unexpected majority of 9,000 votes. The central and northern rural areas gave Nixon a majority of 19,000. If one further isolates the votes of Levittown, it is seen that this new area shifted sharply from its slight Republican advantage of 1956 to a 58-42 division in favor of Kennedy. Considering the county as a whole, Nixon ran about 2,000 votes behind the rest of his county ticket, Kennedy ahead of his by 3,000. This was due to the popularity of the local Republican incumbents.

As for the religious question, careful study of available records leads me to conclude that in the 1960 election the religious factor produced these obvious though sometimes contradictory results:

1. In central and northern Bucks County, Kennedy's Catholicism cost him not less than 4,500 votes, represented by Democrats who switched to Nixon and by Republicans who might otherwise have been won over to the Kennedy banner. This resulted in a swing of 9,000 votes.

2. In suburbia there were two distinct and measurable effects. In the town of Bristol, which has Catholic concentrations, Kennedy's Catholicism enabled him to pick up some votes he might not otherwise have been expected to win. But

in the expensive sections of Levittown he undoubtedly lost, for the same reason, approximately the same number of votes he gained in Bristol. Thus in the southern end of the county the religious issue neither hindered nor helped.

3. If these figures are correct, then had there been no religious issue involved, Nixon would have carried Bucks County by about 1,000 votes instead of the 10,000 by which he did carry it. Thus Kennedy's Catholicism cost him a 9,000-vote differential in Bucks County.

4. However, it seems highly probable that the vicious attacks made upon the Catholic religion in areas like Bucks County directly influenced the large concentrations of Catholics in Philadelphia, where wholly unprecedented Democratic majorities were rolled up. Before November 8 the most realistic hope was for a Kennedy majority of 250,000 in Philadelphia. The actual majority was 331,000. Of this about 95,000 can be attributed to unexpectedly vigorous Catholic voting. Identical factors operated in Pittsburgh, where the Kennedy majority was 110,000.

5. This means that the Republican strategists who wrote to me for help in quarantining the religious issue were correct in their assumption that the issue must ultimately hurt their side. The unwelcomed bigots made it possible for the Republicans to pick up increments like the 9,000 votes in Bucks County, but at the same time helped the Democrats acquire massive windfalls like the 95,000 unexpected votes in Philadelphia.

6. Nevertheless, if John Kennedy had not been a Catholic he would probably have won Pennsylvania by a substantially bigger margin than he actually did. On balance, the religious issue hurt the Democrats grievously.

7. Across the nation the same relationships prevailed. If Kennedy had not been a Catholic it seems likely that he would have gained not less than 53.5 percent of the total vote and somewhere in the neighborhood of 400 electoral votes. That he won at all in the face of the religious odds that faced him indicated a political triumph of enormous proportions.

8. It was ironic that some of the largest concentrations of Catholics happened to be in the largest cities of the states having the largest electoral votes. That this demographic accident enabled the Democrats to win seems obvious, but it must not obscure the deeper truth that if the religious issue

had not beclouded the election in the first place, the Democrats would have won by a much wider margin.

Some facts to support the above contentions might be in order. Haycock Township in the northern end of the county is a rural area containing the county's largest hill, called hopefully Haycock Mountain, and also the most typically Dutch of our small communities, Applebachsville. For some curious reason it has always been a Democratic enclave in the midst of Republican strength and this year had the usual secure registration of 370 Democrats to 262 Republicans. Here Mrs. Eva Horne Derr has long reigned as state committeewoman and cannot recall when she last lost an election. This year the vote was 312 for Nixon to 213 for Kennedy.

After the election I talked with Mrs. Derr about this disappointing showing and with much embarrassment she confessed, "I never thought I'd see the day when I would have to do what I did this time."

"You try to vote dead people?" I asked.

"Worse," she said. "I gave lessons to good Democratic friends on how to split their tickets and vote for all the Democrats except Kennedy."

"You did that?"

"I had to," the committeewoman claimed. "My best friends told me, 'Eva, I'm willing to vote the rest of your ticket, but I won't vote for a Catholic.' So I had to teach them how to vote against my own candidate."

"Was it that bad?" I asked.

"Worse," she insisted. "Because those damned Republicans found out what I was doing and they warned all my people, 'It's very difficult to split a ticket. You vote for even one Democrat and the judges are likely to give Kennedy a vote, too, and you wouldn't want that. So play it safe and just pull a straight Republican lever. Then nobody can mix you up.'"

"Did their argument work?" I asked.

"Not entirely," Mrs. Derr said brightly. "Kennedy trailed the rest of the Democratic ticket by 35 votes. So my instructions accomplished some good." I said it was strange that a committeewoman would find joy in the fact that she had taught her people to cut their own Presidential candidate, but she said, "This was a strange election. We were lucky to salvage any votes."

There are three other districts in northern Bucks County that normally go Democratic, even though they are surrounded by strong Republican areas. This year the combined vote was Nixon 1,358, Kennedy 744.

Now it might be argued that these four specific districts had voted for Mr. Nixon because of economic, social or personality reasons, but interviews in the area fail to support this theory. Ministers preached from their pulpits that a vote for Kennedy was a vote against the basic religion of the area, and parishioners either stayed home or voted Republican.

The figures from normal Republican areas also support the reasoning given above. The prettiest old settlement in northern Bucks County, in my opinion, is Bedminster, where sturdy red-brick homes and carefully tended lawns outline an almost perfect little community, whose German attributes are conspicuous in the cleanliness and orderliness of the village. Bedminster is a gem, and the farms around it are among the best in our county. Several Mennonite churches dot the nearby countryside, and if I wanted to show a stranger my county at its best, I think I would take him to Bedminster.

As the following table shows, Bedminster's registration has always been strongly Republican, but in 1960 Republican registrations increased and in the final election the party took votes away from the Democrats.

THE VOTE IN BEDMINSTER EAST

Year	*Event*	*Rep.*	*Dem.*
1959	Registrations for County election	409	210
1960	Registrations for Presidential election	472	217
1960	Actual vote in Presidential election	465	173

In a non-Catholic part of Bristol one of the hardest-working Democratic workers, Jack Ward, personally saw to it that 938 Democrats registered to 361 Republicans. On Election Day, Jack personally supervised the voting of almost all registered Democrats. Naturally, he felt assured that he had rolled up a strong lead for Kennedy in his district and so reported to me. But when the votes were counted, the official tally showed that only 682 people had voted for Kennedy, whereas 436 had voted for Nixon. Says Ward, "At first it infuriated me to think that I had been driving good Democrats to the polls, and all the time they knew they were going to vote for the other man. But now I'm philosophical about it. I joke with them and I suspect that if we put up good local candidates next time, they'll vote with me because they know they cut my throat in the Presidential. And of this I'm sure. If Kennedy does a good job in the White House, come 1964 they'll be willing to vote for a Catholic, because I know that in their hearts they're Democrats."

Dozens of individual districts could be cited to demonstrate the effect of the religious issue. In Bucks County it is a little easier to trace cause and effect because many voters were willing to state their determination not to vote for a Catholic. And in the later stages of the campaign some Catholics who might otherwise have voted Republican, publicly announced that they were going to switch to Kennedy because of the religious tracts that had outraged them. In my group-discussions prior to the election, I was constantly surprised at the freedom with which people in Bucks County expressed what otherwise would have been private religious conviction, and I was also surprised at the freedom from rancor in which such discussions were held.

Finally, I would like to state for the record, because I have heard what I am about to say controverted many times, that of the four Catholics I knew best, and two of them I knew intimately, all voted for Nixon in spite of my earnest entreaties that they vote otherwise. They did so for social and economic reasons and I believe they represented many other Catholics in this area. Certainly, in my public meetings well over two dozen avowed Catholics claimed they were going to vote for Nixon and gave good reasons why, but none of these were my personal friends so I cannot judge whether they did so vote or not. My strong reformation friends in the northern end of the county claimed that all such public disclaimers had been ordered by the Pope to confuse honest men, and perhaps I was so confused.

The vote in suburbia was reassuring. Levittown, instead of repeating the 51 percent advantage it had given President Eisenhower in 1956, gave Kennedy 58 percent of the votes, a swing of 9 percent.

At Red Rose Gate, for example, where the posh houses are called Country Clubbers ($18,000) and where from outward appearances everybody ought to be a Republican, the vote was only 374 for Nixon and 324 for Kennedy. "A lot of Jews and Catholics live there," a Republican said, explaining the closeness.

At the other end of the social spectrum, in Holly Hill, where the houses are Ranchers ($9,000), the vote even in 1956 had been Stevenson 337, Eisenhower 291. This year, with a somewhat larger registration, the vote was Kennedy 473, Nixon 259.

In Vermilion Hills, where the houses tend to be Jubilees ($11,700) and where the inhabitants seem to be a good cross section of the type of energetic younger people who move into Levittowns and who keep them attractive by tending their lawns and improving their properties wherever possible, the vote in 1956 was as one might expect, a typical suburbia vote: Eisenhower 667, Stevenson 445. This year, however, as a result of intensive campaigning and political discussion, the vote turned out to be Kennedy 852, Nixon 621. Here the Republican vote stayed about the same, but the Democratic vote nearly doubled.

Combining the returns from five high-cost Levittown districts, one finds that in 1956 their vote gave Eisenhower 58 percent; whereas in 1960 the same areas with almost the same people voting gave Kennedy 58 percent. It was this unexpected swing of 16 percent in suburbia that enabled Bucks County to cut the normal Republican advantage in half.

TOTAL LEVITTOWN VOTE

	Candidate		*Vote*	*Percent*
1956	Presidential			
	Stevenson	D	9,689	49
	Eisenhower	R	9,954	51
1956	Senatorial			
	Clark	D	11,840	60
	Duff	R	7,732	40
1960	Presidential			
	Kennedy	D	15,513	58
	Nixon	R	11,364	42
1960	Congressional			
	Hock	D	14,727	54
	Curtin	R	12,748	46

It would thus seem that suburbia, after an exhilarating flirtation with the social respectability of Republicanism, found the experience a bit cloying and remembered the Democratic party of its parents. One of the explanations I heard repeated many times was, "When we moved out here my wife expected the gracious country living of the magazine advertisements, and we thought that the key to this was joining the Republican party. But when we did join all they wanted was our votes. The gracious country living escaped us and we realized with some embarrassment that we had been played for jerks. Or had played ourselves as jerks."

One of the greatest surprises of the 1955-1960 period in the bigger suburbias was the discovery that a community might have enough vital Democrats with reasonably good table manners so that one could vote for Jack Kennedy, retain interesting friends, and still feel as if one were part of a socially acceptable world. Not a little of the credit for this transformation of thinking habits must be accorded to the amazing Kennedy girls, who toured suburbias wearing chic outfits, well-manicured nails and flashing white smiles. I had the humbling experience of addressing several very swanky morning affairs in the various suburbias where hundreds of obviously well-placed women listened in bored tolerance while I gave them the pitch, then filed in excited wonder past one of the Kennedy girls. As one of my captive audience said to me as she came away from meeting Mrs. Peter Lawford, "That girl has real class. It's a privilege to be in the same room with her." Somehow the class of the Kennedy girls rubbed off onto the Democratic party and in suburbia it once more became fashionable to be a Democrat.

Whether the Democrats can hold the prodigals is a major problem for the party. One of the reasons why suburbia was willing to consider the Democratic party this time was Kennedy's youthful vigor. In their own business, professional and intellectual lives, the young suburban families have begun to recognize that a certain amount of raw vigor is necessary if one is to survive. They discovered that the outward appearances of respectability are no substitute for inner vitality. If during its incumbency the Democratic party exhibits no vigor, it will lose these suburban voters. Year by year the average age of voting suburbia is going to increase until a natural conservatism begins to set in. If in the next four years the Democrats do not build strong allegiances, they may lose this powerful voting block forever. It is certainly available to the Republicans and they are going to work hard to win the suburbs back.

In 1956 the four great suburban counties that rim Philadelphia—Chester, Delaware, Montgomery, Bucks—gave President Eisenhower a total of 384,020 votes to Stevenson's 199,617, a massive majority of 184,403. In 1960 those same four counties gave Mr. Nixon only 399,028 votes to Kennedy's 304,192, a majority of only 94,836. The difference is accounted for by the changing patterns of suburbia, and I believe that it has been this shift which has helped the eastern big-city states to swing Democratic. It was not the cities alone that won for Kennedy.

From our vantage point in one of the typical counties we had an opportunity to assess the work of various politicians and various stratagems. For example, we found that clergymen preaching politics from the pulpit were very effective insofar as their own flocks were concerned, but that they aroused bitter antagonisms among those who were not directly committed to them. Thus religion had a terribly divisive power when abused and the end result of any one action could not easily be anticipated. As I said earlier, in Bucks County it cost us about 9,000 votes, but no permanent social damage seems to have been done.

The effect of doctors' being prevailed upon by their medical association to campaign among their patients for one party as opposed to the other was a different matter. A good many of my workers spoke with contempt of this procedure, and there was one sardonic cartoon circulated to good effect. It showed a group of white-masked doctors about to operate on a skinny nude man, and the caption read, "You still determined to vote for Kennedy?" I would suppose that whatever effectiveness the doctors had was in confirming the convictions of people already disposed to vote against what the doctors labeled socialized medicine, just as years before they had so labeled Blue Cross, Blue Shield and social security. Actually, I suspect that few doctors bothered with proselytizing. I would imagine, furthermore, that the effectiveness of the medical anti-Democrat lobby will be somewhat diminished in the next four years, a loss which I can view with perfect equanimity.

The most perplexing problem as to effectiveness on the Democratic side concerned Adlai Stevenson. I have told how I personally encouraged about one hundred dissidents with whom I accomplished nothing into going into Philadelphia to hear the former standard-bearer advise his adherents to support Kennedy whole-heartedly. Other county chairmen, faced by the same problem, must have done the same, for we turned out one of the most excited crowds to hit Philadelphia for a long time. I sat near Mr. Stevenson and was deeply moved by the passionate loyalty he still evoked among his followers, and I could see my wife at one of the front tables rededicating herself to his cause.

But when he spoke I listened in vain for that strong, clear command to unity. His speech was witty, a tribute to a great mind, and thoroughly enjoyable, but I doubt if it convinced one of my wavering hundred. There come times, I think, in any campaign or in any life when one ought to speak out clearly and unequivocally. I am often reminded of long trips that I have taken across country where in the vast empty spaces of our land the radio signals from the big cities fade into a kind of static-filled jargon. One remembers that these are the good stations with the respectable news commentaries and the fine music, but the signal is so weak that one turns with gratitude to the nearest hillbilly station that is emitting a static-free signal. At least one can hear the music, second-rate though it is.

What I have just said is a terrible confession, and as it stands it is probably a self-indictment. But it is how the human mind reacts, and for better or worse, there it is.

The loss of Ohio stunned me. I still cannot understand how it was accomplished. The only reasonable explanation I have heard was that in a fiercely competitive election any party that goes in with disorganized forces stands a good chance of losing, no matter what happens elsewhere in the country. Mike DeSalle and Frank Lausche did not unite, and Ohio was lost. In New York, on the other hand, in the midst of a bitter factional fight between Carmine DeSapio and Herbert Lehman, union to fight the national election was manipulated and victory was the result. But in California, as in Ohio, the Democratic forces did not coalesce and a totally unwarranted loss had to be endured.

The big surprise to many of us in a county like Bucks, but not to me for reasons I have already cited, was the contribution of Lyndon Johnson to the Democratic victory.

When the results were in, a good many of my northern liberal friends were surprised by Johnson's performance in helping to hold so much of the South and particularly Texas, but they were also disturbed over the fact that Johnson probably emerged from the campaign as the single most powerful political force in the party. In mid-September few could have foreseen this outcome. His strength, I think, derived from his being first of all a fine politician. I think we tend to forget how important it is in a democracy to have strong, clever, and able politicians; for the holding together of any federal union or any state with sharply divergent components requires marked skill, and those who have it deserve well of their nation.

I rather think that of all I have written in the last five years, one of the very best things was a series I did for a Honolulu newspaper following the divisive first state election in 1959. It was a series praising politicians and drawing to the attention of the people of Hawaii the remarkable contributions made by a group of men and women not normally hailed as cultural heroes. I selected a millionaire who took time off to whip his Republican party into an effective machine that defeated my side at the polls; a Japanese housewife who took a job so that her husband could carry on an effective campaign for the legislature; a brilliant young governor who started out like the most venal of all spoils politicians, but who got his party organized on a solid base of legitimate patronage; and a young mother who set up an unbeatable headquarters which elected her father to the Senate against what seemed at first insuperable odds.

There are people who merit praise in a democracy, and I am very happy that in Lyndon Johnson I early recognized such an operator. If a complex body like a senate of a hundred prima donnas requires organizing, I want a man who can do it effectively and creatively. Such a man is more valuable to his nation than a scientist, a successful novelist, or a business leader. I have always had the feeling that had I been in the last Senate I might have joined with Senator Proxmire of Wisconsin in fighting Lyndon Johnson as a party leader who was a little too arrogant and dictatorial for my taste. But I am certainly glad he was able to control those attributes and to contribute them to the victory of my party. And I suppose that the Senate, with someone else at the head of the majority party, will be a less efficient instrument than it was when Lyndon Johnson controlled it.

In Bucks County we were still of the opinion that the Republicans should have won the national election. To us it seemed as if they had every initial advantage. The country was at peace; there was reasonable prosperity; there was no great unemployment; their party already held the Presidency; there was a general aura of satisfaction with the manner in which Mr. Eisenhower had operated; an overwhelming percentage of the press favored the Republicans; in a long campaign they could afford more radio and television time; the unanticipated twists and turns of foreign affairs seemed likely to aid them and damage the Democrats; Senator Kennedy was relatively unknown; and he was a Catholic.

For Mr. Nixon, starting with these advantages, to lose would require, we felt, gross mismanagement. To our surprise that mismanagement was forthcoming and what should have been a Republican victory was transformed into defeat. I am not diminishing the extraordinary work of Senator Kennedy and his entire team when I say that good as they were they could not have won had the Republicans mounted a first-rate campaign. It is obvious that under even the most adverse conditions Senator Kennedy would have made a gallant effort, but if the Republicans had been on their toes, his effort would have remained no more than a commendable try. I do not believe that Senator Kennedy won; I believe that Vice President Nixon lost. From what we saw in Bucks County, these were the contributing factors to the Republican defeat.

The enormous prestige of President Eisenhower's position and personality was not utilized constructively. Frequently throughout this report I have indicated points at which we were afraid the President would throw his great weight against some position taken by Senator Kennedy, and I have told how each time we breathed easily when the crisis passed without any Presidential interference. It was also apparent to us that President Eisenhower could certainly have held Pennsylvania and probably New Jersey in the Republican column if only he had campaigned diligently in those states. Finally, if he had gone on television four or five times during the campaign to deny categorically one Kennedy position after another, he would surely have swayed many of the voters with whom I was arguing. In fact, if he had only stated early and unequivocally that he wanted Mr. Nixon to win, he could well have achieved that effect.

In the post-election period numerous news stories have been circulated to the effect that President Eisenhower was deeply distressed at the Democratic victory, and he has belatedly said that he had wanted Mr. Nixon to win in 1960 and that he hoped the Vice President would run again in 1964. I can only say as a common workman in the political vineyard and as a man who followed every twist and turn of the campaign, that during the campaign Mr. Eisenhower failed to convey that impression to the general public. I believe that my strongest argument with Republicans was my constantly repeated statement, "Of course we all know that Mr. Eisenhower is not really happy with Mr. Nixon as the Republican standard-bearer." A single word from the President could have killed that claim. As things stood, however, every time I made the comment, Republicans all over the audience ruefully agreed. When, late in the campaign, Mr. Eisenhower did make strong statements in favor of his candidate, Democrats and Republicans alike interpreted his remarks as those of a man who had been grudgingly maneuvered into the inevitable. It is a curious fact that the man who could have swung the election in October actually damaged his candidate when he spoke out for him too late in November. It seemed to all of us who followed these matters closely that Mr. Nixon was badly treated by his President; but we also felt that Mr. Nixon behaved impeccably in this trying situation. If I and my friends misread the relationship between Eisenhower and Nixon it was not through malice; it was because Mr. Eisenhower permitted this ambiguity to develop and to exist. Republicans remarked upon it more than did we Democrats.

It was symbolic, therefore, that the single event which came closest to being the one vital accident of the campaign concerned Mr. Eisenhower. When the Negro minister Martin Luther King was throw into a Georgia jail in the afternoon of October 25, on a grossly trumped-up charge, it was obvious to me that a critical moment had been reached in the election. At first glance this was a situation that must work to the Democrats' disadvantage, for if Senator Kennedy did nothing he would lose Negro support in the vital northern cities, and if he did something he would alienate the South, where he had to pick up electoral votes. On the other hand, the Republicans would surely gain if they made some strong statement pointing out that this was the sort of racial discrimination against which they had fought for eight years. It looked to me as if Murphy's Law had finally swung into operation, and the inevitable evil had overtaken my party.

What happened is history. Intelligent Republican strategists, seeing a chance to torpedo the Democratic position, drafted an impeccable statement for President Eisenhower to deliver on television. It read: "It seems to me fundamentally unjust that a man who has peacefully attempted to establish his right to equal treatment, free from racial discrimination, should be imprisoned on an unrelated charge, in itself insignificant. Accordingly, I have asked the Attorney General to take all proper steps to join with Dr. Martin Luther King in an appropriate application for his release." For some reason that is not yet known, this striking statement which could have won the Negroes of the North to Nixon was never issued. The fundamental vacillation that characterized the party's use of their President continued, and the great strong voice that should have spoken out and won the election, remained silent.

On the other hand, John Kennedy took the risk and did the gallant thing. He decried the blatant abuse of a Negro's civil liberties and had the courage to phone Reverend King and say so. In doing this he did not lose Georgia or South Carolina or Texas. Instead he won the Negro vote in New York and Chicago and Philadelphia, and thus the Presidency.

The case of Nelson Rockefeller and his relationship to the Nixon campaign is difficult indeed to analyze. That Mr. Rockefeller could have won the election for himself relatively easily is a truism. My guess is that he would have won not less than 53 percent of the popular vote and probably around 390 electoral votes. He and his advisers knew this and they probably suspected that Mr. Nixon could not win. The fight that Mr. Rockefeller had waged for the nomination had been an honorable one up until December of 1959, when he ostensibly withdrew from the competition as it became obvious that the professional Republican politicians would not tolerate an open convention struggle between him and Nixon. I was less impressed with his backing and filling through the spring of 1960, for I felt that he should have enlisted wholeheartedly in support of the man to whom he had surrendered. And his last-minute attempts to influence the party platform, while philosophically proper, were politically maladroit.

It was apparent that a victory for Nixon in 1960 would imply a reëlection in 1964, so that the earliest date at which Governor Rockefeller could hope for the Republican nomination and the Presidency would be in 1968, when either his star might have faded or his age have become a deterrent. It was tempting therefore to adopt the Machiavellian theory that Mr. Rockefeller was conspiring to engineer a Nixon defeat in 1960 in order to make himself the logical nominee in 1964. And if a Democratic speaker believed that this was Rockefeller's gambit, discussion of it certainly sowed dissension in Republican ranks.

I never believed that Rockefeller did undercut the Nixon candidacy, and I avoided the issue. I contented myself with the often reiterated statement, "You know that Governor Rockefeller was not happy with Mr. Nixon as the Republican candidate, and that most of what Mr. Nixon says is in direct conflict with the reports of the Rockefeller brothers." Many of my hearers volunteered the information that the governor was not electioneering whole-heartedly for the Vice President and that was the major reason why Nixon would lose New York. When the campaign was over it was found that Governor Rockefeller had campaigned in 50 of New York's 62 counties and had spoken the astonishing number of 237 times. This surely constitutes "supporting the ticket," but the psychological damage had been done and could not be repaired.

It seemed strange to me both during the campaign and after that the pre-convention attacks on Kennedy by Johnson, Truman and Mrs. Roosevelt really counted for very little once the campaign got under way. They were discounted as the typical Democratic brawling that Americans expect of this vital party, and each of these initial opponents later did yeoman service during the campaign. Mrs. Roosevelt was especially hard-working in our area, and her forthright admission that she had initially preferred another candidate but now supported the convention winner gained many votes for Kennedy. But on the Republican side the philosophical antagonism expressed by Governor Rockefeller before the convention was apparently neither forgotten nor forgiven. He hurt the Republicans enormously and no amount of later hard work could erase that initial impression. Frequently I thought, "That's one of the advantages of being a rough-and-ready Democrat. A man like Truman can blast hell out of Jack Kennedy, then turn around and support him vigorously, and the public brushes it off with, 'That's those crazy Democrats.' But when a proper Republican, in a nice black suit, castigates Richard Nixon, everyone takes it seriously."

As of now, I suspect that Governor Rockefeller may be the Republican candidate in 1964, but then it will be too late. He could have won relatively easily in 1960, but by 1964 President Kennedy and his team will have compiled such a powerful record and consolidated the Democratic position so securely that I doubt any Republican will be able to win. Furthermore, the closeness of the 1960 vote constitutes no precedent for 1964, because by then many who were afraid to elect a Catholic President will have seen how foolish their fears were. They will vote next time where they wanted to this: for Kennedy.

There is a sense of sadness, I think, in reflecting that Harold Stassen was entirely correct in 1956 when he warned the Republican party that Richard Nixon would ultimately prove to be a liability. The 1960 election demonstrated the correctness of Stassen's position, and again the closeness of the vote must not obscure the fact that actually the Republicans should have won rather easily. Of all who tried to predict the outcome of the 1960 election, Harold Stassen proved to be the most accurate. Nixon's candidacy cost the Republicans almost exactly the margin of votes that Stassen had forewarned. And he offered his prediction four years before the event. I suspect that I will endear myself to few Republicans when I praise Stassen's political acumen, but I think it is due him.

But the most perplexing enigma of the Republican defeat was neither President Eisenhower nor Governor Rockefeller. The real mystery centered on the candidate himself, Richard Nixon. At least a hundred times during the campaign I admitted, during question periods, "Mr. Nixon is obviously a much better man than he is allowing himself to appear in this campaign." Up until his sickening homily on swearing, I willingly told my audiences that I was quite satisfied that

Nixon, if elected, would turn out to be one of our better Presidents, and I still believe he had the capacity to become such. But in the campaign he insisted upon parading all the less attractive aspects of his personality and his interpretation of the Presidency. Instead of being strong he tried to be reassuring. Instead of showing an incisive mind he paraded his determination to side-step all major questions. Instead of uncovering the dedicated public servant, he appeared before us a man desperately groping for a prize. In him there was no evidence of fire, no touch of burning inner conviction and no sense of the historical destiny of the moment. He issued no ringing cry to which his followers could vigorously rally, and his campaign was very dull.

Richard Nixon is a much better man than he appeared in the autumn of 1960. How he was trapped into parading before us the shadowy image that he projected onto the TV screens I do not know. His enemies insist, "What you saw was the real Richard Nixon, the man of sawdust." This I cannot believe. I suppose he was tricked by his advertising advisers into believing that what the American people wanted was a bland new father image, a man who never discussed unpleasant truths, a man who looked like a President. If it was upon this basis that he constructed his campaign, I can only say that he was very badly advised. The real Richard Nixon, leading a fighting party and supported by a fighting general already in the White House, could have swept the country. We Democrats can be thankful that he was dissuaded by someone, either his Madison Avenue advisers or his own inner insecurity, from following the hard, clean, clear path that would have led to the Presidency.

There remains the fact that the Republican party as such also failed to wage a very effective campaign. In Bucks County, where the Republicans defeated us, we were never impressed by either the vigor or the intelligence of their effort to gain votes for Nixon. With all the advantages the party enjoyed, it should have given him a majority of 20,000. Throughout eastern Pennsylvania the story was the same. In New York and Connecticut the Republicans also failed to mount that aggressive, committed campaign that might have won. I know there is difference of opinion on this, and one Democratic visitor from California told me, "For God's sake, don't challenge the Republicans to work any harder. In California they ran one of the greatest campaigns I've ever seen and they clawed the victory away from us. They deserve all the credit you can give them."

In the other parts of the nation that I visited this was not so. Their campaign was sometimes effective and occasionally inspired; but the fire that characterized their nationwide efforts in 1952 and 1956 was missing, and the principal ingredient that was lacking was dedication. A great many Republicans simply could not get excited about their candidate, and this indifference was exhibited constantly throughout the autumn.

Many critics, while admitting Republican lassitude, argue, "The Democrats were just as bad. This was one of the dullest campaigns in history and most of the population was plain bored." This is somewhat disproved by the record turnout of voters, nearly 69,000,000 and far in excess of pre-election estimates. At the same time, out of every 303 Americans who did vote, one, while willing to vote for the other offices, refused to cast a ballot for either Kennedy or Nixon. Across the nation a surprising total of 224,931 so refrained, enough to have swung the victory to Nixon had they supported him. In Bucks County about 300 voters rejected both candidates. These may have been disgruntled Stevensonians; more likely they were Democrats who found it morally distasteful to support either a Republican or a Catholic.

In our county we did see some of the general apathy that was supposed to mark the campaign. From the floor people frequently asked, "Neither man is very good, is he?" Others said, "Except for that first debate, there's been no real argument between the candidates." Certainly the fourth debate was about as inept a performance as one could witness, with neither man saying anything new or even repeating the old effectively. But I was never willing to admit, nor am I now, that John Kennedy was inadequate. In everything he did, there was a promise of strong administration and powerful legislative leadership. However, I was quite content to have him say nothing new in the fourth debate. As one leading Democrat exulted with me the next morning. "Wasn't it glorious that this time Jack didn't dig any graves for himself?"

So far as I was concerned, the election could not have been more exciting, and I think that if it had by some fiat been extended for an additional week, I would have had to go into the hospital. For if it lacked the dazzling verbal fireworks that characterized former elections, if there was no commanding figure, if the drama of great events was missing, there was nevertheless, for me at least, a quiet drama of even greater significance. A new dimension was being given to American politics in the election of a man born in this vital century. A new meaning was being added to our democracy in the removal of one more disqualification for the Presidency. Religious bigotry was dealt a crushing blow. But more important than any of these accomplishments, so far as I was concerned, was the conscious choice that America made between a candidate who talked sense and one who took refuge in bland generalities. In political significance, I found this election to be one of the most exciting of my lifetime.

On the other hand, when it was over I was not able to think of it as particularly close, and I believe that the editorialists have been misguided in reiterating that it was. If one considers the religious handicap that John Kennedy carried into the battle, and if one remembers that Nixon should have won easily, one must conclude that Kennedy gained a rather handsome vote of approval for his political and economic policies. I do not understand those critics who preach that because of the narrowness of his plurality he is obligated to proceed cautiously. To me it would seem more proper to advise: "President Kennedy, if your policies won against such formidable odds, the people of the United States must obviously prefer them. Get on with the job."

Furthermore, I cannot accept current estimates of Republican strength, for the party is much weaker than it appears to be. If the Democrats won this time, think what they will achieve in 1962 and 1964 when the religious question is no longer so vital, when inexperience cannot be an issue, and when years of good administration can be pointed to with pride. If the Republicans lost this time, with all the advantages they had on their side, think of the problem they will face in 1964 when they will not be the incumbents and when they will not have the great prestige of President Eisenhower to draw upon. The 1960 election was a tremendous moral victory for the Democrats, and to denigrate it makes no sense.

I wondered what my long-time friends Miss Omwake and Mrs. Dale thought about these matters, so I called on them after the election and they were far from resigned:

MISS OMWAKE: I do have to admit, though, that Mr. Kennedy was very dignified in waiting to claim the election until Mr. Nixon had formally conceded.

MRS. DALE: But I can't ever really forgive him for cheating in the debates. A man who will cheat . . .

ME: How did he cheat?

MRS. DALE: Taking notes when Mr. Nixon didn't.

ME: Are you still convinced that Mr. Nixon was the better man?

MISS OMWAKE: Of course. Mr. Kennedy will bring inflation. He'll bring war. He'll force socialism upon us.

MRS. DALE: And you watch, first thing he'll have his whole family, brothers and all, running the White House. You know what the woman down the street said, "It isn't the Pope I fear. It's the Pop."

MISS OMWAKE: But the really exciting bit is what just came over the radio. It says that Mr. Kennedy isn't elected at all, and that the Republicans are going to get all the votes in Illinois, Texas and New Jersey.

MRS. DALE: I'm sure the Democrats stole about half their states. I'd be very happy to see an honest recount in all the states. You'd find that Mr. Nixon was the real winner.

MISS OMWAKE: If you could take an honest look into the ballot boxes of Philadelphia, you'd find that the Democrats had stolen the election there too.

MRS. DALE: It's infuriating to think that only a few more Republican votes would have won the election for Mr. Nixon.

ME: Did you vote early in the morning?

MRS. DALE: We didn't bother to vote. It wasn't a very interesting election.

In the bars in my district broken-hearted Republicans were saying, "In this election the decent people of America were swamped by the scum. It's really terrifying to contemplate the kind of people who are going to govern this nation." One man garnered a lot of laughs each Saturday by announcing, "Tomorrow attend the church of your choice . . . while you still have a choice."

A woman who wore mink explained loudly, "You know who licked us? The K.K.K."

This was too much and I protested: "That's a silly statement, and you know it. The only time the K.K.K. figured in this election was when some misguided idiot down south said the Klan was for Nixon. And I'm glad to say that Nixon quickly disowned them and said he didn't want their help."

Because I spoke well of Nixon the woman assumed I was a Republican and confided, "Oh, when we say the K.K.K. we don't mean the Klan. We mean the Kikes, the Koons and the Kat'lics."

I backed away and thought, "By God, I'm glad we won."

Earlier I wrote that I saw the Democratic party as a coalition in which people of many diverse types could feel at home: liberals, intellectuals, union people, Negroes, Catholics, Jews, and all who wanted to work for a vigorous new society. After the dreary conservatism of the last eight years, after the anti-intellectualism, after the deification of the country club, I felt that we needed the kind of leadership an entirely different kind of political force could give. I was proud during the campaign that I was working, in even a minor way, for such a force, and when it attained the victory I almost leaped with joy.

I would be less than honest, however, if I did not admit that often during the campaign I was embarrassed by Republican hecklers who charged: "The Democratic party is a coalition all right, but not of the idealistic elements you describe. It's a union of northern radicals and southern reactionaries." After the results were in these same critics pointed out, "You were saved by the arch reactionaries of the South." I do not think that because there were extremely conservative voters who backed Kennedy in some southern states that one need deny that a coalition of liberal groups was mainly responsible for his victory. Politics is the art of the possible, and if the Republicans had won, their victorious coalition would have contained elements just as diverse as ours. Knights in shining armor were not destined to capture this election, no matter which side won. Hard-headed politicians making hard-headed decisions triumphed, and I think that when John Kennedy leaves the White House in 1968 he ought to erect a statue to the man who suggested that he make his urgent phone call to Reverend Martin Luther King in that Georgia jail. Such things win elections and make it possible for coalitions like the one I supported to govern the nation.

During the campaign there was much discussion of the role newspapers were playing, and I tried to read about eight each day. They came from Bucks County, Philadelphia, New York and wherever else possible. Of the eight, seven were strongly for Nixon, about the national average, and I think it would be stretching the metaphor to say that editorially they bent over backwards to be fair to Kennedy. One Philadelphia columnist, whose words appeared prominently on each day's editorial page, was downright ridiculous in much of his pro-Republican ranting, and one of his columns about Adlai Stevenson was despicable. Fortunately, he did more harm than good and in many meetings Democrats quoted his worse effusions for comic relief.

On the other hand, even though the newspapers were commanded by Republican owners, I could find no legitimate complaint against their handling of hard-fact news stories. Senator Kennedy's positions were described and the progress of the campaign was honestly reported. This was largely because in American most working reporters are Democrats, so that no matter how urgently the owners might support Nixon, it was Democrats who wrote the stories and their preference for Kennedy could sometimes be detected.

Furthermore, in this election the role of the independent syndicated columnist was conspicuous. Most were for Kennedy and either said so or implied as much, and Republican papers were rather gallant, I thought, in permitting these men free rein to express their opinions. Alsop, Reston, Childs, Pearson and Lippmann constantly refuted the editorial pages on which they appeared and substantiated the news columns in an admirable demonstration of what freedom of speech means.

After the election Mr. Nixon, perhaps with accuracy, complained that he had lost the Presidency mainly because newspaper reporters had been against him and had slanted their stories in favor of Senator Kennedy. If this was true, and there is some evidence that it was, I can only call the result poetic justice. A great many newspapermen have intellectual interests, and for the past eight years they had watched an administration purposely flout the intellectual life. In those years to be an egghead was to be ridiculous and a thing of scorn. No memorable step was taken by Republicans to modify this national mucker pose, so that at a time when the intelligence of Europe and Africa, to name only two areas, was more prized than ever, the comparable intelligence of America was either ignored or actually denigrated. Everyone who worked in the arts knew this, newspapermen above all, so that if in 1960 most intellectuals of standing ardently sided with Kennedy it was an appropriate revenge.

Belatedly, of course, the Republicans tried to institute committees of college professors and artists for Nixon, but these did more damage than good, because anyone who knew anything about the matter could not look at the resulting ill-assorted rosters without suppressing a laugh. If Mr. Nixon was correct that newspaper reporters stole the election from him, the theft was ironic retribution of an Aristotelian magnitude. Did the Republicans think that they could kick the intellectuals around for eight years and then call upon them frantically for support? It didn't work that way, and any intellectual could have warned them that it wouldn't.

In forming a final estimate of the value of work done by people like me, I am unable to be very optimistic. Of every hundred votes cast for the Democratic party in my county I suspect that 75 percent of the people would have voted Democratic even if the ticket had been composed of Jack the Ripper and Aaron Burr. Of course, about 75 percent of the Republicans would have supported the same ticket if it had represented their side. A critical 24 percent were gotten to the polls solely by the efforts of the organized Democratic party working under the leadership of long-time professionals like Johnny Welsh and Jack Ward. That leaves one percent who might possibly have been modified in some small way by the work of amateur outfits like Citizens for Kennedy, but I doubt if the figure actually goes as high as one percent. To be specific, in Bucks County, where 57,177 people voted for Kennedy, it is possible that my organization influenced 571 votes, but to me that seems about twice too high. I can think of about 250 people that we switched from the Republican column to the Democratic. That's one half of one percent. But of course, a swing of that proportion would have caused a landslide in the 1960 election.

In order to win those 250 votes we spent about $5,800, the unpaid time of innumerable people, the gasoline of many cars, and the full-time energy of about ten dedicated workers. The rewards seemed so very small that I often wondered why we were doing it, and then sometimes as I toured my magnificent county and saw the old houses and the timeless footpaths and the good Germans who were against me this time, and their stout barns, and the bright new suburbs, and the children going to school, I thought: "We're doing it because there is a nation to win." And when the votes were in I added, "And you win a nation by convincing one man at a time, one by one. You win an election by one tenth of one percent. And that's what you're fighting for."

My motives were made clear to me on the final Saturday night of the campaign when I helped in a small way to entertain the final great rally in the Coliseum in New York. It seemed that everyone was there to participate in Senator Kennedy's last major appearance. I sat beside Jim Farley and Carmine DeSapio. Mrs. Roosevelt and Herbert Lehman were there and Lyndon Johnson and Governor Harriman and Abe Ribicoff and John Bailey. And at the appointed time Senator Kennedy made his appearance and took his place before the microphones to address the nation in his last plea for votes.

And I remember looking at the back of his neck and seeing that he had what seemed to be a wart on the right-hand side, just above the collar and it seemed a curious thing to me that the most conspicuous thing about the future President of the United States, so far as I was then concerned, was that he had a bump on his neck. I thought: "Is this the man for whom so many of us knocked ourselves out? Why did we do it? I don't know him. I've spoken to him twice for a total of one minute, so I'm not even sure of what he thinks about really basic issues. He has nothing that I want and I am in no way beholden to him." I watched the wart on the back of his neck as he spoke on in the voice that had become so important to me during the past eight weeks, and I was glad then that he had been so forceful on the night of that first debate when the victory march had started. I thought: "The fact is, I haven't been working for John F. Kennedy, the imperfect man. I've been working for myself and for my perfect vision of what the United States can one day become. The process of selecting a President is confused and exasperating, but after much discussion a crystallization sets in, and the people, in some mysterious way, conclude: 'He's the man.' This man comes to represent justice and equality and courage. It's very doubtful that the man about whom this crystallization begins to coalesce ever had these attributes to begin with, but the nation decides that he embodies them, so pretty soon you're willing for him to be your President, and you're willing to work until your voice is hoarse, because you know that if he doesn't mature into those virtues now, then they probably don't exist anywhere else in your nation."

You look at the thin young man with the reddish brown hair speaking at the microphone and you think: "For eight weeks my wife has been warning me night after night, 'Don't you dare call him "a young man." That's Republican propaganda,' and for eight weeks I've been speaking of him as if he were just a little younger than Adenauer and only a bit less intelligent than Socrates. But he is a young man, and if we hadn't had this grueling campaign he wouldn't be even partially prepared for the Presidency. But no man, young or old, could go through what he's gone through, the awful humiliation of begging 170,000,000 people for their votes, without experiencing the humbling impact that is required before greatness can be attained. I'm for him. I think he now knows what America is all about. I think he has guts."

I heard nothing of what Kennedy said that last night. Maybe I was too tired to listen, but apparently he spoke well, for the crowd roared and went sort of crazy with joy. But something that happened at the end of the speech assured me that John Kennedy knew what it was all about, and when I saw what he did then I felt better.

Between where he was standing and where I was standing were the historic Democrats then living, almost all of them excepting only Adlai Stevenson. Surrounding him were Mrs. Roosevelt and Governor Harriman and Abe Ribicoff and Jim Farley and all the rest. Ignoring them, he elbowed his way across the stage to where I was standing and threw his arms about the tall man standing next to me. Kennedy embraced him in the French manner and thumped his broad back. "We needed you," he said twice. The big man embraced him in the French manner and said, "You're in, Jack."

The man that Senator Kennedy embraced was Adam Clayton Powell, the Negro minister and congressman. In the days that were left in this 1960 election Mrs. Roosevelt and Carmine DeSapio could help John Kennedy no more. Their work was done and appreciated. But Adam Clayton Powell could still do a lot of work in Harlem, where the Negro vote was still touch and go. And if John Kennedy wanted to be elected President he had better see to it that Adam Clayton Powell did all the hard work he could in the remaining hours. As the powerful Negro and the young senator from Massachusetts embraced, I looked over Kennedy's shoulder and saw Lyndon Johnson staring at the pair. He said nothing and moved away toward Governor Ribicoff, and I thought, "If there's any man here tonight who understands exactly the significance of this extraordinary embrace, it's Lyndon Johnson."

Having greeted Powell, Kennedy now rejoined the great figures of the party, and the last roaring rally of the 1960 election ended.

Late that night I straggled into a restaurant and encountered another of those curious coincidences which make politics and life more dramatic than fiction, for seated at the next table was my old friend, Emmett Hughes, the right-hand man and political adviser to Nelson Rockefeller. He already feared a Democratic victory in the nation and was resigned to one in New York. The consequences could only be damaging to his superior, and he reflected glumly, "The tragedy of it is, Michener, that Rockefeller could have won the election so easily. Even the Democrats acknowledge that."

"Some of the ones I've been around do," I agreed. "How did he miss?"

"Republicans were still suffering from the Willkie syndrome," Hughes explained. "They'd rather lose with a regular they can control than win with a newcomer they can't. Yet victory with Rockefeller would have been so easy." To my surprise he recapitulated the analysis I had developed a year before: "The real reactionaries would have had to vote for him, because they had no option. Many of the Stevensonians would have joined up. And he'd have held most of the Democrats who had crossed the line to vote for Eisenhower." He fell silent, then added, "It's maddening."

I said, "A year ago I saw this, too. Why didn't the Republicans see it?"

"They did," he said.

Some minutes passed, then I observed, "Because I'm a strong Kennedy man, I was certainly relieved to see Rocky rejected, because when they turned him down I knew we'd win. But as a good American, I was unhappy to see him passed by. Each party ought to put up its best man. Then everybody wins. Right now, my guess is that he may take the nomination in 1964, but he'll have no chance to win. How do you see it?"

Emmett Hughes, who must have been pondering these things, preferred not to comment.

On Election Night I was invited to the traditional glittering New York Election Eve party given by Tobé, the well-known hostess. From later newspaper stories I found that practically everybody in New York that I had missed for the last two months was there, but I was not. I wanted to be with Sam Thompson and the gang in Bucks County, and we trailed around from one headquarters to another. As soon as I heard that Connecticut had given Kennedy not the expected majority of 30,000 nor the hoped-for 60,000 but an astonishing 90,000, I was satisfied that we had won and bothered no more about the outcome. I drank beer with all the fine people who had worked with me and went to bed relatively early.

The next day Arthur Eastburn, long-time first lieutenant of Joe Grundy, warned me, "This election isn't over, Jim. Nixon's going to carry California and I think he'll get Illinois and Texas on grounds of fraud."

Then I began to sweat. Murphy's Law was back in operation and I counted the agonizing days till December 19, when certification of the electoral votes would formally confirm our victory. I followed each new development with anxiety and foresaw all sorts of contingencies. Each night when I went to bed I said as I had during the last days of the campaign, "Thank God we got through today without anything upsetting the world."

Then, on the last day of November, Sam Thompson came in grinning. "Worry no more," he chuckled.

"How can you be so relaxed?" I asked with some irritation.

"Everything's fixed," he assured me. "The big Democrats are fighting mad over the way the Republicans are trying to steal the election and they've arranged everything, but good."

"You think Kennedy's going to hold on?"

"Well," Sam hesitated, "he's gonna be President, but there has to be just a little finagling first."

"Are the Democrats going to high-pressure some of the Republican electors?" I asked.

"No," Sam explained grandiosely. "Let's suppose that the Republicans succeed in stealing Illinois and those votes are transferred to Nixon. Next let's suppose that Mississippi and

Alabama conspire to throw the election of President into the House of Representatives. On the surface it might look as if the Democrats would have a majority there, and that Kennedy would thus be elected, but we're afraid the Republicans will be able to engineer a stalemate so that neither Kennedy nor anybody else can be elected President."

"So Kennedy loses," I said glumly.

"At first he seems to," Sam agreed expansively, "but the Democrats have arranged a trick which makes him President anyway. This may be hard to follow, but listen. When the House is unable to elect a President, the Senate goes right ahead and elects Lyndon Johnson Vice President, and since there is no President, he takes over. At this point a congressman from an East Boston district made up of one hundred percent Roman Catholics resigns from Congress, whereupon Kennedy resigns from the Senate and in a special election runs for the House and wins. Now Lyndon Johnson resigns as Vice President, and according to perfectly good law Sam Rayburn, the Speaker of the House, succeeds to the Presidency. Of course, when he steps up he leaves the speakership vacant, and who do you suppose gets elected? John F. Kennedy, of Massachusetts, which puts him next in line for the Presidency. As soon as this is accomplished, Sam Rayburn resigns the Presidency and Jack Kennedy takes over."

I was a little dizzy but asked, "What happens to Lyndon Johnson?"

"Same trick. A congressman from Texas resigns, Lyndon runs in a special election, wins, and is elected Speaker of the House, which leaves us Kennedy as President and Johnson as Vice President, just the way every honest man wanted it in the first place."

These intricate shenanigans seemed so typically American that I started to laugh and asked, "What do you think of such manipulations, Sam?"

"Honest men have to protect themselves," he said, starting to go. Then he added as an afterthought, "And mostly against Republicans."

"Wait a minute!" I called. "What happens to Sam Rayburn?"

"In the interests of party loyalty," Sam confided, "he's agreed to take the job of customs collector for the Port of Houston."

Actually, there was much undercover chicanery in November and December, attempts to pervert the Electoral College and to cause confusion throughout the nation. Many observers were frightened by the invitation to fraud which our system encourages and there was much talk of reforming it. Republicans wished to abandon the Electoral College altogether, which would mean that no longer could a popular-vote plurality of even one deliver all of New York's 45 electoral votes to one party or the other. A plan of proportional representation was to be substituted whereby in this election New York's 45 votes would have been divided 23.64 to Kennedy and 21.36 to Nixon. Taking the nation as a whole, this plan would have resulted in no winner, and the choice of President would have been thrown into the House, possibly with the results that Sam Thompson outlined above.

The Democrats would be foolish to permit abandonment of the Electoral College system, for it is this pattern of voting by states that enables a true balance between conservative rural areas and liberal large cities to be maintained. This was the system devised by the framers of the Constitution after prolonged deliberation, and it is about the only system that would protect the rights of all.

For example, our present pattern is sometimes condemned because it favors the big-city states; actually, the truth is quite the contrary. In 1960 it required only 60,762 Alaskan voters to determine three electoral votes, an average of one electoral vote for every 20,000. But in California to determine 32 electoral votes required 6,507,082 voters, an average of about 200,000 for each. Thus in our Presidential sweepstakes, an Alaskan is worth ten Californians.

The virtue of our present system is that a subtle balance between big units and small is maintained. Minority parties are not encouraged. By translating small popular majorities into large electoral ones, and into large blocs of power in both the House and Senate, responsibility is concentrated in one party or the other, and the nation can be governed.

The only change that need be considered is the elimination of the electors, those faceless, unknown men who are not now obligated to respect the choice of the people and who might some day, as some did in this election, pervert the will of the nation. Election officials in each state should certify the results to the state's secretary, who should be required to forward them automatically to Washington. We came perilously close to trouble this time and the temptation to wrongdoing should be eliminated.

I am for our present system for one principal reason: if one considers all the governments that were in being when ours began operations in 1789, the United States alone has escaped the need for major overhaul. All the rest have been substantially modified, usually by revolution. We therefore have the oldest continuing form of government in the world, and it has succeeded, I think, principally because on the one hand it safeguards the exercise of power by hedging it with compromise, while on the other it allocates such power as it does allow to responsible parties and responsible men. When a system has worked so well it is worthy of retention.

During the critical days when the outcome of the election was uncertain I did not so much fear the shifting of enough electoral votes to cause Kennedy's defeat as I did a recounting of ballots that would still permit Kennedy to win but which would cast moral doubt upon his right to the Presidency. In a democracy, even more than in a monarchy, legitimacy of inheritance is a supreme consideration, for it forestalls revolution, and I heard many rumors calculated to question the legitimacy of Kennedy's victory.

I was truly delighted, therefore, when a count of votes in New Jersey, where the Republicans were making a lot of noise, had to be abandoned because in district after district Kennedy's corrected totals were somewhat higher than had been reported. What normal errors had crept in seemed all to have been in Nixon's favor.

But what settled the problem permanently was the Hawaii result. After all the post-election shouting, after all of Thruston Morton's ridiculous charges and insinuations, the only state which had to be shifted from one candidate to the other was Hawaii, and it went from the Republicans to the Democrats. I think we cannot overestimate the psychological importance of this ironic switch, and the men in Hawaii who fought for this recount and who carried it through to a conclusion served their nation well. Imagine the editorial outcry if some one state had been forced to switch from Kennedy to Nixon! A grievous suspicion would have contaminated the election, but as it turned out, the Hawaii shift from Nixon to Kennedy put the whole matter of recounting into proper perspective and tension was dispersed in quiet laughter.

The reader must by now be aware of the fact that I see politics in a democracy as a process of hard fighting to win a nation, conciliation when the election ends, and generous compromise when the office is assumed. I was therefore proud of the manner in which John Kennedy went to see Richard Nixon immediately after the election and of the gracious way in which President Eisenhower put an end to rumors of an eventual Republican victory by inviting the President-elect and his wife to inspect their new home, the White House; but I was even more gratified by a letter which I received from Boise, Idaho. It was written by a man I did not know and said: "At the last meeting of the board of directors it was reported that prior to the last general election you had several persons who were supporting the candidacy of Mr. Kennedy at a luncheon at the country club as your guests. It was also reported that a group of ladies, some of whom were associate members and some of whom were wives of members, conducted themselves in an unladylike and rude manner, embarrassing both you and your guests.

"We have thoroughly investigated the matter and the board has requested that I write to you expressing the board's sincere apologies for the conduct of these ladies. I am also authorized to write a personal letter to each of your guests expressing our regret for any embarrassment which this incident caused them." Such gestures of conciliation make the conduct of politics possible, and I am much indebted to this unknown gentleman from Boise, for his gracious gesture of apology stands in the fine tradition of political campaigning in our republic.

Throughout this report I have several times indicated that my audiences frequently considered John Kennedy less gifted than I did. Many were unwilling to believe that this young man would make a great and forceful President in the tradition of the two Roosevelts. Some doubted that he was a true liberal. Others felt that he was a crusading socialist. To all such doubters I gave my personal assurance that Kennedy was going to be one of the great Presidents. When they continued to doubt I said merely, "You watch!"

It was with real joy, therefore, that I saw the nation slowly swing around to my original assessment of John

Kennedy. There was general applause for his cabinet appointments and admiration for his conciliatory approach to national problems. His mature and reassuring behavior in the ten weeks following the election surprised many; it did not surprise me, for during the campaign I had repeatedly assured my listeners, "John Kennedy will be President of all the people. He'll conciliate political and economic enemies, and at the same time he'll be a true liberal, for he's that kind of man. His only ambition will be to give this nation the responsible leadership it deserves."

When the electoral votes were finally certified, when the inauguration had legally taken place, I could at last relax. More even than when I started I was content that I had worked for a man whom I could respect. That he would make a great President I had no doubt, and I was convinced that I would be increasingly proud of having supported him early and strong.